MAKE ARTS FOR A BETTER LIFE

Make Arts for a Better Life

A GUIDE FOR WORKING WITH COMMUNITIES

Brian Schrag and Kathleen J. Van Buren

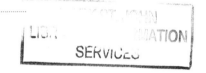

OXFORD
UNIVERSITY PRESS

OXFORD
UNIVERSITY PRESS

Oxford University Press is a department of the University of Oxford. It furthers
the University's objective of excellence in research, scholarship, and education
by publishing worldwide. Oxford is a registered trade mark of Oxford University
Press in the UK and certain other countries.

Published in the United States of America by Oxford University Press
198 Madison Avenue, New York, NY 10016, United States of America.

Library of Congress Cataloging-in-Publication Data
Names: Schrag, Brian, 1962– author. | Van Buren, Kathleen Jenabu, 1976– author.
Title: Make arts for a better life: a guide for working with communities /
Brian Schrag and Kathleen Van Buren.
Description: New York: Oxford University Press, 2018. |
Includes bibliographical references and index.
Identifiers: LCCN 2017057157 | ISBN 9780190878283 (pbk.) |
ISBN 9780190878276 (hardcover) |
ISBN 9780190878313 (oxford scholarly online) |
ISBN 9780190902513 (companion website)
Subjects: LCSH: Artists and community. | Art and social action. | Arts and society.
Classification: LCC NX180.A77 S37 2018 | DDC 700.1/03—dc23
LC record available at https://lccn.loc.gov/2017057157

9 8 7 6 5 4 3 2 1

Paperback printed by WebCom, Inc., Canada
Hardback printed by Bridgeport National Bindery, Inc., United States of America

Contents

CLOSING MATTER

Figures

Preface

MANY OF US can think of a song, a film, a painting, or a story that has transported us to a transcendent reality, one that left our grimy, sometimes mundane lives behind. We know that arts make things happen—solemn vows and rituals forge marriages, colors on a flag inspire devotion and action, a dramatic presentation of lost friendship motivates us to reconnect with our own friends, and certain songs change our mood and lower our blood pressure (Kushnir et al. 2012; Pereira et al. 2011). We can imagine, then, that arts could be powerful components of solutions to problems in the world, even to trauma, hopelessness, and conflict within and across communities. In fact, evidence for the benefits of intentional artistic creativity in community well-being is growing (this will be addressed later in the Guide; see also definitions of health and well-being in *Step 2*). Unfortunately, however, best practices for arts-influenced community development remain widely unknown and incompletely applied.

Our Guide responds to this lack with a groundbreaking model for arts advocacy based on proven methods and sound theory. It describes a flexible method composed of seven steps for arts advocates and community members to work through in developing arts programs aimed at meeting community goals. Goals might include, for example, further educational opportunities for youth, deeper knowledge of relevant health issues, empowerment for marginalized persons, or peace and reconciliation in areas of conflict. The arts alone may not be able to accomplish all of these goals, but they can and are making tremendous differences in many communities around the world. This Guide highlights critical artistic, practical, and ethical issues to consider, and offers examples of some past and ongoing arts programs from around the world.

We invite you to see the Guide as contributing to an even broader enterprise of hope. Prominent voices like Bill Gates (2018) and Stephen Pinker (2018) have begun to promote an evidence-based recognition that aspects of life are getting better (for example, the decrease in child mortality rates worldwide by 50% since 1990; World Health Organization 2018), and that they can continue to do so (see also Easterbrook 2018). For local arts to share a central place with disciplines like medicine and agronomy in this reawakening, we need to significantly expand the body of research demonstrating the utility of the arts. Consider embarking on well-designed projects whose outcomes include convincing case studies and compelling measures of improvement.

History and Acknowledgments

This Guide draws upon centuries of ideas, is geared toward understanding the present, and is directed by a vision of change. We (Brian and Kathleen) wrote or edited most of what you will read in this volume. However, we integrated contributions and feedback from dozens of people. Contributors drew on the historically robust discoveries and methods of academic disciplines like ethnomusicology, folklore, performance studies, anthropology, communications studies, and community development. We also benefited from interactions with colleagues in the Applied Ethnomusicology subgroups of the Society for Ethnomusicology and the International Council of Traditional Music.

We include a number of case studies in the Guide, particularly in *Step 2* but also in other sections of the text. For a few case studies, we break down the processes involved in arts initiatives, showing how these initiatives link with particular stages of the *Make Arts for a Better Life* process (*Make Arts* for short) that we propose. Other case studies are presented only briefly; these descriptions are included to help readers gain a sense of the diversity of arts-related projects around the world, the different types of individuals and organizations involved in such work (researchers, community organizations, nongovernmental and governmental organizations, etc.), and to help spark ideas for new projects. Some case studies have been written specifically for this Guide; in these cases, the authors are identified and their work is referenced as "email communication" with us. We are grateful to these authors for sharing their stories with us. Other case studies are drawn from published literature in ethnomusicology and related disciplines, or from online resources; in these cases, sources are identified so that readers can seek further information if they desire.

We also wish to acknowledge the following individuals (in alphabetical order) for additional contributions to the Guide and encouragement along the way: Dr. Tom Avery, Dr. Kit R. Christensen, Rev. Dr. Tom Christensen, Dr. Neil Coulter, Cory Cummins, Dr. Dan Fitzgerald, Dr. Sue Hall-Heimbecker, Michael Harrar, Dr. Robin Harris, Brad Keating, Dr. James Krabill, Matt Menger, Dr. Andrew Noss, Dr. Philip Noss, Michelle Petersen, Sophie Ravier, Dr. Robert Reed, Dr. Julisa Rowe, Mary Elizabeth Saurman, Amy Schmidt, Eliza Squibb, Glenn Stallsmith, Dr. Julie Taylor, and Denise Wynn. Please forgive any lapses of memory or attribution. A community truly produced this work. We thank Dr. Jacqueline Cogdell DjeDje for our formation as scholars in guiding us through dissertation research at UCLA. For their dedicated work within their communities and the education they have given us, we thank Edward Kabuye, Felix Wanzala, and Kawangware Street Youth Project members. For our families, we feel so grateful and blessed. We are also thankful for the insightful guidance provided by anonymous reviewers of our Guide and by Suzanne Ryan and the staff of Oxford University Press.

Prior to the development of this Guide, Brian Schrag published the faith-based volume *Creating Local Arts Together: A Manual to Help Communities Reach their Kingdom Goals* (Schrag 2013a). The current Guide fulfills our goal to provide a resource that can consider a wider range of contexts and can further explore ethical and practical issues involved in developing community arts initiatives.

This Guide is an imperfect object that will continue to grow and morph, spawning new objects with different shapes in different places. We take responsibility for its current contour and content, including errors and omissions. We urge readers now to take it, play with it, add to it. Finally, join us in celebrating the new bits of artistry that accompany communities' movements toward thriving futures.

About the Companion Website

Oxford University Press has created a website to accompany *Make Arts for a Better Life: A Guide for Working with Communities*. Among other items, we have included many of the book's tables and figures in formats readers can use to analyze their own data. Materials available online are indicated within the text with the visual icon:

We welcome feedback and suggestions for additional content based on readers' experiences with arts programs. Readers can contact us through the following email address: ***[www.oup.com/us/makeartsforabetterlife]***.

Who Should Use This Guide?

THIS GUIDE IS for people who understand that solutions are not always easy. It is not for the impatient, or for those who hold arrogantly to their authority, position, and strength.

We lead readers to reflect on social contexts in which every decision seems to pit one principle against two others—where a solution that helps people thrive in one community falls flat in another; where multilingualism, migration, globalization, urbanization, and ideologies mix in so many unpredictable ways that *any* solution to a problem is complicated. Into these complexities we offer not simple solutions to impose, but straightforward suggestions for how to spark creativity that can last. Seven steps. Seven points of departure that can enable community members to make more knowledgeable decisions about their futures. The Guide is for people who recognize every community's complexity and who will become wiser with a community in learning what "good" looks like in a particular place (see also Foundations, "What Is Good?").

Beyond this crucial attitude, this Guide is for *any* arts advocate: anyone who wants to help communities draw on their artistic resources to improve their lives. An arts advocate may be a community insider, outsider, or someone with a unique combination of characteristics from multiple identities. She may be a professional scholar, or not. However, her primary posture toward a community is one of learning, dialoguing, facilitating, and encouraging.

While ensuring that the Guide is based on robust scholarship, we want it to serve a wide audience. For students, emerging scholars, and community arts advocates outside academic settings, the Guide will provide a clear method for researching arts within communities and for thoughtfully engaging in applied work.

Professional ethnomusicologists or researchers in related disciplines will already be familiar with many of the concepts and processes described in this book, though not necessarily presented in the same format. However, even experienced researchers can benefit from a reminder of critical steps and issues to reflect upon. Furthermore, we hope that the case studies, practical exercises, and supplementary resources will provide effective aids for research, teaching, and community work.[1]

An arts advocate could fill any number of roles. We highlight three: educators, project leaders, and researchers. While we encourage readers to review the full Guide, we provide visual icons throughout the text to help readers in these categories identify information which may be particularly relevant to their work. Note that these categories are not mutually exclusive. One could be both educator and researcher, project leader and researcher, or project leader and educator.

E Educators

As a reader, if you plan to teach a course related to arts and well-being, applied ethnomusicology, or community music, the *Make Arts* process can provide the framework for a class field project. *Step 4* on its own can provide a field research manual for students engaging in fieldwork exercises or in-depth undergraduate and graduate research. In addition, we have included numerous references that you can choose for assigned readings. Look for the Educators icon E throughout the Guide for particularly relevant sections. See also "Suggestions for Educators" (*Closing 7*) for further information.

P Project Leaders

If you have received a grant or are preparing an application for a grant that funds a community development project, the Guide can provide methods for identifying appropriate goals, activities to help reach those goals, and indicators of whether the project has met the goals or not. Look for the Project Leaders icon P throughout the Guide for especially relevant sections. See also "Suggestions for Project Leaders" (*Closing 7*) for further information.

R Researchers

If you are working with a community, the Guide provides well-organized research tools that may be helpful. *Step 4* in particular can serve as a field research manual.

In addition, as ethnomusicologists, ethnochoreologists, and others search increasingly for ways that their research can benefit the communities with which they work, the Guide provides ways to reflect upon and assess community involvement and impact. Look for the Researcher icon **R** throughout the Guide for particularly relevant sections. See "Suggestions for Researchers" (*Closing 7*) for further information.

In addition to providing visual cues for readers in these categories throughout the Guide, we have also provided separate sections in *Step 4* for readers interested in five particular categories of artistic expression: *music, drama, dance, oral verbal arts,* and *visual arts.* Some repetition is necessary within *Step 4* in order to consider similar issues in each of these categories. However, readers who are interested in particular arts may focus on relevant sections, and skim or skip sections that focus on other artistic domains. Remember, though, that often multiple types of artistry are conceptualized and presented together as genres within communities (Stone 2000:7).

We originally envisioned the Guide as a tool for people working professionally in cultural contexts very different from their own. However, as we taught the method to diverse groups, we found that people could apply it to many situations that we would not normally label cross-cultural. This makes sense—every individual human represents a package of experiences, ideas, neurological connections, physical qualities, emotions, and other characteristics that can never be known entirely by someone else. Of course, if you wish to engage with people that group themselves around a language, worldview, geography, diet, and/or social patterns very different from your own, you will need to expend much effort and use many skills; we provide rigorous research and other activities that will help those of you in this situation. But you could also apply the approach to people who are very much like you, your best friend, or your spouse. In fact, you could follow the process outlined in this Guide to learn something new about your own gifts and life goals, and to create something artistic that would improve your *own* future.

Note

1. Readers of this Guide also may be interested in the *Barefoot Guides* (www.barefootguide. org), which focus on various issues related to working with organizations and social change. Writers of the *Barefoot Guides* similarly draw upon extensive experience and expertise but seek to present guides accessible to a broad audience.

MAKE ARTS FOR A BETTER LIFE

FOUNDATIONS

IN 2004, KATHLEEN WAS a graduate student conducting doctoral research in Nairobi, Kenya, on the role of music and other arts in promoting social change. As part of her studies, she visited a number of children's centers and schools to learn about how they integrated the arts into their programs. Each of these centers and schools requested further visits, performances, lessons, or donations of musical instruments or money. There were too many to help all, even if time and funding had not been a problem. One of the organizations that had helped Kathleen significantly in her research was Childlife Trust, an umbrella organization working with children's centers across Nairobi. During her first visit to Childlife Trust, the director commented that the organization had hoped for some time to develop an annual arts festival. Together with her colleague, Ugandan drummer and choreographer Edward Kabuye, Kathleen spoke with Childlife staff to see whether she and Kabuye might be able to offer any help with developing an arts festival. Kathleen stressed that she and Kabuye were not coming to develop their own program, but rather to learn what Childlife Trust and the centers might need and want. It would be up to the centers to decide what would work best and to carry out the program.

Kathleen and Kabuye's offer was enthusiastically received by Childlife Trust staff. Over the next few weeks, they met with representatives from children's centers across Nairobi to ask whether an arts festival or another program would be useful for their children and what form such a program should take. With positive responses all around, center representatives developed a planning committee. Kathleen was nominated as secretary, but declined, noting that it should be their program; rather than taking a leadership position, she served as a facilitator to help bring interested people together and to assist in carrying out committee plans. The committee chose a program name (the Childlife Arts Programme); developed a mission statement; and disseminated a survey to other centers to gauge broader interests. Finally, the committee developed a plan and carried out the first phase of the program: a series of five-day workshops (one day each for music, dance, acrobatics, drama, and visual arts) for each region of Nairobi (Eastlands, Westlands, Southlands, and Central). Later, the group hoped to organize a festival showcasing the children's talents.

Forty-two children from eight centers participated in the first workshop. Although the planning committee encountered some practical glitches during the event, for example due to lack of funding, the workshop participants arrived each day with bright and hopeful eyes. With Kabuye's help, organizers located artists who agreed to teach the children for free. On the last day, Kathleen helped to distribute evaluations to all participants participants (children, the adult representatives/teachers who were present from the centers, and artists). The children all indicated that they would like to participate in future workshops; teachers were highly encouraged by the program and requested that further workshops be held; and artists praised the children's talents and offered to help with future programs.

Despite not having had any formal training specifically in applied ethnomusicology or necessarily thinking about the process in a step-by-step way, Kathleen engaged in particular ways with this project.

- She started by *getting to know the community*. Before developing the program, Kathleen had spent time in Nairobi visiting children's programs, studying their uses of music, building relationships with individuals involved in these programs, and listening to their requests.
- She felt it was important to let community members *define their own goals* for the programs. Her research was focused on arts and social change, for example on how music and other arts were being used in Nairobi to address issues such as drug and alcohol abuse, children's rights, and HIV and AIDS. The participants in the Childlife Arts Programme workshop were all involved in such performances: the artists in creating performances on social as well as other issues, the schoolteachers in composing and leading performances on social themes through their schools, and the children in rehearsing and performing on

such topics at school and national festivals. Kathleen had come to know them through her research on these performances. But participants in the program did not suggest thematic performances as a goal for the workshops; they determined the plan, and in the end only one session at the event included any discussion of social issues, and that was at the artists'—not Kathleen's—suggestion.

- Once the committee was established and the goal identified, organizers worked together to *determine a plan* for the workshop: location, dates, and which artists could lead the various workshops.
- Through the event, organizers sought to work with local artists and to build upon existing resources (e.g., an available school) to *create an event* that was relatively uncommon in those contexts: a series of arts workshops for children coming mainly from low-income communities.
- Organizers developed a framework in which professional artists could work with children to teach them *new skills, spark creativity, and create works* together. The workshops led to much laughter and excitement as teachers and students interacted, performed, and enjoyed being together.
- On the last day of the workshop, all participants were asked to complete evaluations. This was to help organizers critique the event and to offer ideas for *how to improve* future workshops.

We present the preceding story at some length because it demonstrates how Kathleen—like many other ethnomusicologists, artists, people—are already involved in programs within communities, trying to respond to voiced interests within those communities, and engaging in many of the methods discussed in this Guide. In the Guide, we propose an approach that incorporates best practices distilled from experiences like these, from our own experiences and those of many others.

The Guide presents seven steps that can help individuals and communities to learn more about locally accessible arts, and to use these arts to meet practical goals. Briefly, these steps are the following:

1. Meet a community and its arts;
2. Specify goals for a better life;
3. Connect goals to genres;
4. Analyze genres and events;
5. Spark creativity;
6. Improve results; and
7. Celebrate and integrate for continuity.

As a student ethnomusicologist, Kathleen understood the importance of building relationships, of carefully researching performances and performance contexts, and of acting ethically, both in research and in thinking about how to "give back" to community members. She followed many of the steps outlined in the Guide without them being named and listed in quite this format. In fact, she learned many of these lessons long before her ethnomusicology training. Building relationships with people means sharing thoughts, ideas, and cultures. It means learning about each other's needs, and about how these needs are being met or could be met.

The remainder of this section provides the foundations for this Guide. We address concepts such as "a better life," what is "good," and creativity and the arts. We also introduce the *Make Arts* steps. We strongly encourage you to read these subsections, even if you are eager to start engaging with a community. Understanding the concepts and methods on which the *Make Arts* process relies will help your relationships and projects be as rich and fruitful as possible.

A Better Life

In October 2015, the British Forum for Ethnomusicology held a one-day conference on the topic "Ethnomusicology and Policy." The call for papers for the conference highlighted the potentials and challenges in applied ethnomusicology and encouraged "further dialogue around how ethnomusicology contributes to the public good" (https://bfe.org.uk/conf/ethnomusicology-and-policy, accessed September 22, 2017). Many ethnomusicologists do not seem to question that they can contribute to the "public good." Furthermore, for many of us, this is not a choice—it is a responsibility. In discussions at the ICTM Study Group on Applied Ethnomusicology's first symposium in Ljubljana, Slovenia, in 2008, participants argued that applied ethnomusicologists require "professional and ethical dedication to using the knowledge [of music and its cultural context] acquired to 'benefit' individuals, communities and musical traditions" (Harrison and Pettan 2010:7). Svanibor Pettan (2008:97) highlights the potential for scholars to "use their capacities to make our world a better place and to enable applied ethnomusicology to develop its unquestionabl[y] rich potentials." Anthony Seeger (2006:223) advises "that we think about what we can contribute through the knowledge we are privileged to have had the opportunity to learn." Bernhard Bleibinger (2010:37) writes of "our times of globalisation and increasing cultural contact, conflicts and negotiations." He states (2010:38): "We have all come closer, and this means, I dare to say, that we have to take responsibilities. This is the moment when applied ethnomusicology comes in and can develop its potential, when a better world can be created through empowerment." Finally, Catherine Grant (2014:12) writes of her recent book *Music Endangerment: How Language Maintenance Can Help*: "I hope it holds a small place within a larger system of contributions to a better world."

In ethnomusicology, a number of published articles and volumes document the experiences of ethnomusicologists in applied work (recent examples include Pettan and Titon 2015; Grant 2014; Harrison, Mackinlay, and Pettan 2010; and a series of articles in *Ethnomusicology Forum* 22[2] published in 2011; see also Alviso 2003). These publications describe the involvement of ethnomusicologists in areas such as advocacy, medical work, archiving and preservation efforts, and education. Furthermore, ethnomusicologists are not alone in seeking to create "a better world." Anthropologists, folklorists, and communications scholars have long been active in applied arts work (Kodish 2013; Singhal and Rogers 1999; Skinner 2014). Muriel Reigersberg (2010:54) confirms that music psychologists have become more interested in sociological and ethnographically informed approaches, and also in how research findings can be applied to address practical issues. The relatively new field of community music also has an applied focus. Patricia Shehan Campbell and Lee Higgins (2015:640) describe "community music" as involving music leaders or facilitators working intentionally "to engage participants in active musicmaking and musical knowing," with "an emphasis on people, participation, context, equality of opportunity, and diversity." They argue that applied ethnomusicologists and community musicians understand "that music can play a vital role in community development through education, income generation, and self-esteem" (Campbell and Higgins 2015:656). Scholars are sometimes specifically called upon to demonstrate impact outside academia. In the United Kingdom, for example, scholars are under increased pressure to demonstrate the impact of their research as part of the Research Excellence Framework (REF), a national system for assessing the quality of research in higher education institutions. In REF terms, impact is defined as "an effect on, change or benefit to the economy, society, culture, public policy or services, health, the environment or quality of life, beyond academia" (Higher Education Funding Council for England 2016).

The United Nations (UN) also has promoted activity to "transform our world" (United Nations 2016b). Prior to 2015, UN activity focused on eight Millennium Development Goals (MDGs): "eradicating extreme poverty and hunger; achieving universal education; promoting gender equality and empowering women; reducing child mortality; improving maternal health; combating HIV/AIDS, malaria, and other diseases; ensuring environmental stability; and developing a global partnership for development" (United Nations 2016a). Post-2015 UN efforts have sought to not only build upon, but also re-evaluate, strengthen, and broaden previous goals. The UN System Task Team on the Post-2015 UN

Development Agenda titled its first report to the Secretary-General in May 2012 *Realizing the Future We Want for All.* This report "[called] for an integrated policy approach to ensure inclusive economic development, social progress and environmental sustainability and a development agenda that responds to the aspirations of all people for a world free of want and fear" (DESA 2016). Adopted by leaders in September 2015 and coming into force in January 2016, the current seventeen Sustainable[1] Development Goals (SDGs) of the 2030 Agenda for Sustainable Development seek to "end all forms of poverty, fight inequalities and tackle climate change, while ensuring that no one is left behind" (United Nations 2016b). Sometimes the UN has specifically looked to the arts to help meet targets; for example, the UN organization MINUSMA in Mali was founded with a principal aim of using the arts to help promote peace and reconciliation in a conflict area (Ravier 2014).

Despite interest in ethnomusicology and related disciplines in applied arts work, there are limited training materials available for use in the classroom or public sector. Participants in the ICTM Study Group on Applied Ethnomusicology's 2008 symposium discussion recommended two initiatives to help prepare ethnomusicologists for applied work: (1) training programs that draw upon current models of work; and (2) a handbook of applied ethnomusicology that could serve as a resource for new and current ethnomusicologists (Harrison and Pettan 2010:7). Symposium participants suggested that responsibilities might include the following: openness (described as "a willingness to place oneself in positions of vulnerability, discomfort and sometimes even subservience"), self-reflection, communication skills, and broadness (specifically, interdisciplinary approaches; Harrison and Pettan 2010:7). As a written resource that draws upon methods from ethnomusicology and other disciplines to outline critical issues to consider and steps to take for applied work, this Guide responds to these calls. Furthermore, our goal is to make this resource accessible not only to scholars, but also to community members who may wish to promote the arts.

We want this Guide to help us work toward a new reality, one in which *all* cultures are using *all* of their gifts to thrive. People have been integrating the arts into their communities in astounding ways since the beginning of human existence without the help of this Guide. Individuals and communities sometimes create arts with no explicit purpose in mind except "I really want/need to do this!" And sometimes those bits of artistry spread and enliven a community in completely unpredictable ways. Furthermore, some individuals may be exceptional communicator-artists who naturally know how to listen, learn, and help lead. However, many of us will benefit from the reminders and resources provided in this Guide.

We will not tell readers exactly which development issues to focus on. In a discussion about sustainability in music, Richard Moyle argued that ethnomusicologists' jobs "as sympathetic and supportive outsiders [*sic*] is properly that of an on-request caretaker and facilitator, but not as an arbiter of what should be preserved and what should not be" (as quoted in Schippers 2010:156). Our approach in this Guide is to help readers work with community members to discuss what aspects of their lives they wish to see change or flourish, and then to explore that community's resources for artistic genres that might help in the accomplishment of those goals. For one community, it may be enabling emotional and cultural healing after war. For another, it may be improving literacy. For yet another, it may be promoting the use of a vaccine to reduce rates of illness and death. In the Guide, we will discuss some of the main areas in which communities may wish to work, and provide examples of work already being undertaken in these areas. We will describe activities that spark creativity in ways that can help meet a community's goals, and we will demonstrate how readers can join in. But members of the communities in which we work should define new agendas; we will assist. In other words, the Guide will help you—the readers—work alongside local artists to spark the creation of new songs, dances, dramas, paintings, sculptures, and stories that help communities realize their hopes for better lives. We join in *others'* creativity, helping them use their arts for new purposes that will continue into the future. Sometimes conflicts will occur within communities about appropriate goals or arts; we will address such issues too in the Guide.

Working alongside community members also advances what Samuel Araújo calls "a possibility of a new kind of knowledge about social forms such as music and music-making" (Araújo 2006:291). Araújo argues: "The issue at stake here is not quite simply returning something to a community with which one works, out of respectable ethical considerations" but rather about "[subverting] academic knowledge as it has been traditionally legitimated" (Araújo 2006:291). Thus what is at stake is not only the application of knowledge, in the form of end products that meet community goals, but also an alternate method of knowledge production, one which includes and sits within the community, subverting traditional academic boundaries and power relations.

What Is "Good"?

In setting goals for programs, people in communities will likely be making evaluations about what is, or is not, "good" in their lives. They may have an ideal that they are striving for. Yet the concept of "good"—as in a good action, a good product, a better life or closer-to-good life—is complicated.[2] *The English Oxford Living Dictionaries* (2018) provides a range of meanings for the word "good" (Greek adjective *agathos, agathē, agathon*; masc., fem., neut.), including: "to be desired and approved of"; "having the required qualities"; "useful, advantageous, or beneficial in effect"; "possessing or displaying moral virtue" (adjectives); and "that which is morally right" (noun). Different languages have their own words and conceptions of good. For example, in discussing the Gbaya language from Cameroon, linguist Philip Noss (personal communication, June 6, 2017) explains that "to say 'to be good' would most likely begin by saying, ɔ *dee* ('it is good')." Comparison can also be made: "*Dee gan* 'good surpass (someone or something else),' and *dee batɛ* 'good extremely.'" Finally, Noss points out that judgment may be in relation to "not good." An action may be described as "*gbak na*, 'helps not,' 'it doesn't help (to accomplish the intended goal).'" In some cases, an action may even be deemed to hurt a person or community.

Discussions of good can be found in diverse disciplines, including philosophy, theology, environmental and landscape studies, and development work. Central to Western philosophical discussions of "good" are the teachings of Plato and his predecessors. Fritz-Gregor Herrmann (2007:204) explains how Pythagoreans "explained the world by pairs of fundamental oppositions, among them light and dark, good and bad, odd and even." Plato's writings offer the following proposition (*Stanford Encyclopedia of Philosophy* 2017[3]):

> The world that appears to our senses is in some way defective and filled with error, but there is a more real and perfect realm, populated by entities (called "forms" or "ideas") that are eternal, changeless, and in some sense paradigmatic for the structure and character of the world presented to our senses. Among the most important of these abstract objects . . . are goodness, beauty, equality, bigness, likeness, unity, being, sameness, difference, change, and changelessness.

Scholars recognize that defining "good" is tricky and may even be impossible (Rosati 2008:319–320). In an article discussing Ayurvedic medicine, Joseph S. Alter (1999:S43) points out that "the basic idea of all medicine is to fix what goes wrong so as to get back to a predetermined state of good health." But, he asks, what is "good health"? Alter describes how remedial medical systems typically perceive of human beings as starting healthy, becoming ill, and then being treated with medicine in an effort to become healthy again. He argues that Ayurvedic physiology, in contrast, includes a view of the creation of the universe and beginning of human life as triggering imbalance; in other words, human beings are born "unhealthy"

(Alter 1999:S47). Views of healing subsequently may differ. Are people returning to a previous state of existence, or seeking a theoretical ideal state? For Plato, "the form of good . . . is described as something of a mystery whose real nature is elusive and as yet unknown to anyone at all (*Republic*)" (*Stanford Encyclopedia of Philosophy* 2017). Connie Rosati (2008:317) highlights the pull of "common sense"; she asks, "after all, what could be more obviously true than that things can be good or bad, not merely in an absolute sense, but *for us*?" Yet she also points out that there may be differences between a perspective exclusive to an individual versus an absolute good (2008:317, also 314). Furthermore, she suggests that perhaps "actions are never right simply but always right in relation to a context and an agent at a time" (Rosati 2008:344, footnote 79).

In working with individuals and communities, we must seek to learn about local people's perspectives on what is good. Martin Luther King Jr., Nelson Mandela, and Julius Nyerere provide examples of leaders who offered visions for alternative worlds and alternative relationships defined against oppressive and colonial structures. *Buen vivir* offers one example of a movement currently shaping South American political and economic life, based on local perceptions of a good or ideal life. Writing about the *buen vivir* movement, Raúl Alcoreza (2013:145) points out that South American indigenous languages had no equivalent term for "development" or "progress" that shared the Western idea of growth through material possessions. Adopted in the Constitutions of Bolivia and Ecuador as a government objective, the alternative concept *buen vivir* is described by Alcoreza (2013:147; see also 148–149) as "inspired by the indigenous ideal of a harmonious relationship between living beings that ensures diversity, life and the equality of redistribution." Alcoreza (2013:145) comments that "there are fundamental differences between various indigenous languages, but they all share a concept of an *ideal life*."[4]

There is a final level of complexity: sometimes what people identify as good may not actually be the best indicator of good. In a 2015 TED talk, Robert Waldinger, director of the Harvard Study of Adult Development, drew on a 75-year-long study tracking people's development in order to answer the question "What Makes a Good Life?" Waldinger reports that while many people identify money and fame and high achievement as life goals, research shows that good relationships are what lead to happier, healthier lives. He encourages people to "lean in" to relationships, and concludes his TED talk by stating that "the good life is built with good relationships" (Waldinger 2015).

Despite the complexities surrounding concepts of good, we engage with communities believing that most people prefer health to sickness, peace to war, love to hate, hope to despair, gain to loss, and freedom to slavery. We know that increasing these elements will look different in each community, thus we encourage local agency at every step. We hope that the output from this Guide will include not only community arts initiatives but also a broader, more diverse, and more thoughtful understanding of how individuals and communities conceptualize a "good" or "better" life, an understanding built in deep discussion with community members about their perspectives and their visions.

Artistic Vitality and Endangerment

Any "better life" resulting from purposeful artistic activity requires artistic resources. Like the rapidly increasing number of endangered languages (see www.endangeredlanguages.com), more and more such resources are experiencing decline (see Grant 2014; Harris 2017; Schippers and Grant 2016; Schrag 2015b). The amount of scholarship and activity devoted to increasing the health of communities' artistry is growing, some of which we have outlined in Closing 7. We see our approach as complementing these efforts. The Make Arts process starts with a community, exploring how its unique set of artistic genres could be used to meet its unique needs. In contrast, the approaches in Closing 7 start with artistic genres, evaluating and exploring how they might become more resilient.

What Are Arts?

In this Guide, we treat the arts as special kinds of communication. Like all communication systems, the arts are connected to particular times, places, and social contexts. They have their own symbols, grammars, and internal structures. This means that just as you have to learn how to ask directions in a language foreign to you, you must also learn how to move your arms and neck and eyebrows to tell a story in Thai dance. There is no single artistic language that communicates completely across lines of time, place, and culture. Thus, to understand any art form, you have to interact with its practitioners and study it. Getting to know local artists and their arts is an arts advocate's first job.

Artistic and other kinds of communication share common origins in human neurobiology. But artistic forms stand out in several important ways. First, artistic communication places greater emphasis on manipulating form than do everyday interactions. Poetic speech, for example, may rely on patterns of sound and thought like rhyme, assonance, and metaphor that a simple exchange of information will not. Circling a drum while repeating a sequence of foot movements relies on form more heavily than simply walking from one place to another. Adopting the facial expressions of a mythical character draws on form to communicate more than allowing a person's face to remain at rest.

Second, the arts reveal their uniqueness as bounded spheres of interaction. Artistic events have beginnings and endings (no matter how fluid), between which people interact in unusually patterned ways. Ethnomusicologist Ruth Stone (1979:37) describes artistic events as "set off and made distinct from the natural world of everyday life by the participants."

In this Guide we help you—the readers—use these and other characteristics to discover and describe the artistic communication genres in any community you enter, including your own. We keep our discovery parameters broad so that we do not inadvertently miss an important kind of communication that does not fit our existing categories. Thus our view of an artistic act might refer to a concert of Spanish *flamenco*, rehearsals for a Broadway musical, a painting hanging on a café wall, a father speaking a proverb to his daughter, or rhythmic wailing at a grave-site. There are tens of thousands of kinds of artistic communication that people use around the world, an amazing and too often undervalued resource.

How Do Arts and Culture Interact?

The arts may both reflect and influence the cultures in which they exist. Artistic communication reflects the shape of other aspects of culture because it is interwoven with the rest of life. Members of Kaluli society in Papua New Guinea, for example, have a metaphor, "lift-up-over-sounding," that is revealed in several aspects of their lives. This idea underlies music-making in which two singers will alternate in taking the lead role, producing interweaving layers of sound. A similar phenomenon occurs in Kaluli conversation when people "interrupt" each other—they are co-creating, lifting-up-over together. Hence musical form here reflects a more widespread Kaluli communication pattern (Feld 1984).

Artistic communication, however, can also effect change in cultures because of its unique ability to motivate people to action, inspire feelings of solidarity, and provide socially acceptable space to disagree. As an example, women in the African Apostolic Church in southern Africa are able to symbolically take hold of time in a worship service in order to communicate their grievances against men. While they are not allowed to preach to a congregation, women may interrupt a sermon with a song containing lyrics such as these: "Men, stop beating your wives. Only then will you go to heaven." Women-led songs provide symbolic protection for their critical content (Bennetta 1985). Artistic communication has the power to change other parts of culture. Arts may also strengthen existing power structures. National anthems are clear examples of this.

What Is Creativity?

Since the purpose of this Guide is to help you work with communities to spark artistic creativity that feeds into better lives for people, it is essential to understand what creativity is and how it works. Central to an understanding of creativity is the idea of newness. Although everything flows in some way from something that already exists, an idea, painting, rap, or tea ceremony must somehow contrast with other examples of the same thing to be an example of creativity. Many scholars also suggest that for an idea or act to be creative, it must be useful in some way, as in solving a problem or meeting an individual need (Plucker et al. 2004:90; Sternberg and Lubart 1999). Beyond these generalizations, however, how people talk and think about artistic creativity reveals no universally agreed-upon definition. Greek philosophers like Plato thought painters imitated reality, making nothing new (Tatarkiewicz 1980:244). Descartes developed his "I think, therefore I am" philosophy by rejecting all previous thought, whereas Indian thinker Shankara produced his Vedanta philosophy by carefully referencing previous writings (Albert and Runco 2010; "Creativity in the Arts and Sciences" 2015). Europeans and North Americans began studying creativity in earnest in the mid-1900s, focusing on exceptional individuals and psychological processes (Sternberg and Lubart 1999; Wallas 2014), whereas recent Chinese creativy research emphasizes influencing social progress (Niu and Sternberg 2006). In fact, many—perhaps most—languages contain neither words nor concepts corresponding to the semantic range of "creativity" in English (cf. Mpofu et al. 2006:465; Mpofu et al. 2017).

Creativity Flows from Human Nature

Because we want you to have the capacity to enter into the creative processes of any community you encounter, we use an approach that reaches *behind* how people talk and think about these concepts. We identify three drives that undergird the use of patterns and symbols by all humans, then outline ways to discover the unique aspects of each community's creativity.

First, people interact with their environments. Piaget called babies "little scientists" because they explore, and they do things to objects around them to see what happens (Brewer et al. 1998). If healthy, humans *do* things. Second, it is basic human nature to communicate with others. Researchers are connecting people's sociability more and more to neurological and cognitive structures that exist in our brains from before birth (Adolphs 2003; Delton and Sell 2014; Frith 2013; Saucier et al. 2014). Babies are born with complex social concepts in their minds, ready to connect with others. These concepts are refined and expanded through sensory and symbolic interactions with their communities. Pinker describes this common human urge as *The Language Instinct* (1994). The third drive that feeds into creativity is the human attraction to novelty. Since the 1970s, psychologists have used the fact that babies become bored with a repeated visual or auditory stimulus to explore infant cognition. For example, if you want to know if a baby distinguishes between blue and green, show her a blue object, then a series of objects that become slightly greener until she starts sucking hard; vigorous sucking indicates excitement at a new sensory experience (Colombo and Bundy 1983; Franken 1993:396; Roder et al. 2000). Babies attend to the unexpected. As we grow into children and adults, we experience pleasure in novelty in myriad contexts, as when the musical structure of a song sets up expectations, then resolves them in unexpected ways (Jourdain 2008; Levitin 2007). That said, we may not all agree on what constitutes novelty. Discussing musical change, John Blacking (1977:2) reminds us that concepts of change are humanly defined; people within a community decide whether musical features are perceived as part of their existing musical systems, or are perceived as part of a new system.

Human beings, then, are inherently predisposed to make things, to communicate within social systems, and to notice change. These predispositions get realized uniquely as every child experiences her world through all the senses, and learns or assigns meaning to each message. This leads to children developing capacity in particular structured symbolic systems, called languages. Languages are complex, consisting not only of words and grammar guiding simple conversations, but also in stylized forms that integrate melody, rhythm, and word play based on sound and thought patterns, color and shape, and pretending. These special types of language are heightened forms of communication, which we refer to as *artistic genres*. Others have noted the primordial nature of stylized kinds of language, as in *The Music Instinct* (Ball 2012) and *The Art Instinct* (Dutton 2009).

Creativity Flows with Traditions

Every community develops traditions of communicating through artistic genres, and traditions are never static. Tradition is not a fixed body of ideas and practices, but something that is constantly being passed from one person to another, one generation to the next. And every act of transmission introduces small or large changes. The French philosopher Paul Ricoeur describes tradition as "the living transmission of an innovation always capable of being reactivated by a return to the most creative moments of poetic activity. . . . [A] tradition is constituted by the interplay of innovation and sedimentation" (Ricoeur 1984:68; see also Ranger and Hobsbawm 2012).

Traditions, then, are living things. Newness comes through the fluid nature of communication with ever-changing cognitive categories, neural networks, social and physical environments, and our natural attraction to novelty. Thus whenever someone emits a bit of communication that flows from an artistic genre, it is not exactly the same bit as anything anyone has ever emitted before. Each community and individual attaches a different meaning and value to each emission, so we must use a definition and model that accounts for and provides insights into what is produced *within* its unique social context. Also bear in mind, however, that individual artists or members of communities determine how much novelty is desired or allowed. In some cases, community members may identify aspects of artistic genres that are allowed more or less innovation (a master Ewe drummer versus an accompanying bell player), or may identify types of genres in which elements of permanence are important and change is discouraged (for example, in order to retain a connection to historical practices, or for ritualistic purposes). Sometimes permanence in artistic genres becomes particularly important when other aspects of life are unstable (see Impey 2002:19 for one example).

Two examples point to the wide range of ways in which people connect tradition and newness. First, in the Democratic Republic of Congo, Punayima Kanyama composes new songs in the Mono language in the *gbaguru* genre by choosing an existing song and fitting new lyrics. Because Mono melodies follow linguistic tone, the melody changes somewhat, but the accompanying harp ostinato, rhythm, and underlying melodic pattern remain the same (Schrag 1998).

Second, Juniper Hill (2012) discusses creativity with over 100 urban musicians, who described kinds of novelty ranging from "losing oneself in a character's role while singing an opera aria" to improvising bebop solos. The highest value for most of these artists was the level of individual agency they were able to exert.[5]

Creativity Flows through This Guide

We define creativity briefly as purposeful artistic novelty. In slightly expanded form, artistic creativity occurs when one or more people draw on their personal skills, the social patterns of their culture, and symbolic systems to produce an event or work of heightened communication that has not previously existed in its exact form. Thus to understand how people create in a culture, we have to find out who the creators are, what types of novelty they and others value, and what skills, knowledge, and techniques they need to produce something new. We also have to explore the limits that communities place on creativity, identifying the kinds and degrees of novelty they *do not* value. This Guide will help readers do this.

As we get to know particular artists and their communities, we will explore their creativity in two broad ways. First, we will identify the characteristics of actual performances and created objects in terms of the nature of their newness and purpose. How much innovation is internal to the enactment, and how much relates to its context? What are the actual features of the innovation? How did artists modify their processes to produce the newness? And what is the degree of change—barely significant, noticeable, or so extensive that the enactment seems to have no relationship to its genre? Second, we will explore people's concepts and values connected to newness and purpose: What do people perceive as new? How much and how do artists see their output as individual or communal effort? How much and how do communities see creativity as coming from geniuses making arts that may last forever, versus something that anyone can do? Kaufman and Beghetto (2009) call these focii "Big-C" and "Little-C," respectively.

Creativity's foundation in human nature feeds our expectation that every community we encounter creates. The fact that artistic genres emerge through multisensory social interaction helps us identify the features and meanings comprising every creative act. The fluidity and expectation of purpose for acts of creativity promise improved possibilities of reaching goals. And the interaction between individuals and communities in creative processes promises insight into how people can nurture creativity that will help and continue.

We try to assist readers to join local creators in their communities, sparking moments of purposeful artistic activity that have the capacity to effect positive change. Though not every artistic enactment needs to last a long time, we want the *act* of creating to endure so that a community can continue to make arts that help its members. Traditions endure when people are continually motivated to transmit them, with the social structures and resources to support their moments of creativity. Or, as food historian John Edge has said, "Tradition is innovation that succeeds" (2010). Understanding how a community creates increases the likelihood that we can help them generate arts that lead to a lasting, better life.

Finally, succeeding in the *Make Arts* process often requires communities to exercise creativity at a moral and social level, in which they imagine new ways of thinking about their problems and interactions with each other. To break out of cycles of violence, for example, peacebuilding expert John Paul Lederach (2005:173) argues that we must access creative capacity that "lies dormant, filled with potential that can give rise to unexpected blossoms that create turning points and sustain constructive change." And as John Schaar famously said, "The future is not someplace we are going to, but one we are creating. The paths to it are not found but created, and the activity of creating them changes both the maker and the destination" (as quoted in Edwards 2010:149).

The *Make Arts for a Better Life* Process

In its simplest form, this Guide is about conversations. We suggest that developing new arts initiatives should involve the following: meeting people within a community, talking with them about their arts and goals, and exploring together how they can use their arts to meet their goals (see Figure 0.1). Conversations like these can happen anywhere, anytime.

Hidden from this simplified view, however, lie complex interactions and activities that are unique to each community. We have unpacked these conversations for you, resulting in a flexible, replicable process of researching and creating local arts together, as represented in Figure 0.2. The knot in the middle represents an event containing artistic communication and is central to the entire process. This ensures that the community's efforts are grounded in a local reality, based on knowing artists and their arts in context. The artistic event serves as the focus for seven steps (see Figure 0.2):

1. *Meet* a community and its arts
2. *Specify* goals for a better life
3. *Connect* goals to genres
4. *Analyze* genres and events
5. *Spark* creativity

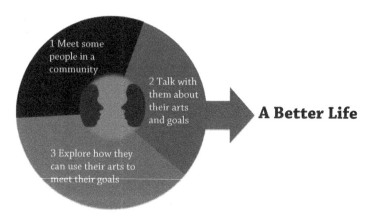

FIGURE 0.1. Conversations centered on local artistry.

FIGURE 0.2. The *Make Arts for a Better Life* process.

6. *Improve* results
7. *Celebrate* and integrate for continuity.

Finally, the words "research" and "relationship" sit under the representation of the artistic event, emphasizing that learning through relationships should be your primary posture.

The following is a quick description of each step of the process.

Step 1: Meet a Community and Its Arts

The *meet* component entails getting to know basic information about a community, first making relationships with people and listing the kinds of arts that run through the community. We draw on research methods from fields such as anthropology, ethnography of communication, and performance studies to help you get to know the community. However, most of those fancy research methods ultimately boil down to building relationships with other human beings.

Step 2: Specify Goals for a Better Life

Which goals does the community you are collaborating with want to work toward at this time? In the Guide, we consider three categories of potential goals: identity and sustainability, health and well-being, and human rights. We recognize that these are broad and sometimes contested terms, and we include discussion of how we understand them in later sections of this Guide. But the Guide is just a beginning—community members will have their own ideas, dreams, and goals.

Step 3: Connect Goals to Genres

Once the community has chosen a goal, you can together decide which combination of effects, art forms, content, and events would likely feed into that goal.

Step 4: Analyze Genres and Events

Creating something in an existing artistic genre for new purposes requires a great deal of knowledge, skill, and wisdom. You will notice that the bulk of this Guide is dedicated to *Step 4*, because it is so easy to assume we understand something, even though our understanding is based on superficial knowledge. We help you get to the details of art forms and their meanings so that you and the community can identify the elements that will have the most impact.

Step 5: Spark Creativity

A person sparks creativity by performing an act that results in a new bit of artistry coming into existence. This can be as simple as suggesting that someone carve a new mask or compose a new song for a celebration, or it may require more complex and time-consuming activities, like workshops, commissioning, apprenticeship, festivals, or developing a new version of an existing ritual or ceremony. In whatever activity is chosen, make sure to include all of the people who have an interest in or control over how new works will be integrated into the community.

Step 6: Improve Results

Evaluation is essential to the co-creative process because we want communities to integrate creativity into their lives that truly results in them meeting their spiritual, social, and physical goals. Evaluation according to agreed-upon criteria helps them make their artistic communication more effective.

Step 7: Celebrate and Integrate for Continuity

Our desire is that communities will increasingly integrate creativity into their daily, weekly, monthly, and yearly lives. To do this, they need to teach newly created artworks to others and to plan for people to keep creating. This means that, at the simplest level, sparking activities like workshops or commissioning should include times to teach new works to other people in attendance. They should also include time to plan for teaching the new works and skills to wider audiences in the future. It may be good to first teach or show them to a small group and receive feedback to evaluative questions before presenting the works to a larger group.

Two Case Studies

To help demonstrate how these steps form part of real-life projects, we would like to share two case studies: one from Uganda and the other from the United States.

The first case study, from Yasuko Harada, offers an example of how the arts have been involved in conflict resolution and in post-conflict healing, both personal and communal, specifically in Uganda. Based on research in Acholiland in 2012, Harada's description is included in the following (email communication, April 25, 2013; see also Harada 2012):

> In Acholiland, northern Uganda, a conflict lasting more than twenty years be-tween the government and the Lord's Resistance Army (LRA), a rebel group, resulted in a number of abducted child soldiers, torn families and internally displaced people, leaving the population with enormous physical and psy-chological distress and trauma. Performing arts, including music, dance and drama, have played important roles in the conflict-affected societies as part of the process of creating a better present and future, in particular for healing, advocating for peace, and achieving justice and reconciliation. During the conflict, local radio stations in Gulu, the central town, ran programs encour-aging the return of the rebels from the bush, playing songs by local artists which appealed to them to come back and calling for the end of the conflict. The radio programs successfully contributed to the return of some of the rebel members, most of whom had also been abducted. Some rebels risked their lives to escape from their bases, while others escaped during fighting between the government and the LRA. Local youth groups, then residing in the displaced people's camps, formed music groups and sang songs to call for the end of violence, using makeshift instruments such as food ration tins and metal spokes. The musical style is called *Aguma*, which was originally a social music event involving dancing and functioning as part of courtship. The performances were recorded and brought to peace talks between the gov-ernment and the LRA.
>
> In post-conflict Acholiland, non-governmental organizations and other stakeholders assisted with collecting individual accounts of war and identifying the concerns of communities at the grassroots level as part of

the transitional justice process. The voices of individuals were put together into drama and dance performances with participation of the community members, and staged in villages. Drama highlighted challenges faced by people in post-conflict situations, and provided opportunities for sharing the consequence of the war among the participants, including both perpetrators and victims of violence.

Dances, in particular traditional ones, are one of the most popular activities for the rehabilitation of the formerly abducted people. A number of rehabilitation centers in Acholiland have performing arts components, not only dances but music and drama, as part of their psycho-social programs. The participants say dance classes are something that they look forward to: they are social and interactive occasions, they allow participants to release their emotional stress and gain confidence, and they can also lead to economic success if participants are trained to become part of a dance troupe (funded by international donors and religious organizations, some participants perform in other parts of Uganda, East Africa, and overseas). Acholi people have expressed concern that their traditional dances had been lost during the conflict along with other elements of traditional culture, and resuscitating traditional culture has been emphasized as a recovery of pride and dignity of the people. These examples demonstrate the wide recognition of potentials and impacts of the use of performing arts in different phases of the conflict in Acholiland.

Several aspects of the *Make Arts* process can be seen in this Acholiland example:

- As Harada describes in the preceding case study, the arts have been used to meet various aims in Acholiland. Community members have had a critical role in *specifying goals* (such as calling for an end to violence), as well as in creating the artistic works (songs in displaced people's camps, radio broadcasts, and dance and drama productions).
- A variety of stakeholders were involved in or witnessed the artistic processes: community members, including both perpetrators and victims of violence; government and LRA leaders; and external funders. To meet the aims of the performances, each of these stakeholders— whether creators and storytellers, listeners, or financial supporters— needed to be considered. Who knew the local arts and could create performances for new purposes? Who needed to listen to the stories told through the arts? Who had the power to change the circumstances in the communities (soldiers to leave the conflict, performers to broadcast messages, LRA and government leaders to reach a peace deal, etc.).

- *Knowledge of local arts* by community members meant that *older styles such as Aguma could be used in new ways, to meet new needs.* The resulting performances both reaffirmed tradition and identity, and also promoted a better life for individual community members healing from their experiences and for the communities as a whole.
- Harada suggests that ensuring *continuity* presents a challenge due to financial and management challenges within communities. Here, community members as well as other stakeholders and arts advocates may be able to dialogue about ways in which to promote artistic sustainability within the communities in order to ensure that the future of the arts does not depend upon external partners. Possibilities include minimizing the cost of performances when possible, sharing resources among community arts groups through informal or formal sharing schemes, seeking recompense for performances when possible, and investigating other local sources of funding. These are big challenges, and certainly are not exclusive to Acholiland.

The second case study offers an example of how the arts can address issues of health and well-being, enabling people to come to terms with illness and move forward positively. In 2008, Brian received news that would change his life: like his grandfather and his mother, he too carries the genetic mutation for Huntington's Disease (HD).

Brian responded to this change through creativity (see Schrag 2015a). His responses included the following:

- He composed the song "Leaves," for his mother, incorporating a gospel song and referencing memories that he shares with his mother in order to encourage her by reminding her of important relationships she has and of her Christian faith.
- He became active in the Huntington's Disease Society of America (HDSA), initially through his local Dallas/Fort Worth support group and also at national conferences.
- In response to experiences described in his support group, he composed the song "HD Blues," with a humorous, empowering take on living with HD. The most visible signs of HD are uncontrolled motor movements, which can lead people to appear drunk. One woman in Brian's support group had twice been accosted by police for public drunkenness: once in front of her house, and another time with her children at the park. "HD Blues" contains this imagined encounter: "No

sir, officer, I am not drunk. I suffer from a genetic progressive neu-
rodegenerative disease causing gradual deterioration of movement,
cognitive function, emotional control, blurring of social boundaries,
and inherited in an autosomal dominant pattern. . . . Are we good?"
To see a video of this performance, go to https://www.youtube.com/
watch?v=BWajNkvnOEs.

- Along with this song, Brian has designed and distributed a T-Shirt with
the lyrics of "HD Blues," as shown in Figure 0.3.
- He has told his story and performed his songs at local, national, and international conferences and events, including in 2015 in Limerick for the HD
Association of Ireland.
- He developed a workbook to help promote creativity among other people
affected by HD.
- He created two websites: www.MakeLifeHD.org and http://www.hdblues.
org/.

Brian's actions demonstrate multiple aspects of the *Make Arts* process, including
the following:

- *Meeting* the HD community was an organic affair. Brian knew about HD
from personal and family experience, but he also listened to the stories of

FIGURE 0.3. "HD Blues" T-shirts.

other people impacted by HD. Getting to know the community meant becoming part of a local support group and later becoming active in national and international networks.

- Brian *identified the goals, determined plans,* and *developed the creative products* himself. However, his creative works were in direct response to needs that he saw or that were communicated to him. The song "Leaves" incorporated musical forms and symbolism which he knew held meaning for his mother, and through the song he sought to encourage her by highlighting relationships that were valuable to her. While a moving song to any listener, its meaning is directed to and will be felt most deeply by his mother. "HD Blues" uses a musical form with which Brian is comfortable but which also will hold meaning for a broader community; especially in the southern United States, where Brian first performed this song, people will know the history of the blues and the challenges but also the resilience that these songs reference. Furthermore, the narrative in the song and the text of the T-shirt provide audible and visible forms of resistance, both to a sense of hopelessness and to a public that may misunderstand and stigmatize people affected by HD.
- By speaking, performing, and distributing a workbook to people affected by HD, Brian is *sparking further creativity*. Furthermore, Brian uses workshops to encourage others to try creating artistic works. For example, at his workshop in Ireland, Brian asked all participants to write down artistic skills that they or someone they knew had; moreover, he asked them to think about how these people could use these skills to create something for someone affected by HD. He also asked a volunteer to name some activities that he enjoyed, and then asked two others to write a limerick for that person referencing those activities. Despite their initial worry about this responsibility, the writers managed in a short time to write a humorous limerick to present to the volunteer.
- Finally, in his workshops and through his websites, Brian encourages feedback and additional stories, so that he can continue to think about *how to improve* his work.

Negative Impact and Conflict in Communities

We want communities all over the world to use this Guide to enhance their lives. However, agreement on the goals that constitute enhancement is notoriously rare. A single individual, following his or her own goals, can instigate brutality far beyond what most of us could imagine—take Joseph Kony of the Lord's Resistance Army in Uganda, for example. Indeed, the histories of interventions by anthropologists, development agencies, religious leaders, national governments, rival factions within ethnolinguistic communities, and others are rife with conflicting aims, methods, failures, and atrocities.

The call for papers for the British Forum for Ethnomusicology's 2010 conference on "The Impact of Ethnomusicology" urged attention to, among other questions (Cottrell 2011:230): "Is ethnomusicological impact usually positive— or at least benign—or are there clear instances of negative consequences? How might one construe the negative impact of ethnomusicology, and should such work necessarily be avoided?" In introducing a set of short papers from the conference and subsequently printed in a 2011 issue of the journal *Ethnomusicology Forum*, Stephen Cottrell gives a number of examples from the work of ethnomusicologists. For example, does promoting one particular music or musician "[risk] upsetting the delicate eco-systems that sustain fragile traditions," and does engaging in AIDS prevention work "[replicate] precisely those colonial relationships we thought we had left behind" (Cottrell 2011:230; see *Ethnomusicology Forum* 20[2], 2011, for the collection of short papers on the impact of ethnomusicology)?

While the preceding examples may be somewhat debatable in terms of impact, there are clear examples of negative impact of applied work. The effects of outside researchers on the Yanomamö in South America, for instance, have drawn worldwide attention through scandalous books, professional reviews, and documentary film (see, for example, Dreger 2011 and Padilha 2010). Muriel Reigersberg (2011) highlights the negative experiences historically in Australia from anthropology, missions, colonialism, and Western capitalism. She reports, for example, that choral singing was used historically in Australia to devalue Indigenous pre-colonial culture and "ridicule the elders who practised traditional initiation customs" (Reigersberg 2011:256, 260). As a result, funding bodies such the Australian Institute of Aboriginal and Torres Strait Islander Studies (AIATSIS) today are careful to review proposals for additional work. The AIATSIS (2000, as quoted in Reigersberg 2011:257) includes the following ethical guideline, among others: "Indigenous communities and individuals have a right to be involved in any research project focused upon them and their culture." According to Reigersberg (2011:257), projects "that actively encourage a positive image of Aboriginality and Aboriginal culture, or initiatives that develop Indigenous leadership, fulfill an Indigenously specified need, and respect local Indigenous knowledge and systems of knowledge production, are more likely to attract funding."

Hofman (2010:23) describes recent understandings of fieldwork as "interactive and dialogic." She highlights Jeff Todd Titon's definition of fieldwork as "knowing people making music" (Titon 1997:91), and stresses that such an approach presumes "respect, equality and reciprocity among the research participants" (Hofman 2010:23). This is also the approach proposed in this Guide; newly developing projects should be underpinned by respect, with all participants able to voice opinions and contribute. John Drummond has argued that part of the work of ethnomusicologists must be to empower communities. According to Drummond, "The help that we give in terms of preserving the past and tradition of a culture is often very useful, but it's no use unless it's given back to the culture to use, so that members of the culture can learn how to use that and renew their own culture in their own way" (Schippers 2010:157). Whether arts advocates are working with communities to help sustain older traditions or are involved in efforts to create fusions or new arts, it is worth keeping Drummond's advice in mind. Arts advocates hopefully can contribute in positive ways to help meet community goals, but they should also be working their way out of their jobs; ideally, community members will gain the same skills through collaborations with arts advocates so that they can continue refining projects and developing new programs as desired.

Such approaches should help prevent potential conflicts that could arise from having researchers (who may or may not be community insiders) or people with greater power and status within communities direct the course of projects without consideration of the interests and needs of other community members.[6] However, conflict can occur also within communities, as not all people will necessarily agree on what issues to address, how to address them, and whether the effects of interventions have been positive or negative. For example, some people praise Christian missionaries in Hawai'i for their roles in helping Hawiian flourish as an oral and written language by the 1890s; others note how many of those same missionaries' descendants became outrageously wealthy and outlawed the Hawaiian language in 1896 ('Aha Pūnana Leo 2016).

Klisala Harrison and Svanibor Pettan (2010:6) remind us that "views and ambitions may differ widely on the basis of intergenerational differences, genders and power structures, or due to differences of personal value and opinion." Furthermore, as is evident in Britta Sweers's 2010 discussion of an applied media project in former East Germany (e.g., 2010:219), producers, sponsors, critics, and audience members may have varying agendas and views. In addition, artists from within particular geographic communities may not be accepted by other people in those communities if they do not share other characteristics such as religion (Sweers 2010:220). Harrison and Pettan also assert that people may have differing opinions on what constitutes music worth safeguarding (to this we could add, issues worth addressing through the arts, and which arts to use for such programs) and how to measure the success of programs. This can create a tricky situation for all involved in developing new programs. From the perspective of an arts advocate, this means that "establishing what can be done with and for a community requires great sensitivity, rigorous research as well as reflection, and dialogue with various stakeholders in any music culture" (Harrison and Pettan 2010:6).

It is critical to keep these issues in mind when working on applied projects. However, it is also important to remember that communities can benefit from well-researched, well-planned projects. In her discussion of work with the Hopevale Community Choir, Reigersberg argues that challenges should not deter scholars from engaging in applied work. Concluding a report about the choir, she emphasizes, "I can report that they are still singing and that for the third time running, they have been engaged by the Queensland Music Festival to represent local indigenous culture" (Reigersberg 2010:71). Sydney Hutchinson (2003:87), in turn, describes a folklorists' roundtable in New York. She explains that participants were invited to bring community scholars along as guests. One guest was a leader of the Indo-Caribbean community in Queens. Hutchinson writes, "After [the leader] had sat through several sessions of papers and discussions, he spoke up: 'I don't know why you people are always whining and worrying. You are *helping* us! You should be happy!'" (original emphasis).

How to use this Guide

A Flexible Framework

We have organized the *Make Arts* process as numbered steps because each flows logically into the next. However, although you and the community might plan these activities in this order, they often will not happen that way. In fact, each step might reveal a need for doing more of one of the others, because each is related to all. For example, to *improve* a newly crafted story, the community may need to go back and do more research on the poetic features of highly regarded local stories, using guides in the *analyze* step (*Step 4*). Ideally, you and the community are trying ideas, learning from what happens, doing more research, trying again, and so on and so on. Act and reflect. Reflect and act. This pattern results in healthy, growing creativity. Think of the steps as a reliable, solid framework you can refer to, but not one that is etched in stone.

Another caveat to this ordered presentation is that some steps include elements of other steps. We will describe some activities in *Step 5* that spark the creation of new works that are bundles of several steps. A workshop to produce woven cloth with proverbial marriage advice, for example, may include *analyzing, sparking, improving,* and *integrating.* As another example, the activity "Help Organize a Festival Celebrating Community Art Forms" includes a larger group in examining and choosing which of their art forms to celebrate—regardless of what genre(s) you choose in *Step 3.* Our emphasis is not on rigidly defining and requiring separate steps, but rather on helping a community make sure that they have considered each component as they have developed arts initiatives.

You will notice a few activities that have "First Glance" in the title. Because artistic communication is maddeningly complex, it sometimes feels impossible to know how to start. The "First Glance" tools are designed to give you a relatively quick grasp of the most important elements of a task. We then show you how to go deeper.

We also include numerous practical activities to help you research local arts and develop arts programs. Visual icons throughout the Guide will help you locate these activities.

If You Do Not Have Much Time

Insights from academic fields like ethnomusicology, performance studies, anthropology, linguistics, and neuroscience show that we can understand the important patterns of human artistic communication. However, every community and its artistic forms of communication represent an unfathomable degree of complexity and variation. Even the most accomplished master of an art form can learn more and increase his or her skills. To make matters more difficult, the physical and social contexts of these communities are in a constant state of change, sometimes dramatically. Because of these complexities, our interactions with communities often are more like explorations and adventures than scientific processes. In short, there is no way you could fully perform all of the activities we describe in this Guide in a definitive way for just one art form, even if you had nothing else ever to do. We recommend that you use this Guide to sharpen and broaden your understanding of artistic communication, but do not feel that you have to complete each activity. Follow the streams of exploration and creating together that seem most relevant and fruitful.

It may also be useful to think about some arts activities that you can start without much preparation. These will get you going and will feed into more complete actions that you may do when you have more time. It may help to think about natural connections you may have with local artists. One connection could be that you are intrigued by a particular art form—you just like it. Or you may have experience or skills related to one of the art forms, such as dance or weaving. Or you may have a personal affinity with a practitioner of an art form.

⚙ Simple Arts Engagement Activities

- Perform part of the "Take a First Glance at a Community's Arts" activity in *Step 1*.
- Attend artistic events and describe them briefly in a notebook.
- Make lists of types of song, dance, drama, visual storytelling, or proverbs.
- Collect instruments.
- Transcribe song texts.
- Do language and culture learning with artists. Spend relaxed social time with them.
- Make systematic audio- or videorecordings of an art form according to song categories, composer, events in a village, or proverbs.
- Learn to play an instrument, sing, dance, act, weave, or tell a story in a local genre.

Some Issues to Discuss with Local Friends and Colleagues

- How did the kinds of arts in the community come about? Who created the things people use or perform?
- What are people's general attitudes toward people involved in different local art forms? Positive? Negative?
- Are there parts of a performance that have special symbolic significance? For example, particular colors, shapes, instruments, or clothes?
- How does the way people do local art forms now differ from how they did them in the past? Are young people learning how to do them? How does someone get good at them? How is good defined?
- Are there certain art forms that only men or only women can do?
- How do people feel when they are involved in different local art forms? Do they ever enter into ecstatic states?
- How are local art forms connected to religious beliefs?
- Are there any taboos related to particular arts?

Notes

1. Definitions of the term "sustainable" will be considered in *Step 2* of the Guide.

2. See also in *Step 6*, "How Do We Assess a Product?"

3. *The Stanford Encyclopedia of Philosophy* (2017) offers a useful bibliography of additional resources on Plato's philosophies.

4. Undergraduates at the University of Florida, Gainesville, are required to take a course called "What Is the Good Life?" (Andrew Noss, personal correspondence, July 15, 2017). Here, too, the emphasis is not on a universal good: students at the University of Florida are encouraged to consider "how different people from different societies across time conceptualize the good life, what meaning and value individuals ascribe to the lives that they live or want to live, and what are the choices, costs, and benefits of the good life" ("IUF 1000: What Is the Good Life" 2018).

5. John Blacking (1977, 1986) discusses concepts of musical change and non-change, critiquing scholars who have focused on musical products rather than musical processes. He defines musical change as involving significant changes to musical systems, and "not simply musical consequences of social, political, economic, or other changes" in communities (Blacking 1977:2). Again, however, he also reminds us that people within communities have their own concepts of change (Blacking 1977:2).

6. The *Barefoot Guide to Working with Organisations and Social Change* (Barefoot Collective 2009) offers a practical discussion about building relationships and types of power. This discussion is aimed especially at practitioners in organizations focused on social change but is also useful more broadly. See especially Chapter 3, "People to People: Creating and Working with Relationships in Organisations" (2009:47–64).

Steps

Step

1

MEET A COMMUNITY AND ITS ARTS

ALL ARTISTIC ACTION exists in the context of more than one person. However original or individual a person's artwork, his or her artistic creativity at some point references and depends on others. In *Step 1*, we guide you through a process of initial discovery and description of a community and its arts. We will help you:

- think about what a community is;
- choose a community and start a Community Arts Profile;
- take a first glance at a community;
- take a first glance at a community's arts;
- start exploring a community's social and conceptual life; and
- prepare to use research methods to learn more.

Think about What a Community Is

"Community" is used popularly to refer to a group of people connected to each other in a wide variety of ways, often evoking positive sentiments such as warmth and solidarity. The term is also used by many organizations dedicated to people's well-being, development, and education (Minkler et al. 2008; Rovai 2002; Wates 2014). Building on both common usage and this literature, we define a community as a group of people that shares a story, identity, and ongoing patterns of interaction, and that is constantly in flux. As we describe each characteristic, think about how it relates to a community you know.

Community Members Share a Story

No group of people exists in more than one point in time, but each sees itself as part of a larger story, a history. On any given day, people may refer to events, characters, ideas, and dramatic elements that have occurred over multiple generations, or that took place much more recently. This shared story provides continuity connections between the past, the present, and an imagined future—and provides impetus to keep gathering.

Community Members Share an Identity

People know they are connected by recognizing and valuing common points of reference in each other. Identity markers tie people in a community together and distinguish them from others. Their shared story may provide a primary marker of this common identity. Other signs of a common identity could include a particular spoken language or accent, food, manner of dress, skills, religion, ideology, geographical location, enemies or allies, taboos, or shared needs and struggles. Artistic forms of communication often provide and reflect key points of identity.

Community Members Share Ongoing Patterns of Interaction

People in a community communicate with each other in patterned ways, times, and places. Contexts for communication may include the following: within a family's living quarters; at meetings designed for rituals, sports, politics, or courtship; during periods of work, business, or education; and at festivals, celebrations, or entertainment. The communication could be face to face, body to body, or may be mediated through radio, telephones, the Internet, or other electronic audiovisual means. Success may be dependent on being geographically close, or proximity may be irrelevant. Whatever the contexts or media, communities depend on common systems of meaning to facilitate comprehension and impact. These systems include, for example, spoken and signed languages, visual and video symbolism, and movement and tactile sign patterns.

Communities Are Not Necessarily What You Think

Although we have been talking about communities almost as static, coherent objects, they are not. They are composed of individuals who each make their own decisions, enter and leave the community, and respond to external and internal factors differently. Every community has internal variation and changes over time. So beware of saying things such as, "Community X tells stories like this." It may be true for a majority of the group today, but some people may be advocating for a different kind of storytelling. In five years, things may be very different. The bottom line is that every community displays both continuity and change, internal coherence and diversity.

Communities in This Guide

The initial spark for this Guide came from a desire to engage better with communities that have strong ethnolinguistic identities and modes of communication; they represent some of the richest, most undervalued, and most endangered artistic traditions on Earth. This remains an important focus. However, the world is urbanizing and globalizing, leading to more and more communities made up of people from more than one culture, glued together by diverse interests. For this reason, we will also provide guidance for working with artists in multicultural groups. Most of the Guide applies equally well to communities marked by significant stability and unity, and to those negotiating with multiple cultures.

Define the Community and Start a Community Arts Profile

Where do you keep what you know? We all store thoughts, facts, feelings, skills, experiences, stories, and smells in our brains and bodies as memories. When we need to drive a car, greet a friend, or dance at a wedding, we call on what we have learned to know what to do. This kind of storage is indispensable to life and artistic action. But memories in the mind and body fade and clutter. Written and recorded data provide a crucial, though imperfect, remedy to this natural loss, especially as you are learning about arts that are new to you. We have developed a tool to help you keep track of what you are learning, called a Community Arts Profile .

A Community Arts Profile is one way for you to gather everything you and the community learn about its arts. It may be in the form of word-processed documents, a database, a website, or a notebook. We have created the outline of such a Profile in .rtf format that you can use. In reality, almost everything you and the community do while creating together will lead to new insights into how a type of artistic activity functions, its meanings, and its place in society; we encourage you to capture as much of this as possible in the Community Arts Profile. This information will prove invaluable when planning co-creative activities, sparking creativity, evaluating artistic output, and integrating the arts into the community.

Our hope is that you will add to and draw from the Community Arts Profile as long as you interact with the community it describes. Open "Community Arts Profile READ ME.rtf" to get started (see companion website and Closing 2).

Take a First Glance at a Community E P R

The Community Arts Profile includes a place to record the first bits of information you gather about a community, including its geographical location(s), language(s), important identity markers, and modes of communication.[1]

From this starting point, you and community members together can decide the scope of your activities. Your scope could be very narrow, restricted to one clan in a village or one multilingual neighborhood in a city, for example. Or it could be very broad, such as everyone who speaks a particular language in a region. "Scope" also refers to how detailed your descriptions will be: you may describe artistic communication from a close-up view (zoomed in), from far away (zoomed out), or somewhere in between.

Questions to Ask

- Where is the community and how many members are there? This includes basic information like village or town, province, and nation. It is likely that community members live in more than one geographical location. It could be that they think of themselves as historically connected to a geographical center, with diaspora in other places.
- What ties the community together? Answers could include factors like language, geography, ethnic identity, and social structure.
- How do they communicate with each other and how often? This question points to languages and modes of communication such as these: face to face, telephone, and electronic social media. It may be that they have frequent face-to-face communication with those nearby but also make regular trips to visit members who live farther away.
- How do they share their artistic creations? This question points to both face-to-face and electronic sharing, cassettes, compact discs, DVDs, cell phones, Internet sites, written notation, or other means.
- How did they get there? Identify important historical events and patterns that have brought the community to its geographical location and have affected its identity.

Opportunities to Ask Questions

Whenever possible, ask these questions of friends, leaders, and other contacts from the community. You can also ask them to point you to other people and resources where you can learn more. In addition, remember that the nearer you live to a community, the more opportunities you will have to learn more.

You can also learn a great deal by reading or watching how members of the community have presented themselves in books, articles, videos, recordings, and other media. Then see how others have described the community through academic research, encyclopedias, or more popular presentations.

Take a First Glance at a Community's Arts E P R

A core feature of our approach is that we help communities create from artistic resources that they already possess. For that reason, one of our first tasks is to list these artistic genres. We will show you how to make a quick survey, then provide two approaches for making it more complete: "outside-in" and "inside-out." You can also develop an Initial Community Arts List (ICAL) by following the process outlined in two files on our website: "ICAL Guide to Making an Initial Community Arts List" and "ICAL Initial Community Arts List for COMMUNITY."

Make a Quick List of Artistic Genres

A productive way to come up with a list of these kinds of communication is to gather a few people together and ask them questions such as the following:

- When do people in this community sing? Play instruments? Dance? Tell stories? Act? Carve? Paint? Use their bodies in unique ways? Play games? Build special structures? Remember that each culture divides up and talks about its forms of artistic communication in unique ways, so learn their vocabulary.
- Do people in this community do anything special surrounding the birth of a child? Someone's death? Someone's passage from childhood to adulthood? For each affirmative answer, ask them to describe what special things happen and make note of the arts involved.

As you list each event, jot down a few basic characteristics of its artistic forms of communication:

- a local name or brief description;
- kinds of people involved (men, women, youth, children, specialists, a particular socioeconomic group, etc.);
- when it is usually done (particular days, seasons, months, times of day, etc.);
- purposes of the genre;
- connotations of the enactments (fun, national or ethnic pride, fertility, religion, health, etc.);
- effects on participants (physical exertion, emotional responses, sense of solidarity, motivation to act, etc.);
- anything else that comes up immediately.

Start a Genre Comparison Chart (Figure 1.1), filling in as much as you know at the moment. You will use the information to help compare the appropriateness of each genre for particular purposes in *Step 3*.

Genre	Brief Description	Event	Participants	Connotations	Effects

FIGURE 1.1. Genre comparison chart.

Do not worry about getting all the details while you are making a survey; we will guide you through a much more detailed investigation in *Step 4*.

Extend the List from the Outside In: Discover Artistic Communication Acts by Researching Likely Social Contexts for Their Performance

In the "outside-in" approach, you begin with an anthropologist's knowledge that cultures often mark important events and transitions with artistically rendered communication. Use the following outline to help identify rituals and special events that exist in a community (modified from Chenoweth 1972). Then explore what arts might be associated with each.

Life-Cycle Events

- birth (birth announcement, lullaby)
- childhood (funny or nonsense games, teasing, taunting)
- puberty (girl's songs, boy's songs, initiation)
- courting (love, courting, proposal of marriage)
- marriage (wedding, men's events, women's events)
- death (funeral, burial, mourning).

Historical Events

- commemorative (disasters, honors, first outsiders, changes in leadership or government, first road, first vehicles, wars, etc.)
- legend (creation, mythology)
- local news.

Activities

- work (cutting timber, hunting, fishing, road making, etc.)
- fighting (preparation for battle, battle, victory, defeat, etc.)
- dancing (male, female, both sexes, social, ceremonial, solo, etc.)
- recreation
- worship.

Ceremonies

- magic (planting, harvesting, fertility, power, prophecy, etc.)
- social (greeting, farewell, wedding, funeral, completion of a special community project, etc.).

Nature

- animals (pets and wild animals, including birds, fish, and reptiles)
- places and things (mountains, rivers, forests, trees, plants, the heavens— including clouds, sun, moon, stars, and sky)
- time cycles (daily, weekly, monthly, annual).

The following is an example of a basic list of artistic genres. This comes from Brian's research with the Mono ethnolinguistic group in the Democratic Republic of Congo:

agbolo: children's play songs
agidi: dance for god of water

ako'ba: dance of women healers

ambala: malice dance

banda: male judges' dance

gaza aga: men's circumcision dance

gaza mbala: men's circumcision elephant dance

gaza yashe: women's circumcision dance

gbaguru: proverbs sung to exhort people

gbanjele: social dance

gbaya: celebratory social dance

gbenge: mourning song when village leader dies

kowo: dance for victory or war

kpatsha: dance from Banda people in Central African Republic

ku'u agbolo: lullabies

kuzu: death celebration dance

nganga: hunters' protection song

ngaranja: male judges' dance

yangba: celebratory social dance.

Extend the List from the Inside Out: Recognize Artistic Communication Acts by Their Special Features

In the "inside-out" approach, you begin with knowledge you have about art forms themselves, often from your own insights as an artist. You will recognize many of a community's arts because they have characteristics of singing, dancing, acting, carving, or other arts you are already familiar with. Sometimes, though, the surface structures of the arts we encounter are so different from those in our own experience that we may not recognize them as being artistic at all. In this section we have listed special features of artistic expression that may help you think beyond your experience and identify more of a community's arts. As you go about your daily life, train yourself to notice these characteristics and ask yourself the questions we have provided. When you recognize something as artistic, ask preliminary questions, write down what you learn, and plan to investigate it further.

Arts May Have a Distinctive Performance Context

Many times, the occasion for artistic communication is different from everyday interaction. It occurs between recognizable boundaries that set it off from "normal" events, and usually it will have distinctive features, such as role changes among the participants (Savile-Troike 2002). An artistic event might occur at a special time of day (often at night), in a special place, may use special language, may involve the participation of a large group of people, or participants might wear special clothing and behave in particular ways.

Many events are what Milton Singer has called "cultural performances" (1972; Bauman 1992:46): scheduled, temporally bounded, spatially bounded, programmed, coordinated, heightened (i.e., more pronounced, extreme) public occasions. You can usually find cultural performances relatively easily because they require planning, gathering and allocation of resources, and the involvement of multiple people.

Where is everybody going?
Why are people wearing those hats today?
What marks the beginning of this event? The end?

Arts May Expand or Contract the Density of Information

In comparison to everyday communication, artistic expressions often convey a great deal in just a few words. This is often true of poetry and proverbs. Other genres show the opposite effect, as in Wagner's operas, where the dialogue and plot unfold almost in slow motion because of the chronological space needed to perform the musical elements. Songs frequently show a great deal of redundancy of texts.

How can those people get so much from that little poem?

Arts May Assume More or Special Knowledge

Jokes are often very difficult to understand for outsiders because insider attitudes and knowledge are assumed by the tellers. It may be important that the assumed knowledge is not made explicit: it spoils a joke if you have to explain it. The implications of references to other artistic works can only be understood if the audience has knowledge of previous works, often of the same genre. Sometimes terminology or alternative meanings of words are specific to a particular artistic genre.

What in the world does that mean?
I understand all of the words of the joke, but I do not understand what is so funny!

Arts Exhibit Special Formal Structure

Artistic expressions are often limited by constraints of form that do not pertain to everyday communication.

> *Why did that person rhyme his last comment? (Clue: maybe it is a proverb.)*
> *Why is this building built differently from others?*

Arts May Elicit Unusual Responses

Artistic expressions often produce a strong emotional or physical response from people who experience them.

> *Why is everybody so excited/upset?*

Arts May Require Unusual Expertise

Artistic expressions often seem to take specialized training to perform; not everyone can do them.

> *How did she sing two notes at once?*

Start Exploring a Community's Social and Conceptual Life

Artistic action interacts with its community like threads and themes in a woven tapestry. To understand an artist and her arts, you have to understand her cultural context. Likewise, to understand a cultural context, you have to understand its arts and artists. This Guide highlights cultural questions especially relevant to arts and artists, especially in *Step 4C*. A broad exploration of a community, however, is beyond our scope. Fortunately, anthropology and related fields have developed a trustworthy set of categories and methods for doing this. If you do not have a background in anthropology, we encourage you to take a course in cultural anthropology or refer to works like Gary Ferraro and Susan Andreatta's *Cultural Anthropology* (2014), Carol McKinney's *Globetrotting in Sandals* (2000), or Kenneth Guest's *Cultural Anthropology: A Toolkit for a Global Age* (2015). Other important resources are Simone Krüger's *Ethnography in the Performing Arts: A Student Guide* (2008), Yale University's *Outline of Cultural Materials* (www.yale.edu/hraf), and the *SIL FieldWorks Data Notebook* (www.sil.org).

If you have already studied anthropology or expect to in the future, you will notice that its different theoretical streams result in different kinds of cultural insights.

For example, functionalist approaches reveal ways in which communities maintain internal coherence, while poststructuralist questions highlight points of dissent and unequal access to power. Interpretive methodologies help researchers identify and decode multiple layers of meaning in what people do and say, and postmodern thought provides insight into the ways that individuals and communities gather and appropriate ideas and images from many places and times. Each of these streams can contribute unique insights into how artistry works in a given community. Our Guide is influenced by these and other theories, but does not reference them explicitly.

We list here several important anthropological themes and a few related questions to stimulate your thoughts.

Language in Its Sociocultural Context

- In what contexts do people use different languages or types of language?
- How do people use silence in their communication?
- What value do people place on different types of speech?

Material Culture and Economics

- How do people use and value objects?
- How do people produce, distribute, and use goods and services?
- How is labor distributed among genders, classes, and ages?

Kinship

- How do people describe their relationships to other people in their community? What are the named categories for blood relatives?
- How do people describe their relationships to their ancestors?
- What social obligations are associated with each kind of relationship?

Marriage and Family

- How do people define the social union between men and women that results in children? How many men and women are involved, and what behaviors define the relationships between each?
- Who can marry whom in the community? Where do married partners live?
- What constitutes a household?
- How do households relate to extended family?

Social Organization

- What roles do gender, age, kinship, locality, and shared interests play in organizing social groups?
- How are social groups ranked by status?
- How do people enter or exit groups?

Power Relationships

- How does a community organize itself politically and relate to government structures?
- How much power does each smaller group hold?
- How do individuals and groups exert, gain, or lose power?

Religion

- What sorts of supernatural beings do people talk about or relate to? Do these include ancestral, nature, human, or supreme spirits?
- What rituals does the community perform regularly, and for what reasons?
- How do people use and control supernatural power?

Worldview and Values

- How do people categorize reality, and what attributes does it have?
- How do people decide what is true about reality?
- What do people say they think is important? How does people's allocation of time and resources reveal what they think is important?

Prepare to Use Research Methods to Learn More

Many of the activities we guide you through in the Guide require basic research skills. Although we cannot teach all the skills in this Guide, we introduce here the most important methods: participant observation, interview, note-taking, audio- and videorecording, photography, and library research. Here is one essential piece of advice, no matter which of these methods you use, especially if it involves equipment: learn to use it before it matters. Practice using a camera, video camera, audio-recording device, even writing in a notebook, before you need it to capture data.

Detailed discussion of software that is useful for gathering, organizing, and analyzing data in ethnographic research is beyond the scope of this Guide. However, here are a few places to start: ELAN, a "professional tool for the creation of complex annotations on video and audio resources" (The Language Archive 2018); Reyero's (2017) exploration of Smartphone Ethnography; and *SIL FieldWorks Data Notebook* (www.sil.org).

Smart phones increasingly are capable of recording all sorts of media for myriad purposes. Compare your phone's specifications with the standards required for each purpose for which you will make recordings. You will need to use specialized equipment for some goals. In addition to recording, smart phones allow access to social media, and apps for planning and analysis. These features support every type of research we discuss in this section: organizing, analyzing, and backing up data; communicating with and paying artists; and making and sharing audio recordings, videorecordings, and photographs. In any case, a smart phone is an exceptional back up recording device that you should have with you in almost all situations.

If we extend these technological supports into the near future, we see that systems integrating electronic devices into global communications, artificial intelligence, virtual and augmented reality, machine learning, multi-dimensional printing, and big data increase constantly in their capacity and reach into human societies. In *Shaping the Fourth Industrial Revolution* (2018), Klaus Schwab paints a compelling and unsettling vision in which artists play a central role: Arts "give us channels to express and to critique our projects before the values and orientations they represent are embedded in technology. In this sense, the role of the arts is not so much to predict the future as it is to provide cognitive and emotional tools to imagine the future and achieve creative breakthroughs" (Schwab et al 2018:189). Arts advocates can help communities imagine better futures during this rapid period of change.

Participant Observation: Learn by Watching While Doing

Painting, playing an instrument, dancing, taking part in a drama, learning to tell stories properly—these are all activities that might be part of participant observation for an arts researcher. In a participant observation model of fieldwork, the researcher lives in a community for an extended period to learn something about how that community functions. For the arts researcher, participant observation often includes becoming a student of a master artist in the community or joining a group devoted to an art form. Learning to perform and create gives the researcher an entry into understanding the artistic system, the artists themselves, and the place of the arts in the community. This deep involvement also communicates respect.

Although it has been a part of research for many years, participant observation became widely popular in the late nineteenth and early twentieth centuries, concurrent with the development of the field of anthropology. American anthropologist Franz Boas and his students employed participant observation techniques in their fieldwork. Ethnomusicologist Mantle Hood (1960) stressed the importance of acquiring "bi-musicality"—learning about a musical tradition by becoming a part of it. Many ethnomusicologists now consider bi-musicality and participant observation as common-sense approaches to fieldwork. We suggest extending our sights by becoming multi-musical, bi-artistic, and multi-artistic.

Participant observation in fieldwork, however, is rarely neat and tidy. Becoming a part of a community means adjusting to the stresses and expectations of daily living. The researcher must be flexible and willing to abide by the schedule offered by local teachers and guides. "Going with the flow" is a crucial, yet frequently frustrating, part of fieldwork. Dance scholar Felicia Hughes-Freeland (1999:120) describes participant observation as "determined by a process of planning and intention, which is disrupted by accidents and enhanced by serendipity." Participant observation often yields the most satisfying results when the researcher is able to spend long periods of time in the field location. Trust also is crucial in the participant observation relationship. The researcher must be committed to being a wise steward of the information he or she is given, abiding by all proper ethical expectations.

The following are two of our personal experiences of learning by doing.

KATHLEEN: I first traveled to Kenya as a college student keen to learn traditional forms of drumming. I arranged to take lessons with drummer Edward Kabuye. When it came time for my first lesson, Kabuye informed me that we would first spend a couple of weeks learning dances, followed by a couple of weeks learning songs. Only after that would we learn the drum patterns that accompanied the dances and songs. "But I'm not a dancer or singer!" I thought. "And I came to learn drumming!" However, I followed Kabuye's instructions. In time I came to appreciate the connections between these inextricably linked art forms, and the fact that you cannot fully comprehend drumming patterns without understanding the attached dance movements and songs.

BRIAN: I was trying in vain to understand how all of the percussion instruments worked together in a Cameroonian dance group. At one of their rehearsals, I played the simplest instrument—the shaker—and moved around the circle with the rest of the dancers. Somehow in the middle of that dance I noticed how one of the men was playing the wooden slit drum, and everything became clear. "Ahhhh! So my foot moves to the right when the shaker goes down and the slit drum hits a repeated pattern." Performance led me to understand connections between instruments.

Becoming an expert in all of the skills, symbolism, and social patterns of most art forms is likely beyond your capacity; artistic communication is complex, as attested by all of the research activities we describe in *Step 4*. Each of us, however, can gain something. This may include learning the appropriate ways to show appreciation during a performance, how to play an instrument, how to sing a song or do a dance, or how to carve a mask. Your research activities in *Step 4* will give you more ideas of what to learn.

Systems of Learning

When you decide you want to learn some aspect of an art form, you can enter an existing social context, devise your own system of learning, or use a combination of both. If you want to learn like people in the community learn, first find out how that happens (see "Transmission and Change" in *Step 4, Part C*). Then you can decide whether it fits your life. Local educational systems can range from informal watching to high-expectation apprenticeships. If you decide to figure out your own learning system, here are some things to keep in mind:

- Find out who in the community is best at the part of the art form you would like to learn. It may be that one person knows all of the songs associated with a social dance, for example, but is not a respected dancer. Ask a friend or two for advice on how to approach your potential teacher, and whether and how it would be appropriate to compensate them.
- Reflect on your own learning style and plan your activities accordingly. One or more of these types might apply to you (Johnston and Orwig 1999):
  - *Relational learner:* Wants to relate to people, have variety, and help others develop.
  - *Analytical learner:* Enjoys working independently and integrating data into theoretical models and solving problems.
  - *Structured learner:* Prefers a systematic and organized approach to learning, a chance to apply concepts in a practical way and to have hands-on activities and practical solutions.

- ○ *Energetic learner:* Likes lots of activity and chances to do things with people, with much variety, adventure, and risk; prefers personal involvement and hands-on activities.
- Watch, imitate, and practice what you want to learn. You may want to audio- or videorecord a performance so you can review it as many times as you want privately. You can also use the recordings for memorization or analysis, transcribing texts, melodies, and movements.

Interview: Learn by Asking

One of the most important aspects of your fieldwork is the relationships you build with other people in your host community. You may be adopted into a family, and neighbors may provide for your daily needs. Obviously, it is difficult to learn much about any of the arts without talking to people and asking questions about what you see around you. But talking can be done intentionally, purposefully, not just casually. When you formally arrange to talk with someone about their expressive arts, you are engaging in *ethnographic interviewing*.

Primary Benefits

- *Information gathering:* Biographical information; descriptions of performance events; emotional, ideological, critical, and other responses to performance events.
- *Clarification:* Confirm or correct information you have previously gathered or conclusions based on other fieldwork.
- *Comparison:* Learn the different perspectives various people might have about the same performance events. What do the differences tell you?

Elements of Ethnographic Interviews

- *Explanation of the procedure:* Tell the interviewee about the purpose of the interview, the recording equipment you will be using, the kinds of questions you will ask, and how you hope to use the information learned during the interview. Also provide the interviewee with a "Participant Information Sheet" explaining these details. Before or after the interview, have the interviewee sign a form giving permission to use the interview and the information for your research project. You can modify the "Sample Participant Information Sheet" and "Sample Permission Form" in *Closing 3* for your purposes.

- *Questions*: Before the interview, create a set of questions that might help guide the interview toward the areas you want to learn about. You may not use all the questions, or that particular order, but it can help to think about where the interview might go. It is important to be aware of the types of questions you use. Closed questions allow for a limited set of responses and stop conversations. "Do you like this weaving?", for example, is closed. Such questions are good for getting the names of people, numbers, facts, and yes/no answers, and to set up for open questions. Open questions, on the other hand, invite dialogue and present multiple avenues for the participant to explore. Questions like, "What are some ways that you prepare for a performance?" often result in finding out what the person really cares about and knows. Remember, of course, to also avoid framing your questions in ways that result in responses you hope to get.

  Another category of questions allows the responder to go in directions you had not anticipated or to guide your interviews of *other* insiders: Is there anything that is important that I have not asked about? Who else should I ask about this? What questions should I ask him or her? Remember that often the best information comes out at the end of the interview after you switch off the recording equipment!
- *Restatements*: At some points during the interview, you may want to restate what the interviewee has said. This helps to clarify that you understand what has been said, and also gives the interviewee the opportunity to say more about what he or she has already said, or to correct you.
- *Audiovisual media*: It may be helpful to have recordings ready to play for the interviewee in order to stimulate thoughtful comments about or reactions to performances.

Ethnographic interviews with groups of people are sometimes preferable to those with individuals. Your questions can spark discussion among the participants that unearths information and issues you had never considered. It is possible to use group interviews to discover genres of artistic communication in a community, to identify and agree on community goals, and to explore the meanings of an event. Be aware, though, of social dynamics in group settings—sometimes group members will defer to a respected or authoritative leader, leaving you with just the leader's opinion.

Note-Taking: Learn by Writing

Writing down what you observe and what you learn forces you to make your impressions clearer, and provides a durable record you can refer to later. Two types of notes are especially helpful, and lead to fruitful analysis (see Spradley 1980:63–72; Myers 1992:38–41):

Jottings: Initial Condensed Account

- Done on the spot, immediately after or during the event. Initial impressions are highly valuable.
- Write short descriptions and keywords and phrases to help you remember the details for later write-up. Do not let jotting become disruptive or distract you from observing.

Notes: Expanded Account

- This is a more descriptive account, when you have more time to write and are away from the event.
- Can be handwritten, typed, or dictated.
- The writer is aware of her or his own perspective, biases, and interpretations.

When writing initial fieldnotes, keep in mind two principles:

The verbatim principle: Record everything in the exact words used by the person you are talking with.

- Write: "You have to swallow the beat to play that shaker."
- Not: "Your rhythm was not consistent."

The concrete principle: Use concrete language.

- Write: "She looked out the window of the truck and started to take sharp, rapid breaths. After about a minute, she leaned her head back, made a high-pitched, loud, prolonged sound without recognizable words that dropped rapidly in pitch. Tears began to flow, and she soon repeated the vocalization."
- Not: "She began wailing."

Codings and Analysis: Processing Fieldnotes

1. Read your fieldnotes. Look for threads that identify larger themes. A cultural theme is any principle that recurs in several domains and defines relationships among sets of meanings (see Spradley 1980:141). Yale's *Outline of Cultural Materials* provides a huge number of possible themes, drawing on categories such as peacemaking, transmission of cultural norms, religious experience, sexuality, life and death, games, and hundreds more (Human Relations Area Files 2018).[2]

2. When you think you have found a theme, choose a short word or abbreviation to identify it. Whenever you find the same theme, write the code in the margins, on a separate piece of paper, or perhaps in a separate book.

3. Do this after you have observed, interviewed, and written a significant amount.

4. Look for patterns, such as themes that often occur together (e.g., food and warfare).

5. You can also code or write about subjects in your fieldnotes, when you start to venture hypotheses.

Audio- and Videorecording: Learn by Reducing Life to Media

"A picture is worth a thousand words." For the fieldworker this is especially true. Verbal description will never show people what the dances look like, or what the storyteller's voice sounds like. An important part of every fieldworker's skills is audio- and videorecording. For more extensive guidance in this area, see *Language and Culture Documentation Manual* (Boerger et al. 2017). *A Manual for Documentation* (Society for Ethnomusicology 2001) provides a small, travel-friendly reference, though its technology content is outdated.

History of Recording

Documentation of audio and visual data is nearly essential in any field project, and the history of ethnomusicology fieldwork is intimately connected with such documentation. Some of the most iconic photographs of early ethnomusicological fieldwork include ethnomusicologists, such as Frances Densmore, using audio-recording equipment. Audio recording and playback began with Thomas Edison's phonograph cylinder in 1877—coinciding with the beginnings of modern anthropology. Audio-recording technology progressed from wax cylinders to magnetic tape, and now to digital recording.

The possibility of recording video and audio together developed more recently, in the second half of the twentieth century. Many fieldworkers feel that audio-only documentation is not complete enough; a high value is placed on being able to see the artistic event (or even an interview), rather than just hearing it. This is especially true of performances in which movement or dance is a significant element. It is also worthwhile to be able to see instrumental performing techniques, facial expressions while singing, and body language.

Choosing Recording Equipment

The pace of change in recording technology makes it impossible to suggest particular products in a printed Guide such as this. However, the following are some guidelines that should be valid for years to come.

When purchasing audio-recording equipment, ask other experienced fieldworkers or look online to find current information about audio recorders. A good recorder should have the following: manual control of recording levels, external microphone input (even if the recorder has internal microphones), high-quality WAV file recording settings, headphone jack, and common media.

For videorecording, you should use a camera with high resolution, a tripod mount, high-quality audio, external microphone input, and headphone jack.

Purposes for a Recording Event

Your purpose in reducing live, human activities to static media will determine how you go about it. We present here four common purposes and their implications for how you record: ethnographic analysis, form analysis, preservation, and production for distribution.

If you would like a record of an event that allows you to later research the meanings of any or all of its elements through ethnographic analysis, then you should capture everything that happens. This means that you will do as much continuous recording of an event as possible, including non-artistic sounds like chickens and babies.

If, on the other hand, you have a particular analytical interest—you would like to figure out the melody of a particular song, or understand how weight shifts in a dance movement, for example—then you will isolate these elements from a normal performance. The benefit of recording sound and visuals in the field is the ability to go back later and look more closely at what happened. Playback on a computer or phone allows slowing down the speed of a musical performance and freeze-framing videorecordings. This can lead to more accurate description. Recordings also make comparative study easier. Different recordings of the same song, for example, can show where stylistic variation is acceptable.

Audiovisual recording is valuable not only for your own needs, but also for preservation. With many of the world's indigenous traditions in decline, this documentation may soon be all that exists to show a variety of creative expressions. Ensure that community members can access the recordings; provide participants with copies of recordings that feature them. Unless the individuals or communities involved request otherwise, your recordings also should be properly archived in local, national, and international collections, with performers' permissions for nonprofit and research uses. Future generations and interested researchers will then have access to them. Many archives have high standards for items they accept: audio files should be recorded at 24 bit/48khz, and video files should be recorded at the highest quality possible (there is no agreed-upon standard as of this writing). Acquire the best equipment you can afford, so that you can maintain a high quality of recordings for preservation.

Finally, the community you are working with may wish to create products from recordings of their arts for sale or distribution. This purpose usually requires using recording standards of existing media in the region. To meet these standards, you may choose to record audio in a studio, and use multiple camera shots for video. Rely on local skills and technology for this as much as possible.

Other purposes of recordings include helping you learn to perform something, or documenting a process, such as making an instrument or weaving fabric. You can modify how you design recording events according to each need.

Documenting Recordings

A recording without accompanying contextual information has extremely limited usefulness, because you will eventually forget what is on it. It is essential, then, to create several kinds of metadata—data about the recording—as you go along:

- Speak onto the medium: If you are working with audio, record, "This is *your name*, recording *so-and-so person*, at *such-and-such place*, on *such-and-such day*."
- Write as much as you can on the outside of the tape, disc, and so on.
- Write in your field notebook: code for the recorded item, date, place, name of the event, participants, instruments used, community(ies) involved, audience description (size, makeup), context, purpose of event, and possible ethical considerations for future use of the recording of the event.

Your notes should have a clear coding system of correspondence with the physical media. Your system may simply consist of the year and recording number: for example, "2017-3" would refer to the third recording (perhaps a CD) you made in 2017.

Planning a Recording Opportunity

- Discuss the event with whoever is in charge—figure out permissions, payment, and so on.
- Step through the whole event in your mind, writing down what you hope to do.
- Choose, prepare, and test your equipment.
- Bring backup equipment and batteries.
- Prepare for equipment failure, batteries dying, electricity going out, hurricanes, and so on.
- Arrange mechanisms for recording metadata—notebook and pen/pencil always work.
- Prepare permission forms or audio recording of authorization (see "Sample Permission Form" in *Closing 3*).

Photography: Learn by Reducing Life to Still Images

Still photographs freeze an object or scene into a two-dimensional image at a precise moment in time. As in each of these research methods, people must give you permission to take photographs of them.

Purposes for Photography

You can use pictures to enrich the research process in many ways, including these:

- Document the existence of kinds of objects, like masks, regalia, props, instruments, paintings, house adornments, ritual aids, and representations of supernatural beings. These could be representations of entire objects in use or in an analytical context.
- Reveal details of objects, especially using multiple shots of the same object from different angles and distances. These can lead to insights into construction, coloring, textures, and other features.
- Document artists, their families, and other community members in performance and at repose. Photos provide an excellent channel for reciprocity: you take pictures, then give copies back to the people you have photographed.

- Encourage community members to take pictures to tell their stories and document the things about a performance that are important to them.
- Ask someone to document your presence and activities in the community by photographing you in action.
- Express your own creative impressions of events.

A Few Tips for Photography

Becoming a photographer with professional skills usually takes training, expensive equipment, and technical and aesthetic gifts. If this describes you, then go take some pictures. For the rest of us, here are a few bits of advice about taking pictures. Remember, though, that you may need to change this advice depending on the purposes of the photographs.

- Your basic kit: a camera (or two), a tripod or monopod, extra batteries, extra lenses if you have them, camera use instructions. Have one or two backup ways to take photos. You may have a fancy camera, but if it stops working (and it will), cheap and lower quality is better than nothing.
- Make sure that the primary element you want to capture is visible and in a prominent place. Many people think that important elements should be off center, and they use the rule of thirds (see *Closing 2: Glossary*). If you can control the focus on your camera, adjust so that anything in front of or behind the object is slightly out of focus.
- Make sure that the light reveals what you think is important. Especially make sure that there is no light shining toward you from behind your subject. Force your flash to flash if there is light behind.
- Consider framing your picture by putting a bit of a wall, tree, or other object at the edge of what the camera captures.
- Ensure that scale is clear. For example, if photographing a small musical instrument, include an object of a known size (a ruler, a person's hand) to demonstrate size.
- Keep your horizon lines (e.g., ocean, land) straight.
- Archive your pictures in different places and on different media to be sure that you will not lose them.

Published Sources: Learn by Getting Others' Written Perspectives

Somebody has probably already written or filmed or recorded something about the community you are working with or a similar group. If so, you may benefit greatly from their experiences and insights.

We use the term "publish" here to refer to anything someone puts into an enduring medium to communicate to an audience beyond one or two people. These could include books, theses, dissertations, articles, films, newsletters, and audio- and videorecordings. The people who produce these resources could be part of scholarly communities or cultural groups, or they could be individuals like travelers, journalists, or missionaries. You will find resources in libraries, archives, bookstores, people's personal bookshelves, and on the Internet. University libraries, archives, and bookstores in the location of the community often prove a rich source of relevant documents found nowhere else in the world. As with anything you hear or learn, make sure you evaluate these resources in terms of the purposes and credentials of the people who produced them.

Respect, Trust, and Law

We want all of our interactions with people to be guided and marked by respect. This means that when we are researching a community and its arts, we are humble, want the best for them, listen to their goals and concerns, and do not promote ourselves or our agendas at their expense. Unfortunately, acting respectfully is seldom simple. You and this community are connected to multiple legal, organizational, and social systems, each exerting moral pressure to act in ways that are often contradictory.

Seeger and Chaudhuri (2004:71–117) identify a number of common actors connected to artistic activity: creators, communities, researchers, organizations funding research, national law, international law, and archives. Each of these advocate at different levels of intensity for ease and control of access to enactments, adequate accreditation, preservation, monetary gain, remuneration, ownership, non-exploitative relationships, and privacy. As your work progresses, find out which of these actors and concerns will affect your context. Put most of your energy into helping the community you are working with benefit from your presence in the ways *they* want to benefit.

Anthropologists and ethnomusicologists have recognized for a long time that social complexity means that there is no universally right way to address rights and ownership (Slobin 1992). Nonetheless, here are a few points that will clarify some important issues before you.

Practice Generous Reciprocity

It is important to give something back for everything you take. Start by providing copies of photographs, videos, and audio recordings to the participants in your research as soon as you record them. Try to be trustworthy, dependable, generous, humble, and concerned about building relationships that will last.

Study Legal Protections for Creators and Communities

Copyright "is a set of specific rights for creators of literary, dramatic, artistic or musical works and the makers of audio, video, photographic and film recordings. It gives them a limited monopoly on making copies (publishing) and otherwise using their original works for a set period of time" (Seeger and Chaudhuri 2004:78). At the international level, the World Intellectual Property Organization (WIPO; www.wipo.int), an agency of the United Nations, administers 26 international treaties and conventions related to copyright and intellectual property, and has a membership of 188 countries. You can explore resources associated with any of these countries at www.wipo.int/members/en/. Note also that WIPO administers the Berne Convention for the Protection of Literary and Artistic Works, one of the most influential agreements related to protecting and promoting artistic production.

In addition to international organizations, countries often have internal systems for applying copyright law. For example, Cameroonian Musical Art Company (SOCAM) follows musicians' production and air time, and makes decisions regarding payment of royalties.

Explore Community Views of Rights and Ownership

Euroamerican systems regulating ownership reflect a high value on the rights of individuals who produce novel works. British copyright, for example, automatically applies "whenever an individual or company creates a work. To qualify, a work should be regarded as original, and exhibit a degree of labour, skill or judgement" (www.copyrightservice.co.uk/copyright/p01_uk_copyright_law). Many communities, however, see artistry as belonging as much to the group that nurtured the individual creator. The questions and activities described in "Ownership and Rights" (*Step 4C*) will help you understand how the community you work with views novelty and rights to artistic production.

A community's history with previous researchers, filmmakers, or recording artists may also impinge on how much people trust you. For example, when Brian began working with the Ngiemboon community in Cameroon, they had already welcomed a European researcher who wanted to record important traditional ceremonies. He made unfulfilled promises to give them recordings and make future visits. This caused some Ngiemboon leaders to view Brian with suspicion until he had proven that his word was dependable.

Openly Discuss Legal and Ethical Considerations with the People You Record

Explain your actions and their purposes to your colleagues and friends, and respond to any concerns they may have. In many situations it will be appropriate—even legally necessary—to let them sign an authorization form. Sometimes such forms can increase distrust if your relationship with the performers is not well established or if they are not accustomed to such documents. In this case, discuss your needs (e.g., to an archive or publisher) with friends knowledgeable of local customs and come up with a respectful solution. Bear in mind that if you are working with an organization or academic institution, or if you intend to publish your research, you may be required to follow a particular procedure for obtaining ethical approval for your work. This may include submitting an ethics application to your institution for review, developing an information letter for participants, and obtaining consent from participants (see *Closing 3* for examples).

Celebrate a Community's Arts from the Start

The overall aim of this Guide is to stir up creativity in local forms that meet community goals. However, we start with the premise that all people and their actions are inherently valuable. Thus, as you document a community's existing arts, celebrate them. The activities "Publish Recordings and Research in Various Forms and Contexts" and "Help Develop Multimedia Collections of Local Arts" (*Step 5*) are great ways to start.

Notes

1. See also *Closing 7: Suggestions for Guide Users. Closing 7* provides suggestions for educators, project leaders, and researchers, linking specific sections of the Guide, such as "Take a First Glance at a Community," with the work they might engage in.

2. An ever-increasing number of paid and free software products are available to do qualitative data analysis. Commercial systems include ATLAS.ti, NVivo, and QDA Miner. Free software includes Coding Analysis Toolkit, Aquad, and QDA Miner Lite. Consult http://www.predictiveanalyticstoday.com for up-to-date lists and descriptions.

ALWAYS when you go on that stage, when you sing, when you dance, it's always to show them what happens behind their back, behind their lives, inside their lives. . . . When you become an artist, you come to the field of looking for a cure for the world. . . . We are the bridge to happiness. That's what I think an artist means. . . . Always when you think, when you compose, you're composing towards the solutions of what is affecting the society.

—KENYAN PERFORMER (interview by Kathleen with Kenyan performing artist, Nairobi, September 1, 2004; also in Van Buren 2010:205–206. Name omitted to protect the performer's identity)

Step

2

SPECIFY GOALS FOR A BETTER LIFE

THE PRECEDING QUOTATION, from an interview by Kathleen of a performer in Kenya, reveals how some artists understand their role primarily as problem-solvers; according to this performer, being an artist means working toward solutions in communities, working toward a better life. In the following sections of the Guide, we present three broad categories of potential goals for communities: identity and sustainability; health and well-being; and human rights.

As ethnomusicologist Jeff Todd Titon (2015:157) states, "Sustainability is a hard concept to avoid these days" (see also Titon 2018). The term is used by environmentalists, economists, and development workers, among others. The United Nations (2018) defines "sustainable development" as "development that meets the needs of the present without compromising the ability of future generations to meet their own needs." The 2008 UN Declaration on the Rights of Indigenous Peoples highlights the rights of people "to practice and revitalize their cultural traditions and customs," including the arts; moreover, it recognizes that local knowledge, cultures, and traditional practices "[contribute] to sustainable and equitable development" (United Nations 2008:2, 6). Here we see not only acknowledgment of the rights of people to practice and promote their local arts, but also the importance of arts and culture to promoting sustainable development in general (see also Impey 2002 on this topic). According to Titon (2015:157), sustainability in applied ethnomusicology "refers to a music culture's capacity to maintain and develop its music now and in the foreseeable future."

Despite its widespread use, scholars have criticized the concept of "sustainability." In her book *Music Endangerment: How Language Maintenance Can Help* (2014), Catherine Grant provides a useful summary of perspectives related to sustainability and culture. Used in conjunction with culture, she notes, terms such as "sustainability," "heritage," and "safeguarding" may promote a conservationist view that relegates the arts (or other aspects of community life) to something of the past, without "freedom to grow and develop" (Grant 2014:10–11, quoting economist Sen in Graves 2005:107). UNESCO's 2003 *Convention for the Safeguarding of Intangible Cultural Heritage* is well known for promoting recognition and support of masterpieces of intangible cultural heritage, yet this program also has been criticized by scholars for resulting in unintended effects, including by relegating them to museum pieces.[1] In his chapter on sustainability, resilience, and adaptive management, Titon (2015:158) asserts that another "[difficulty] with sustainability and its related ideas is that they are ends, not means; they are goals, not strategies." Scholars have suggested a number of alternatives to sustainability: revitalization, transformation, creative regeneration, cultivation, and vitality and viability (Grant 2014:11).[2] Titon (2015:192) highlights the concept of "resilience," defining it as "a system's capacity to recover its integrity, identity, and continuity when subjected to forces of disturbance." He posits that resilience can be strengthened through "adaptive management" (Titon 2015:158). Due to its widespread use and in following the preceding definitions of the term by the United Nations and Titon, we employ the term "sustainability" in this Guide. However, we do so with hesitance and wish to simultaneously emphasize and support the vitality and resilience of artistic and other traditions.

The concepts of health and well-being and human rights in particular resonate with many of the UN's Sustainable Development Goals (United Nations 2016b). We conceive of health and well-being broadly. In their introduction to the *Oxford Handbook of Medical Ethnomusicology*, Koen, Barz, and Brummel-Smith (2008:4) express interest in "the biological, psychological, social, emotional, and spiritual domains of life, all of which frame our experiences, beliefs, and understandings of health and healing, illness and disease, and life and death." Their view echoes the definition of health by the *Journal of Applied Arts and Health* as including "physical, mental, emotional, spiritual, occupational, social and community health" (*Journal of Applied Arts and Health* 2016). We too are interested in the multiple dimensions of life that impact individual and community understandings and experiences of health and well-being. While the full Guide considers well-being in the broadest sense, *Step 2* provides examples of particular initiatives related to health and well-being within communities.

In each of the following sections of *Step 2*, we briefly describe some specific objectives that a community could adopt, explain how local arts might help meet them, and give a few real-life examples of projects that have targeted or are working toward similar goals. We recognize that these examples are brief; while we analyze select case studies in more depth in other sections of the Guide, here our goal is simply to demonstrate some of the breadth of arts activities already taking place around the world and thus to stimulate ideas for further work.

We also recognize that in some cases, it may be difficult to prove the efficacy of the arts in promoting change in a particular intervention. Even if change is evident, how do we prove that a community arts program is directly responsible for reducing cholera infection or HIV rates, for example, when non-arts-based campaigns and advertising may also come into play? First, every intervention associated with improvement results in a hypothesis that can be tested; we should keep building on and evaluating previous experience. Second, we need to design more projects built on scientific standards of validity. Third, whatever the relationship between an activity and changes, the *Make Arts* process requires us to ascertain whether effective communication—a necessary step toward change—is occurring (see also Singhal and Rogers 1999).

Later in *Step 2*, we outline a process that a community can follow to identify the goals they wish to work toward. The UN Declaration on the Rights of Indigenous Peoples (United Nations 2008) highlights the rights of indigenous peoples in defining their own priorities, while Grant (2014:14) emphasizes the importance of communities being "in full control of making their own informed choices about the future of their cultural expressions." What we propose is a model that stems from within communities, involving local knowledge bearers and artistic genres to meet locally defined needs.

Identity and Sustainability

Valuing Identity

In some places, minority groups think more highly of other people than themselves and so denigrate the usefulness, beauty, or intrinsic value of their own culture. Sometimes other groups—often more powerful—have overtly or inadvertently taught this. Missionaries and colonizers are infamous for this. Jan Magne Steinhovden (email communication, May 24, 2013) tells of his experience studying music in churches in Ethiopia. He writes:

"If you want to find a large church which has a clear indigenous sound in their worship, go to Ethiopia." This was the advice given to a student searching for traditional music in a church setting.

The situation has not always been like that in Ethiopia. The early missionaries brought along their own music and musical instruments, so until around 1960 Western hymns (especially English, German and Swedish), most often accompanied by guitar or organ, were the most common sounds in Ethiopian evangelical churches. I have been told that many new believers in Ethiopia thought that this was the "Christian" music, brought to Ethiopia by the missionaries. The new believers thought that their own traditional songs and musical instruments belonged to Satan and to traditional believers, and could therefore not be used in church. At that time, some young Ethiopian singers started to write their own songs using local scales and rhythms. These songs became enormously popular, but they also created many tensions within the churches, especially between older and younger generations. Suddenly the new young musicians gained a position that young people had never before had in the hierarchical feudal Ethiopian society. However, this "Ethiopian" music continued to be accompanied only by "Western" musical instruments, especially guitar and later synthesiser.

In 2000, I visited Awasa, a city in southern Ethiopia, and had the privilege of meeting some young church musicians who dared to bring traditional Ethiopian instruments into the church. They played some beautiful songs on the *krar*, a lyre; the *masinqo*, a one-stringed violin; and the *kebero*, a drum. However, after I had recorded their music accompanied by traditional instruments, they asked me if I could record the same songs accompanied by synthesiser. I am not sure if they did so because they believed Western instruments were more Christian, or if they just liked the sound of the synthesizer.

The synthesizer continues to have enormous popularity within Ethiopian evangelical churches, but lately it has become more acceptable to include traditional instruments in church worship. For example, the church-run music education program at Mekanissa in Addis Ababa has included courses on traditional Ethiopian music.

A community's artistic genres constitute some of the most identifiable and valuable parts of their culture. However, as demonstrated by the preceding story, colonial, religious, and other influences can deeply impact what art forms are supported or rejected within communities. If community members see no good (or are told that there is no good) in their own arts, they will not use them to communicate to each other. Fortunately, again as in the preceding story, the situation can also change; local artists can turn back to older or less popular genres, and can use these independently or alongside newer artistic forms. Arts advocates may work with community members to find ways to affirm local artistic resources and to create works that foster strong cultural identity.

Writing about a different part of the world, Andrew Noss (email communication, January 21, 2014) tells of how community programs can strengthen and promote cultural identity at the same time as providing an economic resource. In this example, cultural identity and economic opportunity go hand in hand, supporting each other. Noss explains:

AMWAE (Asociación de Mujeres Waorani de la Amazonía Ecuatoriana) was legally established in 2005 to represent the Waorani (also spelled Waodani) women. In practical terms this association seeks to promote communication, unity, and culture by generating economic opportunities for women allowing them to remain in their own communities. The first and most important in terms of participants and funds generated is the handicrafts program, which has received financial and technical support from USAID and Peace Corps as well as oil company and local governments and national ministries. Mostly working in their communities in the Waorani territory, but also in towns like Puyo, women make traditional Waorani clothes, jewelry, tools, utensils, and hammocks (with some new models and designs developed among the women with outside ideas and with tourist and buyer preferences) out of natural forest products (beads, palm fiber, and wood). AMWAE holds workshops where Waorani experts (older women) teach the others to make the items, and where they work on design and quality issues. AMWAE also collects the items and sells them principally through a network of shops in towns in Ecuador, with some sales abroad by special order. Each item is labelled with the name of the woman who made it, and the majority of the sale goes back to the maker. They have begun to manage the wild palms for fiber, i.e. planting them near communities so that a supply would persist close by.

One of the principles of the Waorani handicraft program is that it is to maintain culture—not just the cultural artifacts themselves. By producing handicrafts for income, women can remain in their communities, where they maintain the forest (under traditional use patterns, or more active management of plants that produce seeds and fibers for handicrafts) and teach their children their language. Without the forest they lose their identity. Without their language they lose their identity.

Teaching Children

Individuals and groups sometimes choose to leave behind older traditions and develop newer traditions. Other times, however, they may not feel that they have a choice and they may mourn their losses. Speaking of the Waorani, Noss argues that it is vital for community members to be able to teach their children their language, for without their language they will lose their identity. In the next example, Mary Saurman (email communication, July 28, 2011, and October 26, 2017) describes how different generations in a Hmong community in Southeast Asia came together to find ways to actively pass on older songs and dances.

> Members of one Hmong community in Southeast Asia, as happens in many cultures desiring a move towards national education, faced a rupture in their transmission process. This meant there was no passing on of their traditional culture and values. Children no longer worked the fields during the day or sat with elders in the evenings, where transmission of cultural knowledge usually took place. With this shift, a generation grew into young adults who did not have interest in their own traditional songs and dances. Soon the songs and dances would be lost.
>
> Through a participatory workshop, the generations came together and discussed what traditions they valued and what was slipping away from them. Together the older and younger adults interacted and planned how they would actively pass on their valuable cultural wisdom and art forms.
>
> One approach included older expert musicians and artists teaching in the public classes about their art forms and cultural knowledge. Books and other reading materials about the creation process and cultural values were also created. The transmission process that was severed was reconnected through a new creative method within the national education system that initially caused the rupture.

Abimbola Cole Kai-Lewis (email communication, January 25, 2014), in turn, writes about her work in New York City:

> Community School (C.S.) 154, Harriet Tubman Learning Center, is a public school situated immediately behind the Apollo Theater in Harlem, New York. The school has been recognized for its outstanding curriculum and has earned numerous accolades from the New York City Department of Education. The school is also the site of the Apollo Theater Oral History Project at C.S. 154, Harriet Tubman Learning Center, an educational program formed by the

Education Department at the Apollo Theater Foundation, Incorporated. The goal of the Project is to increase students' knowledge of their immediate community through neighborhood excursions, interviews with elders, as well as ongoing research on Harlem with teaching artists and classroom teachers.

As an intern for the Oral History Project for the 2008–2009 academic school year, I offered support to the teaching artists, monitored audio recordings of interviews between the students and the elders, and transcribed each interview. The interview transcripts were used by students to begin developing scripts that would be used for culminating performances. Classroom teachers supported students in the creation of questions for the elders which would help them to unearth details about their backgrounds such as where they grew up, when they moved to Harlem, and what they remembered most about the Apollo Theater over the years. The students also worked closely with teaching artists to construct plays that captured elements of the stories that the elders told and convert them into dramatic enactments. The plays were performed by students on the Soundstage of the Apollo Theater.

Students had the opportunity to learn a substantial amount of information about the evolution of the African-American community in Harlem. They also visited key locations to see many of the places that were described by the elders in their oral history interviews. By the end of the Apollo Theater Oral History Project at C.S. 154, Harriet Tubman Learning Center, many students found that the Project was useful in discovering more about Harlem and its residents. As one student noted, "History helps us connect the past to the present, and the present to the future. It tells where we've been and where we're going."

In this Guide, we suggest that arts advocates and community members select a particular type of event or events that can help them meet their goals. In the examples by Saurman and Kai-Lewis, events promoting knowledge of past history, culture, and identity were incorporated into contemporary educational settings. New and old were blended in unique ways.

Using Media

People around the world are constantly figuring out new ways to communicate with each other. Members of a community with a strong sense of their community's value not only can receive and learn artistic communication from others, but also can contribute recordings of their own arts through local, regional, and global media. Repatriated recordings can also lead to new or renewed creativity. In the following example, Samuel Kahunde describes his experience in Uganda, where traditional kingdoms were abolished and then reinstated more than 20 years later. As a member of the Bunyoro-Kitara community, but also a researcher able to access recordings housed outside Uganda, Kahunde was in a unique position to study what had happened to cultural traditions with the loss of the kingdom and to assist kingdom officials and musicians who wished to bring back the older arts. Kahunde explains (email communication, February 11, 2014; see also Kahunde 2012a and 2012b):

After the kingdoms of Uganda were abolished by the Ugandan government in 1967, the royal music and dances of the Bunyoro-Kitara kingdom of western Uganda were rarely performed. When the government reinstated the kingdoms again in the early 1990s, the people of Bunyoro-Kitara had difficulty reviving the older traditions because most of the elderly people who knew much about them had died. Many of the traditions, including musical ones, had not been locally preserved because the people did not expect the kingdoms to be revived.

In 2007, as a graduate student at the University of Sheffield in the United Kingdom, I initiated a study about the musical traditions of Bunyoro-Kitara kingdom. During my fieldwork in 2009, Boazi Wandera and Ben Mulimba, who participated in the restoration of the kingdom, informed me that before restoring the king they had to carry out a program for creating awareness among the people of Bunyoro about the revival of kingship. This was done partly through the performance of the royal *Empango* dance and by having musicians hum older trumpet songs. The performances would excite people, and seemed to assure the community that the revival was a reality. Wandera recalled that some people would exclaim, "Oh, the kingdom may get revived!" However, I observed that the royal musicians were still struggling to revive their music and dance fourteen years after the restoration of the king. Performers had few repertoires, and new performers either learned by observing others or were trained to play instruments and to dance while performing on the stage. Furthermore, several youths who could have participated in the royal music and dance inside the palace yard opted to participate in popular music staged immediately outside the palace yard.

While in England, I acquired royal recordings by Klaus Wachsmann and Hugh Tracey from the British Library Sound Archive and the International Library of African Music, respectively. In consultation with the British Library Sound Archive, I decided to support the revival of the royal music and dance of Bunyoro-Kitara kingdom by giving out some songs to the royal musicians in 2008. I was glad to find the royal musicians playing them during the 2009 coronation anniversary celebrations. As I write this, the kingdom officials and the leader of the royal music are requesting more songs to enrich their repertoire. Indeed I will soon burn a CD of more songs and pass it on to them.

Health and Well-Being

Healing

Artistic activity can play a crucial role in increasing health and well-being. Studies discuss the benefits of arts, for example, for decreasing levels of anxiety, depression, and perceived pain; counteracting the decline of cognitive functions; and providing a sense of community and social support (Clift and Camic 2016:3–10; Sadler and Joseph 2008:3; Staricoff 2006). Music and dance therapist Mary Saurman (1995) offers personal insight into her experience with one woman:

> One birth-mother's heart rate began soaring beyond control during delivery. The nurses refused my assistance to let her listen to her favorite music, even though I had explained how helpful it would be. Finally, in desperation, they consented. I turned on the *heavy metal music* (the birth-mother's favorite) and immediately her heart rate and the baby's (still in her womb) began dropping and quickly returned to a normal state.

The following example comes from Kathleen's work with the NHS Centre for HIV and Sexual Health on a World AIDS Day 2007 event in Sheffield, United Kingdom (see also Van Buren 2010). On 1 December 2007, the Department of Music at the University of Sheffield and the NHS Centre for HIV and Sexual Health hosted "World AIDS Day: Hope through the Arts" in Sheffield, United Kingdom. The aim of this event was to remember those affected by AIDS and to celebrate what can be done—particularly through the arts—to stem the spread of the pandemic. Features of the event included: a march on the streets of Sheffield; a diversity of musical performances (including performances of samba, English folk music, jazz, rock, mbira, and sitar and santoor among others); short talks, stories and poems by people impacted by or working on HIV-related issues; a keynote by Carol Brown, independent curator attached to the art collection at the Constitutional Court in South Africa; and informational and visual arts displays by local charity organizations and Department of Music students.

A questionnaire distributed in hard copy at the event and also online provided feedback on various aspects of the event and its impact upon audience members. Participants were asked, for example, to rate their knowledge of the following issues before and after the event: (1) basic facts about HIV and AIDS; (2) the impact of HIV and AIDS in the United Kingdom; (3) the impact of HIV and AIDS globally; and (4) the role of the arts in addressing HIV and AIDS. Answers from all participants except one indicated that individual knowledge increased as result of the event. Responses to a short-answer question on whether the event changed participant perspectives on HIV and AIDS were mixed. Some participants stated that the event did not change their perspectives, in at least one case because the person was already knowledgeable about HIV and AIDS before the event. Other respondents, however, noted that they had become much more aware of the seriousness of AIDS, particularly in the United Kingdom. As one person remarked, "I am more aware of it existing within my own community and of the bias/discrimination against sufferers here." Another person commented, "The event really brought home the enormity of HIV/AIDS in Britain."

Participants also were asked to rate the value of the arts in addressing a variety of HIV-related issues. The results showed that participants placed a high value on the role of the arts, particularly in promoting awareness about HIV and in decreasing stigmatization. However, participants seemed less confident that the arts could shift personal behavior sufficiently to result in decreases in infection rates. One person, for example, remarked, "The arts will only be helpful in decreasing the spread of HIV if the people who observe it take away with them what they've learned and act upon it. It's one thing learning something and gaining knowledge but another putting it into practice in personal situations." This response demonstrates participant awareness that increased knowledge does not necessarily result in changed behavior. Changing behavior can be more complicated, as a person or community must be both willing and able to make a change.

There are a wide variety of community programs around the world that draw upon the arts to promote health and well-being. Many programs are well documented by scholars and community organizations or non-governmental organizations (NGOs). Here, for example, Matthew Davis tells of his experience in Benin, where song was used to help raise awareness about cholera. This experience demonstrates how song can immediately engage an audience and help to communicate critical information on how to stay healthy. Davis (1999:38) writes:

In Benin, I met a community nurse who had realized that singing about health can inspire people to change their behavior. Yerima, the nurse, told me that he started to sing about health issues out of frustration. He had noticed that the women who came to his village's two-room health center for prenatal care paid little attention to his lectures on topics such as nutrition and childhood vaccinations. Yet when he composed and performed songs with the same information, he found that his audience became much more interested, and they sang with him in the common call-and-response form of the region.

Given the threat of a cholera epidemic at the time of my visit, I asked whether he could write a new song to communicate fundamental ideas about water hygiene. Yerima disappeared into the back room while the clinic director gave a lecture on cholera, which received scant attention. Five minutes later, Yerima returned and began to shout that cholera causes diarrhea. The crowd responded with sounds of disgust. Yerima then began to sing, repeating a response line for them: *kolera baradarorwa* (cholera will kill you). Gradually, he began to sing lines of information between the response lines, advising the women to boil their water and urging them to wash their hands and those of their children before eating. In less than ten minutes, a new song had been learned and a new message communicated: simple, fast, effective, memorable.

While the song in the preceding example was effective, using fear to promote change also has been criticized widely. Fear has featured in campaigns against illnesses such as AIDS and ebola. One example is "Ebola in Town," a piece that became popular in Monrovia's nightclubs in May 2014 as people began to pay attention to the disease (see also Stillman 2014).[3] The use of lyrics such as "don't touch your friend" may have been effective in some ways, but has troubling social implications. Lyrical content must be carefully considered in developing projects.

Uganda often has been identified as a success story in managing to decrease HIV rates; there, community members have used music, dance, and drama to educate about HIV and AIDS. In his book *Singing for Life: HIV/AIDS and Music in Uganda* (2006), Gregory Barz chronicles some of their stories. Here are the words of one Ugandan, spokesman for the Meeting Point organization, who expresses his view of the power of the arts (Barz 2006:168):

We communicate our messages primarily through music, dance, and drama. Counseling on our site is also done through music and drama. When we organize a play or music, we don't just compose any song or meaningless drama. First we recognize the experiences and needs around us. If we pass along those experiences in drama we find that we help people enormously. We can show a drama demonstrating how younger girls acquire HIV because they want to get rich, to become "smart" at an early age. We can show what happens when women go to witchdoctors instead of testing centers. We can pass along some songs in places where AIDS has hit aggressively. Music is our most powerful tool, Gregory, for affecting change in Uganda!

A final example from North India shows how community health NGOs worked together with local actors, singers, and dancers to create an anti-tobacco DVD that would be effective for use in a particular remote mountain region. Working together meant that NGOs could pool resources. Furthermore, participants involved state health program directors in promoting the DVD, thus acknowledging and receiving support from state officials, and used numerous channels for distribution. The following is based on information reported by Nathan Grills, Robert Kumar, Rajesh Kumar Dongriyal, Bhagat Pun, and Evy Pun (email communication, April 17, 2013, and January 14, 2014; DVD can be viewed at www.chgnukc.org/dvd.html):

> Tobacco control activities in the mountains of North India are in their infancy with tobacco usage rates estimated to be 65% for males and 14% for females. In 2009, twenty-four community health NGOs linked to explore if cooperating would allow them to produce an effective and culturally appropriate anti-tobacco DVD for this remote mountain area. Through pooling resources and expertise, staff members from these programs were able to create an innovative DVD to raise awareness about the harms of tobacco. Each program provided a small donation towards the production of the DVD. Depending on their specific skills, individual NGOs contributed expertise including technical assistance, medical expertise, drama skills and musical input. The DVD was produced locally, drawing on local actors, singers and dancers. The DVD was launched at a large community event with two state health program directors presiding. Since the launch it has been shown as part of tobacco control projects at schools, clinics, melas and other community events. Furthermore, the campaign has been covered in ten newspapers and on two TV channels.

Reconciliation

Human beings do not always get along. We fight, denigrate, mock, disdain, undermine, exploit, deceive, enslave, and exclude each other. We justify our actions through appeals to self, ethnicity, class, religion, ideology, and pleasure. Yet artistic forms of communication may lead to powerful moments of repentance, forgiveness, solidarity, love, hope, and reconciliation. Singing and dancing can help us to heal individually. Watching others sing and dance can help us to recognize their uniqueness and their value. Singing and dancing together with others can require us to mold our individuality into coordinated sound and movement. The joy, pleasure, and solidarity that the arts evoke can pull us out of patterns of distrust and hopelessness.

Arts are being used in a variety of communities to help promote reconciliation. For example, following 30 years of war in Aceh, Indonesia, Nadine Hoover of Friends Peace Teams to Indonesia has developed an advanced-level "Alternatives to Violence" workshop to help community members learn the skills they need to recover from the trauma they have experienced (https://avp.international.org, accessed May 17, 2018). Through role-playing and games, the workshop focuses on the following: safety and self-care; companionship and accompaniment; facing traumatic incidents; stress, trauma, and reactions to trauma; remembering without reliving; loss, grief, and mourning; and rebuilding social relationships.

Much of recent world news has been dominated by stories of refugees fleeing war-torn regions of the world. Such tensions are not new, yet leaders in receiving regions continue to argue about how to handle newcomers, while community members argue about whether and how to receive refugees as well as other migrants. Displaced persons, already often dealing with the trauma of war and related losses, must learn to adapt to a new life and home. Here, too, the arts are being used to help. Jan Magne Steinhovden reports on one arts program from Norway (email communication, 24 May 2013; see also http://fargespill.no/):

The Norwegian program *"Fargespill"* ("Play of Colours") is an example of how art can become a major resource when people who have left "everything" meet people who seem to have "everything." Shortly after arriving in Norway, one of the economically richest countries in the world, some of the most vulnerable of all refugees—children and youth who seem to have lost everything they have, including their fundamental need for security—are invited to take part in a program that leads to a high quality show which merges performance arts from all over the world. "Fargespill" focuses entirely on people's resources. Refugee children are told that they are not arriving with empty hands. All of them have brought a few words from a song or a melody which reminds them of something beautiful. They have all brought themselves and their voices. These are the valuable elements of "Fargespill": the sum of voices and sounds and actions that were not present before these children arrived. Through the artistic adaptation of "Fargespill" founders Hamre, Saue and Erdal, these components are developed into a show that helps break down conceptions of difference and facilitates acceptance.

Social acceptance may be the most important resource that can enable immigrants to grow strong and secure in a new country. But social acceptance is not just something they can acquire themselves; rather it is something those who have already lived in a society have to be willing to give. "Fargespill" is a wonderful example of how this sense of community and recognition can be transmitted. I brought my seven- and nine-year-old children to one of the shows and we were astonished by what we heard and saw. We were touched beyond words by a performance of a children's song with rhythms and movements from other cultures. Great artistic expectations and hard work on behalf of the performers led to a standing ovation from people who had the rare opportunity of communicating what is often too hard to say directly: "You are fantastic. Thank you very much that *we* could come witness your gifts."

Rest and Play

Artistic forms of communication can provide exceptional opportunities for playful restoration; they can contribute to reduced stress, heightened hope, and improved emotional and physical health. The world's communities engage in an astounding variety of sporting activities that can display artistry in themselves, can promote a sense of identity, and can be integrated into larger events full of arts (see also Lipónski 2003). Cory Cummins (personal communication, June 20, 2016) describes the nonprofessional sport *castells* from the Catalania region of Spain:

Games and sport can energize a community, help develop identity, and transmit cultural values in ways that might not otherwise occur. A prime example of such a game is *castells* (human towers). *Castells* are found in the Catalonia region of Spain and have been in existence since the eighteenth century, generally occurring during festival times. These human structures are visually impressive, sometimes with ten levels of people standing on each other's shoulders with a supporting base of hundreds of assistants. Variations of these towers not only add to the complexity of the tower and success of the *castell* team but also to the visual beauty. As a nonprofessional sport, participants wear specific clothing to indicate their regional identity, and unique songs are played while the *castells* are being built. UNESCO has recognized the value of the *castell* and placed it on their list of the Intangible Cultural Heritage of Humanity.

Creative use of sports can also help meet broader goals within communities. For example, Uncharted Play (http://unchartedplay.com) was founded in 2011 by Jessica Matthews and Julia Silverman. Matthews and Silverman believed that forms of play could be harnessed to reach practical goals within communities. They invented the SOCCKET, a soccer ball that generates electricity every time it is kicked. Thirty minutes of playing soccer can power a lamp for three hours. According to Matthews, their goal was to "[amplify] existing enjoyment to make the world a better place" (Noble 2013). Today their soccer balls are enabling children to study and parents to work in the evenings in communities where electricity is not available or is unstable.

Human Rights

Social Justice

Communities often marginalize people in certain categories. Orphans, widows, foreigners, the poor, prisoners, the homeless, non-elites, and others often lack access to what they need for social and material health. Artistic communication can be used to work toward equal rights for all due to its abilities to instill hope, speak unwelcome truth to those in power, and encourage solidarity.[4]

Here is one example: The Kawangware Street Youth Project in Nairobi, Kenya, is one of hundreds of rehabilitation programs for street children and youth across Nairobi. In addition to income-generating activities such as bag making, participants also engage in a variety of artistic and sports-related activities. During Kathleen's research in Nairobi in 2004, one of their main activities was weekly music and puppetry shows performed by the youths for younger children in the community. These shows combined songs in English and Kiswahili with puppet shows on a variety of themes, including children's rights, alcohol and drug abuse, various diseases, and the environment. Puppetry performances were followed by question-and-answer sessions, during which members of the project asked the children about the characters and events in the skits. The following week, children were asked to recall the key lessons. During conversations with group members on one occasion, Kathleen was told how one show had focused on alcoholic fathers who use family income for alcohol and leave their children without shoes or school supplies. After the show, a child had confronted his father, asking him why he would waste the family income and leave his child without necessary items. The angry father came to project staff members to complain. However, it was precisely this type of empowerment of young people that the project members wished to encourage.

Ranjita Biswas (2010) describes the work of the organization Kolkata Sanved (which means "sensitivity" in Bengali) in another part of the world, India. Kolkata Sanved is a local NGO that uses dance to help transform the lives of trafficked girls and women. The founder, Sohini Chakraborty, initially used classical Indian dance and contemporary dance with the girls. Biswas explains that when the girls did not respond to this teaching method, Chakraborty began asking the girls to create body movements that imitated everyday actions, such as sweeping or making tea. Chakraborty later realized that this method was a recognized form of therapy called Dance Movement Therapy (DMT). Biswas writes, "As Chakraborty explains, the women she works with often feel a deep inferiority and have extremely low self-esteem. 'DMT encourages them to think, "I am creating my own body through my own expression."' By taking control of their bodies, they are able to rebuild their confidence and begin to cope with mental trauma."

In addition to working with trafficked girls and women, Kolkata Sanved also collaborates with NGOs working with street children, young people living in red-light areas, people living with HIV, and people with mental health issues, among others (Biswas 2010). Through dance, this organization is able to boost the confidence of marginalized and traumatized groups, enabling individuals to feel empowered within their communities.

Education

Rapid social change—when new economic and political realities devalue previous knowledge—can result in weakened educational systems. Because the arts are such penetrating and memorable systems of communication, communities can integrate them into all educational subjects and teaching contexts. This may be valuable both in community education campaigns and in programs linked with formal schools. Here Samuel Kahunde (email communication, February 11, 2014) describes how the arts are used widely in Uganda for educational purposes:

> In Uganda, music and drama are widely used as tools for bringing together people so that a particular message may be delivered. I have observed government departments and non-governmental organizations in Masindi, Uganda, use music and drama not only to bring people together, but also to convey messages. For example, in the late 1990s the Department of Health in Masindi contracted a local group, Masindi Black Actors, to use drama and music to mobilize people and convey anti-malaria campaigns, especially about using treated mosquito nets. The Department of Community Development in Masindi also used music, dance, and drama to promote

adult literacy. Today, The AIDS Support Organisation (TASO) in Masindi has supported the formation of voluntary groups to promote services such as HIV/AIDS counselling and testing; safe male circumcision; encouraging positive living with HIV; prevention of mother-to-child HIV; and other methods of HIV prevention. The groups move around the target villages staging free music, dance, and drama performances. Finally, every year in Uganda the Ministry of Education and Sports organizes music, dance, and drama festivals for schools and colleges. Participants compete in a variety of categories, including in thematic performances on topics such as constitutional changes and HIV and AIDS. It seems that the use of music, dance, and drama is perceived as being very effective in mobilizing and educating communities in Uganda.

Abimbola Cole Kai-Lewis (email communication, January 25, 2014), in turn, describes how an afterschool program for elementary and middle school students in New York City supplements the formal school curriculum by providing alternative educational methods, content, and performance opportunities to students:

Established by the Schubert Foundation in conjunction with the licensing company MTI International, Broadway Junior is an afterschool theater program for elementary and middle school students. It has been adopted by over 30 public schools in New York City, including Public School/Middle School (P.S./M.S.) 4, the South Bronx school where I work. The program has been hailed as a major achievement for theater education in schools. Broadway Junior provides students with opportunities to perform 60-minute adaptations of popular Broadway shows. Moreover, students sometimes take to the stage of a Broadway theater to perform one of the signature songs from their school's play before an audience of their peers and a celebrity host.

I have worked with the Broadway Junior team at P.S./M.S. 4 for two years. While my primary duty is to teach English Language Arts (ELA), I have also been able to witness how Broadway Junior contributes to students' development in ways that complement the standard P.S./M.S. 4 curriculum. Unlike the prescribed standards-based classroom learning that students are accustomed to, Broadway Junior exposes them to different learning approaches and content. Students must learn complex sequences of choreography, memorize all of their lines from scripts, grasp the basics of staging, and familiarize themselves with theater terminology. Amid all of this, students have attested that Broadway Junior helps them to nurture a range of talents that they do not ordinarily use at school. One student summed up his participation in the program by saying, "The thing I like about Broadway Junior is that I have the chance to show what I can do."

Literacy

Since many decisions affecting people's lives in private and government relationships involve written documents, the ability to read and write can provide minority communities with tools to help protect their interests. Literacy goals relate to both technical (e.g., understanding language structure) and social issues (e.g., wanting to read and write in a language, and feeling capable of acquiring these skills). This makes it likely that artistic forms—not only those with heavy language components (e.g., songs, drama, storytelling, proverbs, and riddles), but also those without (e.g., dance, visual arts)—will feed into these goals.

English speakers may be familiar with the alphabet song often taught to primary school children. In the following example, Michelle Petersen (personal communication, June 20, 2016) describes how an alphabet song was created as part of a Sango literacy program in Central African Republic. Petersen writes:

A literacy specialist in the Central African Republic felt that an alphabet song was needed to strengthen the reading readiness component in literacy efforts in the Sango language. She commissioned a local choir director to set a poem to music. It was to accompany a one-page alphabet chart which teachers distributed to learners and posted in their classrooms. A local artist had illustrated it. The chart had a key word and illustration to go along with each letter. "The Sango Alphabet Song" used alliteration, and Sango literacy teachers taught the song to help students learn the sounds of each letter. Here is part of it:

a A	âgara tî âta agä,	*Grandfather's cow came,*
b B	lo buba bongö tî babâ.	*It ruined father's clothes.*
d D	Deku adö dödö tî lo.	*The mouse did his dance.*
e E	Ë te lê tî këkë sô.	*We eat fruit from this tree.*

As well as serving as a learning tool, this song helped students' motivation. Their community also liked the song. When learners completed the reading program and received reading certificates, their community would sing them this song. Seeing a group of people receive certificates was in turn motivational for the next group of learners to desire to begin learning when the next opportunity arrived.

Economic Opportunity

Artistic communication can enhance commerce through advertising, and can motivate and coordinate people who are laboring. Artists also benefit from their activities when people pay for performances or objects. For example, the charity Voices from the Nations has produced a CD and DVD entitled "Sing to the Well" of performances by the Wagogo people of Tanzania but aimed at a Western audience. Martin and Rebekah Neil (Neil 2010) describe the results of the production: "The recording is a collection of songs taken from everyday life in a beautiful but harsh environment, where famine and drought are often just around the corner. Through an agreement between the local community, musicians, and the producers, sales of this production have provided water sources, a clinic, and other emergency help to the Mnase area implemented by a local development committee."

In Cambodia, finally, the arts have provided both emotional healing and economic opportunity. Martin and Rebekah Neil write (adapted from Neil 2010):

In Cambodia during the 1970s, under Pol Pot and the Khmer Rouge, some of the first people who were taken, tortured, and murdered were the creative people who carried the story and the heartbeat of the land. Even instruments were destroyed during this time, and ultimately an estimated total of 1.7 million deaths resulted from Khmer Rouge policies. Cambodian Christian Arts Ministry School (CCAMS) was started by Noren (a survivor of the Pol Pot regime), and an American lady, Gioia. Former street kids, gang members, orphans, and children being used in slavery and prostitution are rescued into a loving home where they are loved, fed, sheltered, and educated. Alongside its regular schooling, the CCAMS family has an emphasis on the arts (music, dance, drama, visual art, and literature). By teaching the children at CCAMS the arts, they not only give the children incredible skills and a means to express their emotions, but they are also restoring something that was stolen from the nation.

The Ling family offers one example of the impact of CCAMS. Noren met the Ling family at a very crucial time and took the children into CCAMS, where they have flourished. One girl became their lead dancer and, together with her sister, earned enough money performing to help their parents build a house in their home village and farm the land successfully. The mother

makes many of the beautiful costumes for the children of CCAMS while another sister teaches them to dance.

Steps to Specifying Goals P

As this whirlwind tour shows, the arts are used in incredibly diverse ways around
the world. In this section, we outline a process that you and a community can follow
to choose one or more goals for artistic programs. We want this procedure to be
marked by maximum participation of the community. This means that everything
we do should demonstrate respect for local knowledge and intelligence; emphasize
discussing, listening, and building consensus; help community members become
agents of change; and advance sustainable changes. This mindset plays a crucial
role in deciding what goals a community wants to work toward. You may be familiar
with some formal methods people use to specify community needs and goals in
participatory ways, with names such as Appreciative Inquiry, Force Field Analysis,
Stakeholder Analysis, and Participatory Action Research. We draw on a few of these
here, outlining an activity that you can modify to fit different situations.

Creating together will include a continual process of specifying and refining
community goals. This section provides a place to start. Before presenting this approach, however, we must note that it will not work in every community. In fact,
many participatory approaches to decision-making assume that participants will
esteem individuality and equal opportunity as their highest values. Many societies
instead focus more on hierarchical systems composed of people who fill clearly
defined roles. In these contexts, voices at the top of a hierarchy may silence those
further down. Because of this, we include a planning stage before implementing
this process.

1. 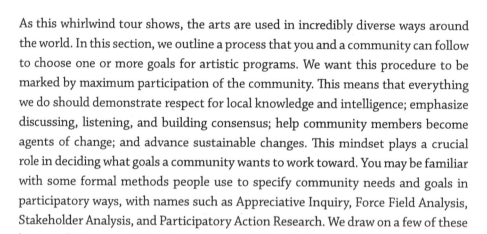 *Plan Decision-Making Activities*
    - Meet with a few friends or other trusted members of the community you
      are working with.
    - Ask for stories of how people normally make decisions among family
      members (nuclear or extended), a school, a religious group, or other
      common social groupings. Ask initial questions like these, then follow up
      on answers: What clear signs of a hierarchical or egalitarian approach are
      there? Is there a method for everybody to give input? Are some people
      excluded from decision-making? Do people need to follow protocols of

politeness or respect in interacting about a decision? Write themes you notice during this discussion in your Community Arts Profile.

- Discuss elements 2, 3, 4, and 5 (in the following) with your friends. Ask questions like these: How well would this work in your community? How might we change it so we receive everyone's input? Or the best result?
- With your friends, plan the decision-making process, identifying the following choices: participants, when and where, who takes various roles during the process, and what resources are needed to hold this decision-making event.

2. *Gather Voices*

Your first task is to talk with and listen to people. Here is one example: Between 1986 and 1991, artist-animators from the University of Dar es Salaam helped to organize a series of two-week "Theatre for Development" workshops in Tanzania. They led participants through identifying local art forms, elicited problems in the communities, and helped participants address these problems through communication in local performance genres. Problems included many particular to women, such as frequent cases of being beaten by men (Mlama 1994).

You may join conversations about goals that people already have in social structures such as traditional or government organizations, rotating savings and credit associations, churches, mosques, or temples. Goals may be clear; if not, the following section may help identify priorities and opportunities. You may have this conversation as part of an event that is already happening, such as a conference or workshop. Work toward including people from as many parts of the community as possible, especially those not usually given a voice.

3. *Explore Strengths*

All communities have strengths and weaknesses. Identifying strengths and aspirations gives people courage and may lead to solutions to problems. Ask people questions such as these:

- What is your community known for doing well?
- What hopes do you have for your children? For yourself? For the community as a whole?

Strengths and Aspirations	Goals for a Better life
Respect between generations	Identity and Sustainability
Celebration	Identity and Sustainability
Hospitality	Health and well-being
. . .	. . .

FIGURE 2.1. Sample list of strengths and aspirations.

List answers to these questions, then think together how they relate to goals for a better life. Here is a reminder of the goal categories we used earlier:

- *Identity and sustainability*: valuing identity, teaching children, using media
- *Health and well-being*: healing, reconciliation, rest and play
- *Human rights*: social justice, education, literacy, economic opportunity.

List the most closely related goal category next to the strengths, or make up a new one. You may come up with something like Figure 2.1.

4. *Explore Problems*

Ask people questions such as these:

- What issues are difficult for your community?
- What causes you significant worry?
- What is worse in your community now than five years ago? Ten? Twenty?

List answers to these questions, then think together about how solutions would relate to goals for a better life. List the most closely related goal category next to the problems, or make up a new one. You may come up with something such as Figure 2.2.

5. *Choose a Goal*

Needs may be linked within communities. Speaking about the community of Kawangware in Nairobi, Kenya, for example, social worker Augusto Githaiga explained to Kathleen (interview with Augusto Githaiga, Nairobi, August 12, 2004):

You see, you have so many AIDS organizations. As I was telling you, they want to change this habit of AIDS. You know, why are people dying of AIDS?

Problems	Goals for a Better life
Disease: HIV/AIDS, malaria	Well-being
War, crime, violence	Well-being
Intergenerational conflict, loss of traditions	Identity and Sustainability
Exploitation: slavery, prostitution	Justice
Inability to read or write	Justice
Poor education	Justice
Hunger	Justice
. . .	. . .

FIGURE 2.2. Sample list of problems framed as goals.

Why are people not changing their habits, and yet the disease is killing hundreds? But just because of the sense of poverty, people want to live as the days come. . . . Because they don't have hope for tomorrow. So everything has been eclipsed by poverty. You see, you want to build [address] . . . the environment. Who'd care about the environment, [when] they don't have food on the table? Who'd care about . . . security, and yet they don't have food on the table? . . . And then illiteracy as well. Illiteracy has really affected our community.

According to Githaiga, programs that address AIDS as an isolated issue are doomed to fail. AIDS is not the only problem within his community. There are numerous challenges, many of which affect people's behavior and attitudes toward AIDS. What does this mean for arts advocates working within communities? Working alongside community members, we may need to respond to multiple needs within communities. Addressing one problem may involve recognizing and tackling other issues, too.

Ask community members to decide which problems they would most like to address, or the strength they would most like to build on. If you are not a decision-maker in the community, your role in *Step 2* is now complete. The goals must emerge from and be owned by the community, not inserted from outside.

Notes

1. For discussion of problems related to UNESCO's intangible heritage designations, see Grant 2014:36–37. Titon 2015:168 discusses terminology related to this initiative.

2. For additional discussions of arts and sustainability, see Schippers (2015), Titon (2016), and resources in *Closing 7* in this volume.

3. To listen to this example, go to https://www.youtube.com/watch?v=loEBQKdQyyM.

4. Additional examples are available through the Society for Ethnomusicology's Music and Social Justice Resources Project (2018), a repository of resources on how people are using music to address social conflict, exclusion/inclusion, and justice (https://ethnomusicology.site-ym.com/page/Resources_Social).

Step

3

CONNECT GOALS TO GENRES

ONCE A COMMUNITY has identified goals that they want to work toward, it is time to figure out how their arts can help them achieve those goals. Each genre is particularly apt for communicating certain kinds of content and producing certain kinds of effects. In *Step 3* we explain a process that you and a community can follow to

- choose the desired effects of new artistry;
- choose the content of new artistry;
- choose a genre or genres that have the capacity to communicate the content and produce the desired effects (note that multiple genres may be integrated into the same events);
- imagine events that could include enactments of new works.

You may wish to have this conversation with the same people you gathered for *Step 2*, or you may wish to include others. We present the path of gathering elements in *Step 3* in a linear, logically ordered way. We recommend that you address all elements of the process, but you can experiment with alternating the order of activities or incorporate other participatory methods that may be more appropriate to your context. The community also may be innovative both in terms of genres and types of events.

Choose the Desired Effects of the New Artistry

The first task to connecting goals with local arts is thinking through the effects that you want those arts to produce in the community. These are possible ways in which people may be impacted by artistry:

- They understand an important message.
- They act differently.
- They change an unhelpful or dangerous behavior.
- They do something new.
- They think differently.
- They feel solidarity with others.
- They experience hope, joy, anger, remorse, elation, peace, satisfaction, relief, empathy, surprise, or other emotions.

So together, ask the following:

- How do we want people to change in ways that move them toward our goals?
- Then enter the results of the discussion in the Community Arts Profile.

Choose the Content of the New Artistry

If the desired effects depend on people learning ideas through the arts, then it is crucial to make sure that those ideas are trustworthy. It is important to study the content to be taught so that an accurate message is conveyed. If the message is about how malaria may be prevented, make sure you know the facts about how malaria is actually prevented; talk to your health-care professional. Together discuss these questions:

- What content do we want to communicate?
- How can we make sure that the content is reliable?
- Enter the results of the discussion in the Community Arts Profile.

Choose a Genre That Has the Capacity to Communicate the Content and Produce the Desired Effects

Every artistic genre has characteristics that affect the messages it conveys and the effects it has. So together discuss the following:

Genre	Brief Description	Event	Participants	Connotations	Effects

FIGURE 3.1. Genre comparison chart.

- Show the list of artistic genres you produced in the activity "Take a First Glance at a Community's Arts" in *Step 1*. This could be on a big piece of paper, a chalkboard or whiteboard, an overhead projector, or a digital projector.
- For each genre, ask:
  - Would a new artistic work in this genre have the effects we have chosen? If not, why not?
  - Would a new artistic work in this genre communicate the content we have chosen well? If not, why not?
  - Do resources exist that allow enactment of the genre? For example, are there people who know how to do this? This genre may not be practically feasible.
  - Fill out the information in the Genre Comparison Chart you began in *Step 1* for the genres most likely to work, reproduced here as Figure 3.1.
- Narrow the list to one or two genres that would be the best for effecting these changes and communicating this content now.
- Perform "Take a First Glance at an Event" (*Step 4*, Part A) for each of these genres. This new glance might cause you to reconsider genres you have chosen or rejected. The rest of *Step 4* will then lead you through more detailed exploration of the genre or genres you finally decide on.
- Be sure to include artists in this process. Avoid treating artists only as "messengers" rather than colleagues and creators; they will have significant knowledge to contribute to this decision-making process.
- Put the results and important factors of this discussion in the Community Arts Profile.

Imagine Events That Could Include Performance of New Works in the Genre That Would Produce the Effects in Its Experiencers

When an individual or group acts artistically alone, it can be deeply satisfying, cathartic, or healing for them. This is of great value. The focus of this Guide, though, is artistic action in the context of community. This means that a new dyed cloth, play, or poem has limited value if it remains hidden. It has no effect on anybody else unless it is part of an event where communication happens.

Before we start planning how to create new works in a genre, then, it is important to start imagining the contexts for their presentation and how they work as communication. We started thinking about events with artistic content in *Step 1*. To expand our concept of what could constitute an artistic event, here are some more examples of an infinite number of such communication contexts: weddings, funerals, baptisms, harvest celebrations, courting rituals, birth rites, rites of passage, teaching contexts, listening to an audio recording, watching a videorecording, transmitting live audio or video to other locations, viewing a sculpture in a museum, looking at a skyscraper in a city, concerts, rehearsals, gigs, awards ceremonies, sporting events, intimate family discussions, smoking a peace pipe, court, and war.

Each of these examples has certain components that typify communication events, illustrated in Figure 3.2. Figure 3.2 reveals how people interact by directing messages through various artistic genres to other communicators at particular places and times. The place and time could be one evening in a concert hall, or spread out such as when someone watches a film created previously by someone else in a different location. The people involved in the communication event consist of at least two individuals or groups who may or may not be physically close, and may or may not exist materially; humans often perform for spiritual beings.

We represent artistic genres in Figure 3.2 by the tubes enclosing and connecting the communicators. Note that some genres are more regular and predictable than

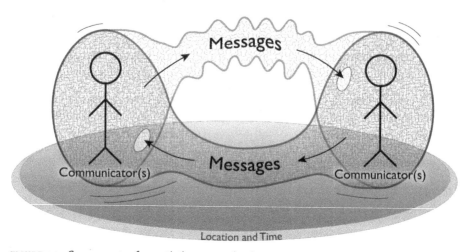

FIGURE 3.2. Components of an artistic communication event.

others—these are depicted in the front with smooth lines. Others include more variability or improvisation, which we have indicated by the curled edges. Messages are the ideas or feelings that take form when mediated by a genre. People at the event experience this content when they hear, see, feel, smell, or taste whatever other communicators produce with their singing, dancing, painting, cooking, and the like. Finally, you will see that communication happens in particular directions (indicated by the arrows), but is always eventually reciprocal. People who experience a bit of artistry may respond with verbal, physical, or visual encouragement or discouragement, by joining in a performance, with notable silence, or in many other ways. It is this response that so often feeds back into the performance, resulting in more energy, pleasure, and creativity. See "Cultural Dynamism" (in *Step 4*, Part C) for activities exploring how a particular community draws on this communication feedback to increase energy.

Together, do the following:

1. Make a list of kinds of events of which new works in the artistic genre could be part. Let your minds run free with possibilities at this stage. Include both presentations where performers and other participants are in the same place, and those in which people experience the arts through sound, visual, videorecording, or broadcast.
2. Remind yourselves of your choices thus far: effects, content (messages), and genre.
3. Choose a few of the event types you came up with and briefly describe them in terms of their communication components: Who are the communicators? When and where might such an event happen? What senses will participants use in experiencing the content? How will the genre affect the messages that people experience? When people experience the artistry, will it have the effects that you would like? How will people respond to the communicators?
4. Choose one or two events that would be likely goals for co-creative activities. You can always choose other events in the next steps, but this will help you plan.

Put the results of this discussion in the Community Arts Profile.

A Note on Tourism and Other Repurposing

Every time someone enacts a bit of artistry, it differs from every other time it was enacted. The difference may be very small, as when an actor inflects a word slightly differently on one day to the next because of her emotional state, humidity affecting her voice, a considered choice, or a whim. Or the change may be large, as when a singer has laryngitis and invites audience members onto the stage to sing his songs for him. We explore how performances can differ in some depth in *Step 4*.

An increasingly common form of change results when communities reframe their arts from an internal purpose to an external purpose: entertaining outsiders. When the Cameroonian DAKASTUM dance association decided that they wanted to become famous throughout all of Cameroon, for example, they modified their performances. From singing and dancing at all-night death celebrations for someone in their Ngiemboon networks, they wanted people to listen to their songs on the radio and attend concerts. So DAKASTUM shortened each song from 10–15 minutes to 3–4 minutes; added French lyrics to Ngiemboon texts; regularized the percussion and call-response forms; and highlighted their flamboyant drum improvisations (Schrag 2013b).

Touristic performance brings attractive benefits: employment, affirmation of identity, and sometimes the reinvigoration of a disappearing tradition. However, reframing an artistic genre for outsiders may also result in the loss of many crucial elements and its separation from the values and social structures that produced it. In addition, when minority communities perform for wealthier outsiders, they usually conform to outsiders' tastes, possibly reinforcing a dominant-subservient relationship redolent of neocolonialism (for more on tourism, see Ó Briain 2014; Krüger and Trandafoiu 2014).

Since the *Make Arts* process almost always includes local arts being put to new purposes, it is crucial that the community reflect on the implications of such a move. *Step 3* has provided some ways to evaluate what may happen. *Step 4* allows you to explore genres and events in many more ways, resulting in more information to evaluate.

Step
4

ANALYZE GENRES AND EVENTS

YOU AND THE community have stepped through first meetings, have explored dreams and goals, and have begun to connect the arts to a better life. Now you have reached the crux of creativity: the artistry itself—the complex, intricate processes and objects that move us to cry, laugh, dance, resolve, remember, forgive, understand, and imagine. Artistic communication affects us because our previous experience leads us to expect certain things to happen. These expectations are sometimes completely satisfied, sometimes pleasurably tweaked, and sometimes startlingly overturned.

All of this energy is wrapped in an extremely complex package, thus *Step 4* takes up almost half of the Guide. But do not most people in communities implicitly know the information we are trying to tease out in this step? Do not master artists know how to subtly modify a vocal timbre to bring a tear to one's eye or a spring to one's step? Yes. And are not others sometimes able to express this knowledge explicitly, using their own or outside analytical vocabulary? Yes. So why do we have to put such time and energy into learning what others already know?

Here are two good reasons to research artistic genres. First, even within our own communities, most of us do not have the perspective or categories to understand everything that is important in our artistic actions. Second, by enabling you to better understand artistic practices, this research will help ensure that you—in collaboration with, or as a member of, a community—develop artistic initiatives that are effective in meeting community goals. *Step 4* is critical in leading a community toward designing sparking activities (*Step 5*), improving new works (*Step 6*), and integrating new creativity within the community (*Step 7*).

To help you access these benefits, this introduction will show you how to

- think clearly about genres and events;
- understand *Step 4*'s structure;
- decide what analysis to do.

Think Clearly about Genres and Events

An artistic event is something that happens in space and time that includes artistry. Artistry is anything someone produces from knowledge and skills related to an artistic genre. For the analyses in *Step 4*, it will be helpful to explore these terms further. So, more precisely, we define event and genre as follows:

An *event* is something that occurs in a particular place and time, related to larger sociocultural patterns of a community. It is divisible into shorter time segments. An *artistic event* contains at least one enactment of a genre. Communities have types of events that include social expectations and patterns. Examples of events include festivals, church services, birthday parties, rites of passage, watching and listening to a music video on an electronic device, and studying a painting in a museum. Figure 4.1 represents the kind of complex artistic event that could exist. Its multiple, intertwined artistic features include character and plot (drama), etiquette and frame (storytelling), balance and color (visual art), texture and scale (music), and phrasing and effort (dance).

An *artistic genre* (which we often shorten to *genre* in this Guide) is a community's category of artistic communication, characterized by a unique set of formal characteristics, performance practices, and social meanings. A genre enactment is an instantiation of a genre during an event. Examples of genre include: *olonkho*

FIGURE 4.1. Sample artistic event with intertwined artistic features.

(Siberia), Broadway musical (New York City), *kanoon* (Cameroon), *huayno* (Peru), *haiku* (Japan), praise and worship (Euro-America), and *qawwali* (South Asia).

The following are some implications of thinking in this way:

Events may contain enactments of more than one genre: A commemoration of the death and life of a Bamiléké (Cameroon) king may last a month—one event with many sub-events. During this time, performers from other kingdoms visit to pay their respects, usually including performances of one or more genres, each with unique combinations of music, dance, drama, and visual elements (like royal stools).

Events are longer than enactments of a genre: At a wedding, for example, you may perform a solo that is in a love song genre. Enactment of the love song genre is just one part of a larger event that includes rituals and other elements.

Enactments of genres may be found in more than one kind of event: Certain kinds of acrobatic feats, for example, may appear both in circuses and gymnastics competitions.

Many events entail strong expectations of what kinds of genres they can include: For example, a raised fist or performance of "We shall overcome"—visual and sung examples of resistance genres—would jar an Olympic awards ceremony. There may be an inflexible association between a certain type of event and a certain genre, or participants in an event may have the freedom to switch out elements from different genres. In *Step 3*, we already have explored this a bit. We will help you think about it more in *Step 5*.

Genres and events are always changing: Old ones die, new ones are born, creative people innovate. Genres like Kiswahili rap have multiple origins wrapped in unique ways; such fusions are common. Hence do not hold your definitions too tightly. As you describe more events and genres, you increasingly will be able to understand their boundaries and flexibilities.

Understand Step 4's Structure

Step 4 is devoted to exploring an event that has actually occurred in time and space. We emphasize this because we want to make sure that everything you do with a community is based on reality, not a disembodied idea. All of the research activities we include require either your direct experience with or recorded elements of an event. We augment these with secondary research, often in the form of interviewing people with more direct experience. The knotted shape in Figure 4.1 represents the artistry in such an event.

After helping you choose which event to analyze, we guide you through three kinds of analysis of an event and its artistry:

- Part A: Describe the Event and Its Genre(s) as a Whole
- Part B: Explore the Event's Genre(s) through Artistic Domain Categories
- Part C: Relate the Event's Genre(s) to Its Broader Cultural Context

Here we show you a small sample of the kinds of information you would learn from each of these analyses, using Brian and his wife Barb's wedding as an example event. We focus on one genre enactment: performance of a love song. A breakdown of this information will be provided in more detail shortly; the following sample is simply to give you a taste of the types of information you can gather about an event.

Choose an Artistic Event to Analyze

You may explore anywhere from one to hundreds of events—each will make your understanding of a genre richer. Here are a few guidelines to get started.

Essential Elements

- You need to be able to witness the event or objects firsthand, or have a good videorecording of the event. Any event at all is better than people's words about something you cannot experience.
- The event needs to contain an example of the genre or genres the community has chosen to work with.
- The event must be done by people in the community.

Elements That May Make Your Analysis More Immediately Fruitful

- A typical example of this type of event will help you understand more quickly the normal elements of such an event.
- An example of the event performed by artists whom the community states are the most skillful will help you understand aesthetic and enactment values.

Part A: Describe the Event and Its Genre(s) as a Whole (discussed in depth on pp. 96–114)

Take a First Glance at an Event: Brian and Barb's Wedding

The questions in this section lead you to basic information such as: it is the coalescing of a bi-family community; California (US); May 18, 1985; inside a church; ornate regalia; kin and fictive kin of bride and groom; stylized walking; organ, piano, voice, oratory; joy and sadness; affirmation of marriage; much time, money, and activity invested.

Look at the Event and Its Genre(s) through Lenses on Forms and their Meanings

This section helps you take a closer look at the forms of the artistry in the event through the *seven-lens view* of *space, materials, participant organization, shape of the event through time, performance features, content,* and *underlying symbolic systems* (to be discussed more later). Doing a few of these research activities on the wedding would lead to the following kinds of insights: the front of the church sanctuary was reserved for the most sacred activities; the bride and groom exchanged rings that symbolized love and eternity; the groom's brother had the role of bringing the groom's ring; the event's ritual expectations were followed closely; performance of the love song genre included the groom's three siblings as singers, and the brother as pianist; the song emphasized romantic love in the context of God's love.

Part B: Explore the Event's Genre(s) through Artistic Domain Categories (pp. 114–198)

The guided research in this section is divided into five Euro-American artistic domains. You only need to delve into those that the genre in question contains. The wedding event contained several artistic genres: classical organ music; love song; processional and recessional instrumental music; oratory; blessing; and storytelling. For this example, we will learn more about the artistic features of one of these genres, the love song. The primary artistic domains that this genre draws on are music and oral verbal arts.

From examination of the song through a few of the research activities in "Music in an Event" (later in *Step 4*), we discover a strophic form of verse/chorus/verse/chorus/gentle, floating outro; the groom's brother played the piano (a struck chordophone) and sang, and his sisters sang; they used narrow vibrato at the end of phrases; the chorus was contrapuntal; the song used a divisive meter of ¾; quarter note equals 94 beats per minute; and the tonal center was G.

From examination of the song's lyrics through some research activities in "Oral Verbal Arts in an Event" (later in *Step 4*), we discover phrase repetition, metaphor, lexical substitution, rhyme, and that overall form parallels song form.

Part C: Relate the Event's Genre(s) to Its Broader Cultural Context (pp. 198–214)

This section leads you to connect the artistry in the event with other elements in the community. Applying a few of these research tasks to the wedding leads to the following kinds of knowledge: the performers and composers of the love song are siblings in a family with historically notable singers and instrument players, rooted in Mennonite choral traditions; the performers enjoyed a transiently high status in the eyes of many experiencers during the event; the new love song resulted from collaboration between two siblings; high aesthetic value was placed on new lyrics and melody, with highlighted vocal harmonies; the creativity components—creators, language and other symbolic systems, and gatekeepers—were all within the family; and many in the audience experienced a combination of pleasure and melancholy.

Figure 4.2 shows the categories of insights each of these three kinds of research produced in this genre example of a love song. Note that you only have to investigate the artistic domains (music, dance, drama, oral verbal arts, visual arts) that the genre under investigation contains. This love song genre, for example, has primarily musical and verbal features, with few or no dance, drama, or visual features.

Figure 4.3 depicts the analysis process as looking through a series of differently shaped or colored glass lenses. Although we look through all of the lenses at the same event, each lens reveals aspects that the others do not uncover.

Each kind of analysis will help you understand what goes on in the others. Allow your mind to roam from detailed information about minute features of an event to broad cultural themes and back again. We never know whether a single note, vocal timbre, feather, facial expression, eyebrow movement, color, or any number of other elements could help enable a better life.

The more you and the community know about the range of art forms available and how each one works, the more you can reflect together on how to best

Enactment of Genre 1: Love Song		
Unique form and meaning description through seven-lens view (Part A)	Unique set of musical and verbal characteristics (Part B)	Unique set of relations to broader cultural context (Part C)

FIGURE 4.2. Three types of research.

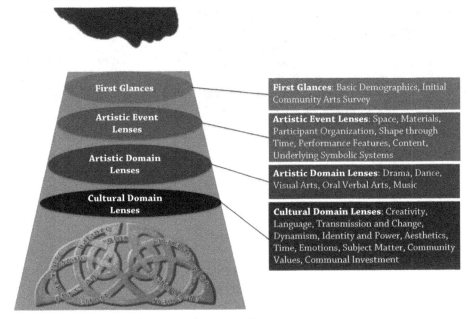

FIGURE 4.3. Analysis as looking through a series of lenses.

use them. We provide research activities in this step, but they are only a start. If you are not learning anything interesting from our directions, think about these questions: What other questions could I ask? What other ways could I find out about this phenomenon? What is true about this genre that does not fit any of the categories here?

Another Way of Organizing the Analysis Process

The table in Figure 4.4 provides a model you can use to organize your observations about an event in a way that highlights connections between features from different artistic domains. We will discuss these artistic domain categories in turn shortly; it may be useful to keep this figure in mind as we move forward.

Decide What Analysis to Do

Not every research activity we include in *Step 4* is relevant to the artistry you are investigating. Even if it were, you do not have enough time to do it all. Here, therefore, are a few ways you can focus your research.

Artistic Domains	Event Lenses	Space	Materials	Participants	Shape through Time	Performance Features	Content	Underlying Symbolic Systems
	Drama							
	Dance							
	Visual Arts							
	Oral Verbal Arts							
	Music							
	Other							

FIGURE 4.4. Organizing observations about an event by event lenses.

First, always do anything that starts with "Take a First Glance at. . . ." These sections provide much insight requiring a relatively small amount of energy and time. Second, we have created indexes of these activities that you can peruse with a community friend, to see what seems most pertinent. Third, notice that many of the sparking activities in *Step 5* describe research someone needs to do to complete the activity. While performing these activities in *Step 5*, go back to *Step 4* to do the recommended research. Fourth, if you have an advisor or more experienced arts specialist available, work with him or her to design a research plan that includes strategically chosen activities. Fifth and finally, we offer targeted guidance in the introduction of the section "Some Advice on Choosing Research Activities for Artistic Domains."

Part A: Describe the Event and Its Genre(s) as a Whole

In this section, we lead you through an exploration of a complete event containing artistic content.

Take a First Glance at an Event

Use these journalists' questions to capture your preliminary observations, brief interviews, and assessments of an artistic event. You will explore each category in more detail later.

Context

- Name of community:_____
- Location (country, region, city/village, place):

  _____
- Date(s):_____
- Your name: _____

What happened?

Where did it happen?

When did it happen?

Who was involved?

How did the event progress?

Why do people say the event happened?

Look at an Event's Forms

Identifying the unique attributes of the form of an artistic act of communication allows you to enter more accurately into its creation, integration, and celebration. Any small element of the form may evoke significant symbolic or emotive meaning. Because of the potential importance of details like these in meeting a community's goals, it is crucial that we have a way to notice them. In this section, we do this by helping you look at an event through specially chosen lenses.

In physical terms, a lens is a piece of glass that has been polished or otherwise changed in a way that alters any light coming through it. Depending on its maker's goal, someone who looks through a lens at an object may see that object as closer, farther, or perhaps with one color intensified. A lens, then, is a way of looking at something to make one of its aspects clearer. We are using this same idea metaphorically to guide research in the arts. In particular, we present a method that will direct your eyes, ears, and bodies to reveal seven categories of detail: *space, materials, participant organization, shape of the event through time, performance features, content,* and *underlying symbolic systems.* All lenses can reveal elements that carry meaning. To describe the lenses, we answer the following questions:

- *Space*: Where does the event occur? In what ways do performers use their space?
- *Materials*: With what?

- *Participant organization*: Who has responsibility for doing what?
- *Shape through time*: In what order?
- *Performance features*: How?
- *Content*: About what? To what imagined time and place does the enact-ment take us? What people, events, and ideas is the enactment about?
- *Underlying symbolic systems*: By what rules?

The first six lenses (*space, materials, shape through time, participant organization, performance features*, and *content*) are transcribable. The *underlying symbolic systems* lens describes the rules by which the other six lenses function well in a genre.

Note that each of these seven lenses may interact very closely with others, describing the same thing from a different perspective; do not be surprised if you come up with recurring patterns. Also, each lens may not reveal insights equally well in any given event, so if a lens does not seem to help much, move on to another.

Discussion of each of these lenses contains the following parts:

- *Basic description* of the lens.
- *Research questions* to guide your exploration of the event through the lens under discussion.
- *Research activities* that are particularly relevant to answering these re-search questions. Put the results of these activities into the description of this event in your Community Arts Profile.
- *Artistic domain connections*, a discussion that highlights common impor-tant connections between each lens and arts domains. You can follow up on these connections by performing exploratory activities in the next section's discussions of music, dance, drama, oral verbal arts (especially storytelling, poetry, oratory, and proverbs), and visual arts.
- *Meaning connections*, a reminder to relate your findings to meanings, sym-bolism, and broader cultural themes.

We have designed these lenses to help you understand more about a particular event with artistic content. If it is the first event you have seen of its type, you will not know yet if it is a normal example or if it differs in significant ways from what usually happens. As you use the lenses to describe more events of this same type, you will see patterns and points of divergence. Remember to focus your inquiries on the genre you chose in *Step 3*.

Space

Basic Description

Space is the location, demarcation, and physical characteristics of the area used, which can affect the form of artistic communication. Space is the canvas upon which the event is painted. It affects the movement of participants and their relationships to one another, lengthening or shortening the time it takes for participants to move around it, and other elements of an enactment.

Write what you learn about how this event uses space in the Community Arts Profile. Include drawings, photographs, and other representations to help explain what is going on.

Research Questions to Help You Know What to Explore

- Did it occur inside, outside, or both? If inside, give the type and size of the building.
- What are some characteristics of the place where it happened (shape and size, for example)?
- What parts was the space separated into? Were there physical and/or conceptual markers to separate these parts?
- What activities were associated with each part?
- Who designed, controlled, or owned the space for this particular event?
- How did each participant's location in the space and proximity to other participants affect his or her contribution to the event? How did it affect other participants' experience of their contribution?
- What meaning(s) do people attach to these elements of space?
- From what you know of the genre of this event, did people use space in usual ways? Uncommon ways?

Research Activities to Help You Answer the Questions

- Draw a floor diagram, including boundaries and demarcations.
- Take photographs of the place and its surroundings.
- Ask questions of participants and other cultural insiders about what happened. You may want to do this while watching a video of the event.
- Make a list of local names for the elements of space used in the event.

Artistic Domain Connections

In an artistic event, features that interact most closely with space are often associated with drama and dance. In addition, creators of art objects manipulate space to create formal structure through features like proportion, rhythm, balance, and the like.

Meaning Connections

Explore how what you have discovered by looking at an event through the lens of *space* relates to meanings, symbolism, and broader cultural themes. "Relate the Event's Genre(s) to Its Broader Cultural Context" (Part C) will provide direction for this.

Materials

Basic Description

Materials are all of the tangible things associated with an event, like clothing, regalia, instruments, props, and lighting. Some objects are more important to the execution and experience of the event than others. They may be made by humans (as in a mask) or appropriated to fill a function (as an eagle feather marking regalia as royal). Objects may serve multiple purposes, conveying meaning at many levels. For example, the Atumpan drum (Ghana) serves as a functional member of the musical ensemble, while also indicating royalty by its shape, colors, and construction; it plays both a functional and symbolic role. As another example, *kanoon* dancers in Cameroon move shakers in patterned ways that both add to the dance (experienced through visual channels) and produce sounds integral to the rhythm (experienced through auditory channels) (Schrag 2005:177–r230). Note also that some objects in the space where an event takes place may be incidental to what is going on.

Write what you learn about how this event uses materials in the Community Arts Profile. Include drawings, photographs, and other representations to help explain what is going on.

Research Questions to Help You Know What to Explore

- What objects were involved in the event?
- What is each object like physically?
- What meaning(s) do people attach to these objects?
- From what you know of the genre of this event, did people use objects in usual ways? Uncommon ways?

⚙ **Research Activities to Help You Answer the Questions**

- Make a list of objects associated with the event. Do this by observing and asking yourself and others questions like these:
  ○ What objects were present, including structures (such as buildings)?
  ○ What objects did people bring expressly for the event?
  ○ What did people wear?
  ○ What did people hold? Kick? Otherwise manipulate with their bodies?
  ○ Were there objects on surfaces, like walls, floors, or ceilings?
  ○ Were there technologies that produced atmospheric effects and performance enhancements, such as lighting, sound amplification, smoke, incense?
  ○ Were there live objects, like animals or plants, in the event?
  ○ Were there foods or drinks involved in the event?
  ○ Were there man-made or natural objects that were repurposed for this event?
- Describe each object by examining it and asking questions like these:
  ○ What are the object's physical characteristics? This may include materials, design, construction, weight, and length. Kinds of source materials include fibers (from plants or animals), minerals, metals, plastics, and wood.
  ○ What are local and other names for the object?
  ○ Take photographs that reveal details of objects (close-ups, from various angles).
- Describe the functions and interactions of objects in the event through observation, interview, and other activities:
  ○ Draw a floor diagram, showing placement of objects.
  ○ Take photographs of the objects in their locations.
  ○ Describe who interacted with each object, and in what ways.
  ○ Imagine and ask how participants might have modified their actions because of the presence of objects. You can also ask how the presence of an object might have constrained the participants' use of space. For example, a short microphone cord limits the range of movement of an actor.
  ○ List all of the ways in which an object contributes to the execution of the event.
- Learn and document how to make or use an object.
- Ask questions of participants and other cultural insiders about the uses and construction of objects. You may wish to do this while watching a video of the event, looking at pictures of objects, or interacting with the objects themselves.

- To whom does each object belong?
- How old is each object? Was it created especially for this event or kind of event?

Artistic Domain Connections

In an artistic event, objects can play significant roles in all of the artistic domains. Drama uses costumes and props to show characterization and provide dramatic settings. The most common objects used to produce musical features are instruments. In dance, costumes and props may highlight motion. A storyteller might use a prop to symbolize an event in her story, and visual artists use all sorts of materials to create objects. Finally, cooks gather and process ingredients and spices to create food. Remember that each object can play roles in multiple artistic domains.

Meaning Connections

Explore how what you have discovered by looking at an event through the lens of *materials* relates to meanings, symbolism, and broader cultural themes. "Relate the Event's Genre(s) to Its Broader Cultural Context" (Part C) will provide direction for this.

Participant Organization

Basic Description

At an artistic event, virtually everyone present (and sometimes people who are not even there) participate in some way. We focus here on the people involved in the event in terms of the roles they play, the ways they interact with each other through time, and how they use the space around them. Each participant in an event plays a role (given by genre and personal proclivities) that affects the form of the enactment. Roles can include creators, performers (e.g., singers, instrument players, actors, dancers, storytellers), audience (e.g., aficionados, mass, cognoscenti, hecklers), helpers (e.g., set builders, stage managers, gaffers, ticket takers, bouncers, ushers), producers, directors, and so on. Also relevant to the formal characteristics of an event are participants' histories, skills, kin and other relationships to each other, status and role in everyday life, and ethnic, religious, and social identities. For example, a king or queen may be the only ones who can play certain roles in a royal ceremony.

Write what you learn about participants in this event in the Community Arts Profile. Include drawings, photographs, and other representations to help explain what is going on.

Research Questions to Help You Know What to Explore

- How many participants were there (be sure to include ancestors or gods that are not physically present)? What were each of their roles?
- How did the participants use performance features to interact with each other? Were there obvious patterns (etiquette)?
- How did participants interact with different sections of the event space? Were any roles associated with particular places?
- Which participants exerted creative control and to what degrees?
- Are there local names for the roles that participants played in the event?
- Who is fulfilling each role?
- Why and how did each participant come to fill his or her role?
- What are the salient characteristics of each participant, in terms of his or her training, ability, reputation, and professional/caste status?
- What meaning(s) do people attach to each participant's role?
- From what you know of its genre, were the number and roles of participants similar to those of other events of this genre?
- Did any participants receive payment in goods, services, or money for performing their role?

Research Activities to Help You Answer the Questions

- Make audio, video, and photographic recordings of the event.
- Ask a friend involved in the event what role(s) you might be able to fill in this type of event. Note what background and competencies you need or would have to acquire to fill different roles. When appropriate and possible, prepare to perform a role for a future event of this type.
- Draw a floor diagram, showing where participants were at different times, or what roles were associated with certain places.
- Make a time line, noting participants' actions and interactions.
- Ask questions of participants and other cultural insiders about what happened. You may want to do this while watching a video of the event.
- Make a list of local names for participants' roles. Ask what privileges or obligations are associated with each named role.
- Take photographs that reveal details of participants' clothing, props, pertinent facial expressions, gestures, and the like.

Artistic Domain Connections

Many roles in artistic communication are associated with the artistic domain categories we have included in the following sections. Essentially all artistic events require an audience of some sort, someone to experience the communication. Beyond that, some typical dramatic roles include actor, spect-actor (someone who both watches and enters into a drama), set designer, and director. Musical performance may have singers, instrument players, and composers. In dance, people fill roles of choreographer, soloist, and ensemble. Various oral verbal arts performances may include a teller, listener, sidekick, crafter, and affirmer. Visual arts require at least one creator, manipulator, and experiencer. Food creation roles commonly include recipe maker, chef, food manipulator, and presenter. Research these roles in more depth in the artistic domain chapters, and remember that one person could fill various roles in multiple artistic domains.

Meaning Connections

Explore how what you have discovered by looking at an event through the lens of *participant organization* relates to meanings, symbolism, and broader cultural themes. "Relate the Event's Genre(s) to Its Broader Cultural Context" (Part C) will provide direction for this.

Shape of the Event through Time

Basic Description

One way to describe the shape of an event is by splitting it into sequential segments in a hierarchical fashion. You can identify the time at which one segment ends and the next begins by noting significant changes in elements of the event as viewed through each of the other lenses. These changes are called markers. For example, markers could include pauses, sudden contrasts in features or participants, beginning and ending of participants' activities, beginning and ending of songs, and the like. The shortest segment we are interested in for this lens is the *motif*: the smallest meaningful collection of performance features.

Write what you learn about the shape of this event in the Community Arts Profile. Include lists, time lines, and other representations to help explain what is going on.

Research Questions to Help You Know What to Explore

- What were the segments of the event?
- How did you know when one segment ended and another began? What marked these transitions?
- Were there parallel segments happening at the same time? How were they related?

- What were the important parts of each segment (onset, nucleus, coda)?
- What meaning(s) do people attach to these segments at each level?
- From what you know of its genre, was this event longer or shorter than normal? Did it have the same number and size of segments as normal?

Research Activities to Help You Answer the Questions

- Make audio- and videorecordings of the event.
- You may use one or more of the following approaches to create a time line of the event:
  - From a top-down perspective (in other words, macro to micro):
    - While watching or listening to the recording, make a time line of the event, highlighting its major segments by listing the transition markers with the time they occur.
    - While watching each major segment, make a time line of its sub-segments, listing the transition markers with the time they occur.
    - Continue dividing sub-segments at finer timescales, down to the level of your research interest. This may be at the level of the motif.
  - From a bottom-up perspective:
    - While watching or listening to the recording, make a time line of the event, identifying the smallest meaningful chunks (sequences of performance features), their beginning and ending times, and how they are assembled to create larger segments.
    - See how these small segments are in turn assembled into larger ones.
    - Continue assembling super-segments at longer timescales until you have described the whole event.
  - From a basic level-out perspective:
    - While watching or listening to the recording, make a time line of the event, identifying the most salient activities and how they are assembled to create larger segments or divided to create smaller ones.
    - Continue this process.
- Create a Hierarchical Segmentation Time Line showing a basic level-out perspective, as in Figure 4.5.

- Make a list of local names for the segments of the event.
- Ask questions of participants and other cultural insiders about what happened. You may wish to do this while watching a video of the event.

Step One

Time	What Happened
13:30	Storytellers began to arrive
. . .	. . .
. . .	. . .
14:27	Everyone left the area

Step Two

Segment 1 (5 min.)	Segment 2 (12 min.)	Segment 3 (10 min.)	Segment 4 (3 min.)
. . .	. . .	. . .	. . .

FIGURE 4.5. Sample Hierarchical Segmentation Time Line.

Artistic Domain Connections

Artistic domains each have traditions of splitting their enactments into smaller and smaller chunks. Drama may start with a genre like a play, broken into acts, scenes, and eventually to gestures and movements. An example of music's highest hierarchical level could be a concert or song, split into movements, phrases, and notes. Dances may consist of pieces, motifs, and gestures. An oral verbal art like a poem may contain stanzas and lines and beats. Visual and culinary arts normally do not change perceptibly through the same time frames, but how people view objects and eat food can be split into subparts. You can explore more relationships between the shape of the event through time and these art domains in the chapters that follow.

Meaning Connections

Explore how what you have discovered by looking at an event through the lens of *shape* relates to meanings, symbolism, and broader cultural themes. "Relate the Event's Genre(s) to Its Broader Cultural Context" (Part C) will provide direction for this.

Performance Features

Basic Description

Performance features are observable, patterned characteristics of an enactment that emerge from an event's unique combination of physical and social context and participants' actions. They are the skills, processes, and conventions that the performers in an event must master to make the event successful. In more detail, a *feature* is a characteristic of an enactment that

- is produced by participants (e.g., singers, dancers, storytellers, hecklers, playwrights),
- who choose embodied actions (e.g., sing, move, gather together, play instrument, wear a certain color)
- that derive from formal systems (e.g., movement, vocal production, conceptual development, color symbolism, social interaction)
- and temporal patterns (e.g., metricity, flow, timing).

The performer(s) chooses his or her actions by taking into account the

- intended messages, content, and subject matter;
- other participants (seen and unseen) and their responses;
- location;
- genre expectations: for example, acceptable variation and source materials (e.g., written forms, orature);
- and the performer's abilities and preferences.

Each feature

- is experienced by participants (e.g., performers, observers, audience)
- through communication channels (e.g., auditory, visual, tactile, spatial, olfactory).

In short, performance features are things people do that can be transcribed. Transcription is reducing elements of a communication act to writing and graphics. Performance features are our attempt to name the elements most useful for understanding the structure of an event; it is impossible to focus on everything, so this vocabulary and process help us to begin finding out what is important. Transcription can draw on existing notation systems such as Time Unit Box System (TUBS, for rhythm), staff (melody, harmony, and rhythm), Laban (movement), and writing down verbal content. It can also consist of prose descriptions of performance features using specialized vocabulary.

Note that transcribing the verbal features of an event requires access to knowledge of a language not immediately necessary with transcriptions of other kinds of features. This Guide does not teach transcription; you must learn specialized notation systems elsewhere, perhaps in the classroom with an expert. Depending

on your interests, search for schools or programs accessible to you that teach notation for music, language, dance, visual arts, or drama.

Write what you learn about performance features in this event in the
Community Arts Profile. Include prose descriptions and notation to help explain
what is going on.

Research Questions to Help You Know What to Explore

- What do people do to send messages through communication channels?
- How are performance features or clusters of features patterned?
- What meaning(s) do people attach to each performance feature or cluster
  of features?
- From what you know of its genre, did participants produce performance
  features in ways similar to other events in this genre?
- What are the stock motifs, or clichés that emerge? These are memorized
  bundles of performance features.

Research Activities and Artistic Domain Categories

Make Audio, Video, and Photographic Recordings of the Event

- There are several ways to train yourself to attend to features of people's
  performance: (1) focus on the communication channels through which
  you perceive the features (sight, sound, smell, touch, taste); (2) focus on
  the common producers of features (voices, bodies, objects, and minds);
  and (3) focus on similarities and contrasts between clusters of performance features (dynamics and rhythm).
- To access each of these three windows onto performance features, watch
  and listen to a video of the event multiple times, answering the following
  questions.

Feature Perception (Through Communication Channels)

Write a free-flowing account of your answers to the following questions, noting
patterns as well as unique occurrences. Make educated guesses on what seems
important, based on what you have learned by looking through the other lenses.
This is just a start.[1]

- What sounds did you hear?
- What movements, colors, lights, and shapes did you see?
- What aromas did you smell?

- What sensations did you feel?
- What flavors did you taste?

Feature Production

- What did participants do with their voices? Common vocal actions include singing, acting, orating, narrating, or producing sound effects.
- What did participants do with their bodies? Common bodily actions include acting, instrument playing, and dancing.
- What did participants do with their words? Common word-related activities include poetry, singing, acting, orating, and narrating.
- What did participants do with objects? Common actions with objects include instrument playing, acting, spectacle, dancing, oratory, narrating, and presenting a communicative object.

Similarities and Contrasts between Clusters of Performance Features

- How did people express intensity, weight, flow?
- How did people organize time?

Advice on Knowing What Features to Attend to

- Look for repeated actions.
- Look for actions that seem to provoke a strong reaction in participants.
- Note heavy contrast between bundles of features and the next set of bundled features.
- Use your own imperfect intuition to notice what might be important.
- Note where participants are focusing their attention.
- Remember what participants and other knowledgeable people have told you is important.

Other Research Activities

- Listen to an audio recording of the event, noting any patterns that you hear.
- Stare hard and long at a photograph of the event, noting patterns of colors, shade, size and shape, balance, and lines.
- Note when certain feature combinations occur. These co-occurrences may provide clues to underlying symbolic systems that participants all refer to explicitly or implicitly during the event. To learn about some common kinds of combinations, ask these questions:

- How did people advance the plot through dancing or singing? See the "Drama in an Event" section (in Part B of *Step 4*).
- How did people relate their movements to melody or rhythm or create movement motifs? See the "Dance in an Event" section (in Part B of *Step 4*).

- Make a list of local names for performance features or clusters of features. You can describe these using the analytical vocabulary in this chapter.
- Ask questions of participants and other cultural insiders about what happened. In particular, ask about meanings and emotions evoked by certain actions or points in the event. You may wish to do this while watching a video of the event.
- When appropriate and possible, learn to perform part of this kind of event. Write down what people tell you to do when teaching you, how they correct you, and insights you gain and questions that arise by attempting to produce features with your own body.

Other Kinds of Socially Meaningful Actions and Their Performance Features

- Participants may produce features not associated with a particular artistic domain, in order to express opinions and emotions. These opinions and emotions could be to affirm or reject, encourage or discourage, express pleasure or displeasure, attract or repel, assist or impede, unify or divide, goad or hinder aspects of the enactment. Examples of such features include hand clapping, stomping, cheering, ululating, heckling, "the wave," throwing rotten fruit or candy, and holding up lighters or cell phones.
- Participants may express basic emotions by crying, laughing, screaming, or wailing. These expressions often take on artistic form.
- People may produce other bits of communication with their bodies that contribute to an event that you may not have categories for. These could include actions like snapping fingers, belching, whistling, or producing vocal overtones. Keep all of your senses open to bodily communication.

Artistic Domain Connections

We have grouped the way performance features relate to artistic domains in these categories: vocal, body movement, object manipulation, visual, rhythm, narrating, and poetic.

Participants manipulate *vocal features* in drama to help them act, in music to help them sing, in dance to coordinate breath with movement patterns, and in oral verbal arts to create effects by changing the pitch or timbre of their voices.

Participants *move their bodies* in ways that contribute to acting, characterization, and space organization in dramatic aspects of performance; instrument playing in music; movement dynamics, phrasing, and body and space organization in dance; and gesturing in oral verbal arts.

People manipulate *objects* to help them act and produce spectacle, both related to drama; to help them play instruments and modify their voice in music; to support or facilitate movement in dance; to emphasize oratorical elements in oral verbal arts; and in making or presenting a communicative object in visual arts.

Visual features play important roles in dramatic elements like costuming, makeup, puppets, and spectacle; in dance, such as costuming and makeup; and in visual arts, such as design and composition.

Rhythm features contribute to musical characteristics like poly-, proportional, or free rhythm. How does external rhythm (e.g., music experienced through auditory channels) affect movement in dance? What about meter used in oral verbal arts?

Narrating features play significant roles in presenting or recounting events in drama and oral verbal arts.

Finally, participants may use *poetic devices* for acting in drama, song lyrics in music, and throughout oral verbal arts. You can research these and more relationships between performance features and artistic domains in the sections that follow.

Each of these artistic domain categories varies according to its proportional focus on referential meaning versus form qualities. Traditions that rely more on referential meaning (e.g., storytelling, singing, drama, Thai classical dance) will normally have more features that require a greater understanding of a language to recognize and understand.

Notes about Performance Features

- Any specific artistic event will likely draw on multiple features, each of which may exist within different groupings in other performance traditions.
- Performers may add unexpected features, purposefully or accidentally, and with varying degrees of skill and social license.

Meaning Connections

Explore how what you have discovered by looking at an event through the lens of *performance features* relates to meanings, symbolism, and broader cultural themes. "Relate the Event's Genre(s) to Its Broader Cultural Context" (Part C) will provide direction for this.

Content

Basic Description

Content is the subject matter or topic of an artistic event. It is most closely tied to symbols such as words, and movements in signed languages or dances. There may be multiple layers of meanings, which may be implied or explicit. While all the lenses expose meaning, the *content* lens describes most saliently what the enactment is about.

Write what you learn about the content of this event in the Community Arts Profile. Include transcriptions of language and other content signs to help explain what is happening.

Research Questions to Help You Know What to Explore

- How did participants communicate the subject matter at different points in the event?
- What was the event about? What else was it about? What was its most important point? Second most important point?
- What assumed background knowledge does an experiencer need to understand the subject matter?
- Ask a bilingual friend to explain the meaning of the content to you. Ask the following: Who was this about? What happened? What are some of the most important reasons for performing this or creating this?

Research Activities to Help You Answer the Questions

- Record the event. Ask a friend to write down important words that people uttered, and meanings of any symbolic motions that occurred.
- If you do not speak the language, ask a bilingual person who speaks a language you understand well to summarize the content for you and/or transcribe and translate the oral verbal content in full. Even when you understand the words, you may not understand the reason for some of the words. Ask your friend to explain any humor, puns, or metaphors that you do not understand.
- Ask participants what they intended to communicate during the event.
- Ask participants what emotions or actions they hoped to elicit in other people because of the event.
- Ask participants what topics were angering, humorous, boring, or rousing.

Artistic Domain Connections

In an event, features that interact most closely with content are commonly associated with drama, oral verbal arts, and songs in music.

Meaning Connections

Explore how what you have discovered by looking at an event through the lens of *content* relates to meanings, symbolism, and broader cultural themes. "Relate the Event's Genre(s) to Its Broader Cultural Context" (Part C) will provide direction for this.

Underlying Symbolic Systems

Participants draw on all sorts of rules, expectations, grammatical structures, motivations, and experiences to decide what to do at any given moment of an enactment. This is their cognitive and emotive environment, the hidden set of knowledge that participants share that allows composition and interpretation. *Underlying symbolic systems* describe the rules participants use to create an instantiation of a genre.

Some underlying systems are simple and easily discoverable. For example, the cyclic pattern of an Indonesian *gamelan* piece is quickly discernible by noting the regular interval at which the big gong in the ensemble sounds. Similarly, the metric division of a Strauss waltz into groups of three beats, with an accented first beat, does not require extensive analysis. As another example, stock characters in Thai *likay* drama are easily recognizable after a brief description of their behavior and costume conventions.

However, deriving some systems may take intensive, methodologically rigorous analysis, interview, and participation. For example, grammatical rules governing melodic or rhythmic structure of a song, the permitted movements in a dance, or the use of space in a painting are often not immediately evident. Though much of this complex analysis is beyond the scope of this Guide, the sections in Part B on music, drama, dance, oral verbal arts, and visual arts provide some tools to explore underlying systems.

One underlying system that is common to each artistic event is the degree of variability that its genre allows. Some features may be malleable from instantiation to instantiation, while other features must be present or the work would no longer be representative of the genre. After having begun a list of features, you can research variability by asking a wide variety of people questions such as these:

- Which characteristics do people state must exist in order for an event to be a useful example of this genre?
- What features of this genre are appreciated?
- What features are acceptable but not necessary?
- What features are not permitted?
- Is any of this contested? In what ways do participants innovate? In what ways do they seek for features to remain stable?

Part B: Explore the Event's Genre(s) through Artistic Domain Categories

Each genre of artistic communication consists of a unique set of characteristics: how, when, why, where, with whom they happen, and their formal features. Because of this uniqueness, our first goal is to describe each community's genres in their own terms. But it is also true that we humans share a great deal—bodies, cognitive structures, patterns of interaction, and so on. It is therefore not unusual to find similarities in the ways we communicate, even in different cultures. Mehr et al (2018) began a project to determine whether people from 86 diverse cultures could recognize the functions of songs from all over the world merely by listening to them. They found that participants could reliably identify lullabies and dance songs. Although there are conceptual and methodological weaknesses in this pilot study (see, e.g., Marshall 2018), the idea that helping a child sleep might normally require softer songs than those meant to energize a dancing group makes sense.

Music researchers have worked with neuroscientists to know with more precision the biological aspects of musical understanding and response. David Huron (2008), for example, has conducted laboratory research in the area of *expectation*, investigating whether all humans share common perceptions about "what happens next" as they listen to music. Ethnomusicologist Judith Becker (2004) researched *deep listening*: the almost trance-like neurobiological engagement with music listening, which is seen in many parts of the world. *The Oxford Handbook of Music and Emotion* (Juslin and Sloboda 2010) collected chapters by these and other researchers in the field of aesthetic and artistic universals. Such research has also informed books for general audiences, such as John Powell's (2010) *How Music Works* and Daniel Levitin's (2007) *This Is Your Brain on Music*. It seems inevitable that our understanding of universals will continue to grow.

In this section we draw on these commonalities to show how deeper investigation into five categories of artistic expression provides more detailed knowledge that can inform processes like sparking creativity (*Step 5*) and improving new works (*Step 6*). These five categories are *music, drama, dance, oral verbal arts*, and *visual arts*. You could perform similar investigations into other artistic domains with specialized features that we have not included in this Guide, such as food arts, games, architecture, and film.

Note that we are not claiming that disparate communities express themselves in the same musical or verbal ways. Rather, we are leveraging the fact that people integrate musical and poetic features into their communication to identify each community's distinct patterns.

In each artistic domain section, we lead you through activities that will help you discover artistic elements of a genre. Note that we have grouped these activities in the same way that we grouped your event analysis earlier in "Look at an Event's Forms": *space, materials, participant organization, shape of the event through time, performance features, content*, and *underlying symbolic systems*. This grouping provides continuity with what you have already learned, but it also means that some repetition is necessary. While we feel that the deep focus on each genre in turn is important, we also recognize that reading straight through all the sections may feel tedious. You can jump to particularly relevant sections; however, bear in mind that genres often are combined in enactment.

As we show in Figure 4.6, each genre has a unique set of interrelated artistic features: dramatic features like character and plot; visual features like balance and color; musical features like scale and texture; dance features like phrasing and effort; and oral verbal features like etiquette and frame. The research tasks we suggest for each domain consist mostly of participant observation, dialogue with practitioners, written description, and transcription. Write what you discover in the Community Arts Profile.

As you look at the artistic characteristics of an event through the lenses, keep in mind what you have learned about it earlier in "Look at an Event's Forms." Artistic characteristics are always interwoven with other realities in communities; you will not be able to fully understand the music, drama, dance, oral verbal arts, or visual

FIGURE 4.6. Sample intertwined artistic features in an event.

arts without a more complete picture. In particular, locate the event in its broader physical context relating to the *space* lens (nationally, regionally, and locally), and its broader temporal context, connecting to the *shape* lens (month, day, hour, season, and occurrence in the overall event).

You should also remember that arts are complicated, and you cannot be an expert in everything; there are aspects of analyzing artistic production that you will not be able to understand using just these sections. For you to make the most of some of these activities—especially those related to *performance features* and *underlying symbolic systems*—you will need to study their specialized vocabulary with an expert.

Some Advice on Choosing Research Activities for Artistic Domains

It is likely that the artistic activity the community has chosen does not have equal parts of musical features, drama features, oral verbal arts features, dance features, and visual arts features. One or two or three of these might play more prominent roles than others, occurring more frequently, or perhaps exhibiting more complexity. You can exploit this fact to help focus your research. Perform this activity, then start exploring the most prominent artistic domains.

Activity: Make a Rough Comparison of the Prominence of Each Artistic Domain

You have probably thought in terms of most of the five domains we are choosing, so you will be able to recognize some elements from each. We have added a few common features to each to jog your memory and focus your attention.

Watch a video of an enactment of the genre that you and the community are investigating and estimate each domain's prominence, using Figure 4.7. Watch the video as many times as it takes to focus on each domain.

Interrelationships between Formal Elements of an Event

Each event lens in our treatment of artistic domains begins with a section titled "Summary and Relationship to Other Lenses." These brief comments point to common connections between lenses in a particular artistic domain. For example, we note that *materials* in dance (e.g., floppy grass rings attached to the ankle)

Domain	Common Features	Prominence in the Enactment: None, some, much
Music	melody, rhythm, beat	
Drama	someone taking on someone else's persona; showing participants in the present either the past or a hypothetical time	
Dance	patterned body movement	
Oral Verbal Arts	has words, poetic features, discourse features	
Visual Arts	shape, line, color	
	add other categories you notice, such as architecture, food, or sports	

FIGURE 4.7. Artistic domain prominence workspace.

interact primarily with dance *performance features* (accentuating a dancer's forceful stomps on the ground). Figure 4.8 can help reveal some of these connections.

Event Lens	Music	Drama	Dance	Oral Verbal Arts	Visual Arts Other	Effects
Space						
Materials						
Participant Organization						
Shape of the Event Through Time						
Performance Features						
Content						
Underlying Symbolic Systems						

FIGURE 4.8. Artistic features by event lens summary.

Record Similar Artistic Events

Before we consider artistic domain analysis, we will offer some general recording and collecting advice that may come in handy.

Some Purposes for Different Kinds of Recordings

We introduced these concepts in *Step 1* but will now expand them for applications to analysis.

Integral Performance Contexts

An integral enactment is one that is familiar to the participants and has a high number of normal social and artistic components. Here are some reasons to record arts in integral settings:

Videorecording
- to discover overall flow of an enactment through time, including subdivisions;
- to see how sounds are produced and by whom;
- to see how movements, dynamics, phrases, and relationships are produced;
- to see how artists create visual objects.

Audio recording
- to transcribe melodic, rhythmic, movement, plot, and other patterns in simple performance.

Analytical Performance Contexts

An analytical enactment context is designed by the researcher in order to isolate features of artistic production. One important purpose for such recordings is to collect components of an artistic genre for analysis and comparison; these might include songs, proverbs, dances, or stories. Here are a few other reasons to design recording events in analytical settings:

Videorecording
- to enable subsequent feedback (performers and others can watch and verbally annotate the videorecording of a performance with the researcher);
- to describe playing or movement or acting techniques;
- to document movement in the clearest manner for future viewing.

Audio recording
- to transcribe melodies, rhythms, and texts.

Recording Artistry

Some of the research and analysis activities we describe in the following sections will benefit from a collection of basic products of an artistic genre. Such collections will help you find patterns, contrasts, themes, and limits to variation in the genre.

They will also be key in contributing to archives of the artistry for protection and sharing.

How to Collect Songs

Songs are a nearly universally occurring type of artistic object composed of musical and verbal characteristics.

1. Discover an artistic genre that includes songs (see "inside-out" and "outside-in" in *Step 1*).
2. Ask people you know: Who are the best performers of this kind of song? Who knows the most songs? (Often older people.) Ask to be introduced to this person.
3. Create an analytical recording context: meet the person, describe what you will do, receive permission to record.
4. Slate the recording: at the beginning of the recording, say, "This is *your name*, recording *so-and-so person*, at *such-and-such place*, on *such-and-such day*, singing in *such-and-such genre*." Then, before each song, say, "This is song number *one*, etc."
5. If the lyrics are in a language with limited geographic usage, then consider recording someone translating the lyrics into a language of wider communication after each song.

How to Collect Proverbs

The vast majority of languages include condensed, specially formed bits of wisdom that we call proverbs. To truly understand a proverb, you need to learn what its words mean, and other cultural information it refers to. You also need to know how it is performed in a social context: Who can use it and for what purpose(s)? There may be an important place for you to perform integral audio- or videorecordings, in order to record them in natural use. This is hard and usually time consuming, but possible.

However, there are many analyses that benefit from an analytically recorded collection of proverbs. Here are a few tips to making such a collection (for more ideas, see Unseth 2008):

1. Gather people together, turn on a recording device, have everyone speak in the vernacular if possible, and ask people to think of as many proverbs as possible.

2. Suggest situations in which proverbs might be used. These could include what a mother might say to a daughter who is angry with a friend, or a father to a son who is misbehaving. You can also suggest topics that proverbs might address, like laziness, animals, children, or food.

3. Suggest kinds of people that proverbs might mention, such as debtors, merchants, old people, midwives, children, hunters, or ancestors.

4. Listen to the recording with someone who knows local proverbs well and can help you translate them into a language of wider communication (if relevant). When a proverb occurs in the recording, stop the device, and have your friend(s) help you write and translate it.

How to Collect Plays, Dances, and Other Bits of Artistry

You can apply similar steps to collect photographs of woven bags, videorecordings of dances or plays, and many other bits of artistry.

1. Go before the event begins and ask who would need to give their permission for the event to be recorded, or ask who needs to give permission for an object to be photographed. Ask them to record a verbal consent form or sign a written consent form.

2. Record the event or photograph the works. If there is oral verbal content, transcribe and translate the recordings. To understand the content, work with a member of the community who can translate the verbal content and explain the meanings of the work to you. You may ask for either a summary explanation or a detailed line-by-line transcription and translation. Even when you understand the words, you may not understand the reason for the words in context without asking about the intentions of the performers. What do participants hope to convey, or what do viewers of the recording understand from it? What do they enjoy about it? What causes people to laugh or experience emotions? In some cultures, it is not polite to ask these questions directly; you may find it more helpful to bring up topics for discussion, saying, for example, "I notice that . . ." or "I did not understand why . . ." and your friend may comment helpfully about the topics you bring up.

Music in an Event

This section will help you describe more completely the patterned, stylized sounds we describe as music in an event. To understand this section best, you should first work through some of the activities in "Look at an Event's Forms" (Part A). We use the same seven lenses here, but introduce descriptive categories that are particularly pertinent to music. You will gather your discoveries about the musical characteristics of this event and others like it in the Community Arts Profile.

Musical aspects are primarily experienced through auditory channels, though visual channels play important roles in helping the experiencer understand auditory information. Isolating the part of a single drum in a percussion ensemble, for example, may require visual attention to the drummer's playing. Watching a person play an instrument may also be the only way to understand playing technique, as in a rattle rhythm produced by complex, multidirectional movement.

Actions that produce the sounds most frequently include singing and other vocal production, and participants' interaction with instruments, their own bodies (e.g., in clapping), or other parts of their environment (e.g., in stomping the ground).

The conceptual systems that participants draw on when performing these actions structure sound through time and frequency relationships (e.g., in rhythm and melody). Musical systems interact most commonly with systems in verbal (e.g., in song texts and speech surrogates) and movement (e.g., in dance and instrument playing) domains.

Research activities most helpful in understanding the musical aspects of performance include audiovisual recording, ethnographic interview, and participant observation.

Space

Space is the location, demarcation, and physical characteristics of the area used, which can affect the form of artistic communication.

Summary and Relationship to Other Lenses

Space relates to musical action primarily in how performers place themselves to affect the sounds they produce and hear. Performers may choose to be near each other in order to hear and respond to each other more clearly and quickly. In addition, physical characteristics of the performance space will affect how participants produce and experience musical sounds. Singers, for example, may generate more strident and louder sounds in a larger space. Finally, space is closely related to participant organization in musical production. Groups using antiphonal ensemble structure, for example, may dedicate two separate areas of a performance space to create a stereophonic effect.

⊗ Activity: Explore How Participants Change Their Musical Behavior in Response to Their Physical Space

Video record an event and arrange a meeting with participants. While watching the video, ask questions such as:

- Why were you that distance away from other performers at this point? How would your experience of the music have changed if you were farther apart or closer?
- Would you have changed how you sang/played if the space had been smaller? Larger?

⊗ Activity: Explore How Participants Design or Use Space to Affect Musical Sounds

Building designers may create physical spaces to enhance acoustic characteristics of musical sound. Roman amphitheaters, for example, were designed to carry sound from the stage through the audience. In addition, Gothic cathedrals were created to accentuate reverberation of organs and choirs. Designers may also demarcate areas for specific types of performers.

If someone designed the space in which they performed, ask him or her: Why did you design the performance space this way? Did you think about how your design would affect the sounds produced by the performers? How so?

Materials

Materials are all of the tangible things associated with an event.

Summary and Relationship to Other Lenses

The most important materials related to music are instruments. The presence of musical instruments and the way they are designed affects the creation of music performance features. Also, elements of their design may reveal some of the genre's underlying symbolic systems. For instance, instrument tuning may reveal musical scales or harmonic systems. Alternatively, an instrument may be "sight tuned"; for example, the finger holes on a flute are drilled where the fingers naturally fall on a flute, rather than according to the pitch the hole makes.

✪ Activity: List Musical Instruments

Using each genre in the Community Arts Profile as a starting point, ask friends and experts to tell you all of the sound-producing objects. Write down the name of the instruments in the local language and any other languages used in the area.

✪ Activity: Describe Each Musical Instrument in Several Ways

You can base your descriptions of an instrument primarily on interviews with knowledgeable people, personal observation and handling, and insights you gain from learning to play it. You can also take photographs of the instrument in use and from different angles to expose physical features. Here are a few approaches to get you started:

1. *Construction and materials*: Interview someone who has made an instrument to find out what materials they use (include local names) and the construction process. You can also document someone making the instrument with video or still photography.

2. *Sound production*: The Sachs-Hornbostel organology system groups instruments by the part that is activated in vibration to make a sound. *Aerophones* (such as flutes, trombones) use a resonating vibrating column of air to sound. *Chordophones* (such as harps, guitars) sound from vibrating strings. *Membranophones* (such as drums) have a membrane stretched over a frame and are often struck to make a sound. *Idiophones* (such as cymbals, xylophones) vibrate the entire material of the instrument. Decide what category the instrument you are working with fits in.

3. *Playing techniques*: Participants blow, suck, hit, scrape, pluck, bow, shake, and do other actions with objects in order to produce sounds that relate to melody, rhythm, texture, and text. Describe these interactions according to body parts, action types, instrument parts, constraints the instruments place on potential actions, resulting sounds, and their relationships to other aspects of performance. These techniques often come with local vocabulary. Note that people will modify their techniques to change the qualities of sounds that their instruments produce, such as timbre (see "Performance Feature Categories" in the following).

4. *Musical function*: Another way to classify instruments could be according to musical function in the texture: melodic or rhythmic, solo or ensemble. Note that it does not necessarily follow that aerophones and chordophones are for melodic/harmonic use and membranophones and

idiophones are for rhythmic use. To explore musical functions of an instrument, begin performing the activities in "Performance Feature Categories." Then note which instruments produce each feature category.

5. *Visual design*: Instrument design also often includes shaping or adornment using visual art features. Describe and analyze these visual art features following the research activities in "Visual Arts in an Event" later in *Step 4*.

6. *Tuning*: Using a fixed pitch producer like a pitch pipe, melodica, or electronic tuner, write down the note names that correspond most closely to the pitches produced by the instrument. Note if a pitch is slightly higher or lower than that on the fixed pitch producer. There are software programs and devices that can identify the exact frequency of a pitch, including freeware Sonic Visualiser (www.sonicvisualiser.org) and Audacity (www.audacityteam.org). Also be aware that the relationship between pitches is more important than the pitches' individual frequencies; different players may tune their instruments differently, and the community may tolerate a fairly wide variance in an instrument's tuning.

7. *Cultural integration*: Ask for names of different parts of the instrument. Sometimes a part will have a human attribute (e.g., male and female strings on a harp) and reveal cultural values (e.g., the male and female strings should follow a prescribed structure to sound pleasant). You can also ask whether there are conventions for who should play an instrument (e.g., male, female, child), how it is constructed, all the genres it is used in, and whether there are connections to broader cultural themes.

Participant Organization

Participant organization highlights the people involved in an event, in terms of the roles they play, the ways they interact with each other through time, and how they use the space around them.

Summary and Relationship to Other Lenses

Common roles of participants in musical production are singers, instrumentalists, and composers. *Participant organization* interacts with musical structure at two main levels: texture and song form. In terms of melodic or rhythmic texture, roles relate to the horizontal and vertical relationships of participants' contributions.

For example, a solo singer or a group of singers performing the same melodic line will produce monophony, while multiple singers performing different melodic lines will produce polyphony or homophony.

In terms of song form, participants' roles may be directly related to sequential segments required by a genre. For example, hocketing requires each participant to produce a small number of notes in the formation of a larger melodic line, as in a bell choir, *anklung* ensemble, or a Mamaindé Toré puberty ceremony. As another example, participants in some African choirs create call-and-response form by dividing into the roles of leader and chorus.

⚙ Activity: Identify the Roles of Musical Production

Watch a videorecording of an event with people who participated, either as performers or observers. Point out someone who is singing, playing an instrument, or otherwise making sound, and ask them questions such as:

- Who is that person? What is he or she doing? How did he qualify to do this? What path in her life did she follow to get there?
- Does what he or she is doing have a name? What would allow someone else to be able to do this?
- What does this role add to the event? What would be missing without it?
- Repeat this, asking about others who are making other sounds.

Note that individual performance genres associate participant roles with characteristic musical output. These genre-defined roles may be based on musical structure, difficulty of parts, and social status associated with the roles. For a given performance, individual participants may occupy these genre-defined roles based on their own abilities and social status. In a trombone quartet, for example, there may be four named roles: first, second, third, and bass trombone. The first trombone part may be the most difficult to perform, and the player with the greatest ability may fill this role. However, in a particular performance event, someone may play the bass part because he or she is the only one who has a bass trombone.

Shape of the Event through Time

Shape of an event refers primarily to its constituent segments, organized hierarchically.

Summary and Relationship to Other Lenses

In "Look at an Event's Forms," you may have described an event with musical content such as a concert, festival, political rally, or ritual. In this Guide we focus on two closely related types of musical segments that are often part of such events:

Song: A composition consisting minimally of rhythm, melody, and text.

Piece: A composition consisting minimally of rhythm and melody. Be aware that some cultures do not have a meta-term to distinguish a song with text from a piece of music without text.

We describe the shape of songs and pieces in terms of their form. Form is composed of smaller segments of phrase and motif, which in turn consist of notes and beats. Definitions of these segments from highest to lowest place in a hierarchy follow:

Form: The organization of musical materials. Songs and pieces consist of patterned combinations of textual, rhythmic, and melodic segments. Assigning these segments letter names can reveal the overall structures that their combination produces. We use the following naming conventions:

A, B, C, etc.   phrases

a, b, c, etc.   motifs, or subphrases within a phrase

a^1, B^2, etc.   the original motif or phrase with one element changed

b^a, C^b, etc.   a motif or phrase based on another motif or phrase, but differing by more than one element. It is different enough from its referent to earn its own letter.

Phrase: A brief section of music, analogous to a phrase of spoken language, that sounds somewhat complete in itself, while not self-sufficient (Shelemay 2001:358). Phrases consist of motifs, which may be elaborated or varied.

Motif: A salient combination of notes.

Note: A minimal structural unit of pitch or rhythm produced by a voice or instrument.

Beat: A single time unit, sounded or not.

Activity: Determine the Form of a Song or Piece

You must first identify a song or piece. You can do this by choosing a segment you have already elicited and recorded as part of a collection. Another method is to look at a time line of an event that you created following guidelines in "Look at an Event's Forms," noting the beginning and ending times of a song or piece. Listen to a recording of this segment many times, marking repeated sections and points of change. If you can, transcribe its melody. Direct observation or watching a videorecorded rendition of the song or piece may also help.

After becoming familiar with the song or piece, note in the Community Arts Profile whether its form follows any of the following common patterns:

Call and response (responsorial): Singing in which leader and chorus alternate; ABAB (e.g., much African song).

Antiphonal singing or playing: Music in which two groups sing or play alternately (e.g., Renaissance choral music, Mamaindé song teaching).

Strophic: "Designation for a song in which all stanzas of the text are sung to the same music, in contrast to a song with new music for each stanza [through-composed]" (Apel 1972:811) (e.g., hymns are songs with strophic structure; they often also have a refrain).

Through-composed: Melodic structure with no large-scale repetition; ABCDEFG.

Progressive: Each section has completely different material. Differs from through-composed in that it allows a fixed number of immediate repetitions of sections when they appear. After this contiguous repetition, a section will not repeat; AABBCCDD, and so on.

Theme and variations: A basic theme is presented and then different variations of it are subsequently presented. Each variation pertains to the whole theme, not merely phrases or other smaller elements; $T\ T^2\ T^3\ T^4\ T^5$, and so on.

Litany-type: Consists of only one short phrase that is reiterated throughout (Nettl 1956:69).

Performance Feature Categories

Performance features are observable characteristics of a performance that emerge from an event's unique combination of physical and social context and participants' actions.

Summary and Relationship to Other Lenses

Performance features associated with music relate primarily to how participants organize sounds through time, frequency, and volume.

⚙ **Activity: Describe Instrumental and Vocal Timbres**

Performers manipulate their voices or instruments to produce various timbres.

> *Timbre*: The quality ("color") of a tone produced by a voice or instrument. This is determined by the relative loudness of the harmonics, the presence of accompanying noise, and the noises occurring at the attack of the note. Initial descriptions of timbre might include rough, smooth, raspy, breathy, nasal, or creaky.

To begin to understand how singers produce the sounds they do, first watch and listen to how they do it. Then ask them how they produce the sounds, how they learned to do it, and how they describe good sounds. Finally, you might ask someone to teach you to do it. Write the results of your explorations in the Community Arts Profile, using the terms from the following list when appropriate. Note that vocal timbres are most often determined by gender (e.g., male/female, soprano, alto, tenor, baritone, bass) and the ways in which singers modify their voices. Here are some techniques you may come across:

> *Vibrato*: A minute fluctuation in volume and/or pitch in a sustained note.
> *Yodeling*: Singing style in which the performer alternates frequently between the natural chest voice and falsetto tones.
> *Sprechstimme*: A vocal style in which the melody is spoken at approximate pitches rather than sung on exact pitches.
> *Overtone singing*: A vocal technique in which a single vocalist produces two, three, or four distinct notes simultaneously. This is accomplished by separating and manipulating the voice's natural harmonic overtones, which we typically hear as "color" or timbre, but not as individual tones.

⚙ **Activity: Determine the Number of Notes per Speech Syllable in a Song**

Write down the text of a song. Transcribe the melody associated with the text if you can. If not, listen to a recording of the melody and mark on the text when more than one note is associated with a single syllable. Note in the Community Arts Profile whether any of the following types describe its relationship of note to syllable:

> *Syllabic*: Usually one note per syllable (e.g., "Happy Birthday" or "Twinkle Twinkle Little Star").

Pneumatic: Usually two to three notes per syllable (e.g., "Amazing Grace" sung "folk" style).

Melismatic: Frequent use of one syllable sung on two or more notes (e.g., much North African vocal performance).

✪ Activity: Determine and Describe the Texture(s) of a Piece or Song

Texture describes the horizontal and vertical relationships of musical materials, comparable to the weave of a fabric (Apel 1972:842). To find out the texture of a song or piece, listen to a recording of it several times, focusing your attention each time on different pitched sounds. Then note in the Community Arts Profile whether any of the following types describe its texture:

Heterophony: Musical texture in which the same melody is played by all voices and instruments but with variations and omissions depending on the particular nature of each (e.g., Javanese *gamelan*).

Polyphony: Musical texture composed of two or more voices sounding on different notes (not octaves).

Parallel organum: Polyphony composed of a melody and a second part that parallels it (e.g., Maxacalí, Medieval Organum).

Drone: Polyphony composed of a melody supported by one or two unchanging pitches (e.g., Scottish bagpipe, much South Asian music).

Homophony: Polyphony composed of a melody supported by chords (e.g., most hymns and popular songs of European derivation).

Homophonic parallelism: The melodic voices move parallel to each other (e.g., in parallel thirds or fourths) (Nketia 1974:161). The emphasis here is on horizontal movement rather than the vertical building of chords.

Independent polyphony: The melodic voices move in different directions. (The term "independent polyphony" is not necessarily recognized as standard, but it is useful to illustrate a point. Some scholars restrict the term "polyphony" to mean "independent polyphony.") For example, any of Bach's harmonizations of "O Sacred Head."

Imitative polyphony: The melody of one voice is based on another; it imitates it (e.g., Baroque fugues, Oiampí songs).

Canon (or round): All or almost all the material of the first voice is repeated by one or more following voices (e.g., "Row, Row, Row Your Boat").

⚙ Activity: Determine and Describe the Rhythm(s) of a Piece or Song

Rhythm describes the whole feeling of movement in music, or the pattern of long and short notes occurring in a song. To find out the rhythm of a song or piece, listen to a recording of it several times. As you are listening, try to clap a regular beat that coincides with patterns you hear. If you can do this, the rhythm is likely to be polyrhythm or proportional. Otherwise, it may be based on speech or have free rhythm. Note in the Community Arts Profile whether any of the following types describe its rhythm:

> *Proportional rhythm*: Smaller rhythmic units are simple proportions of larger units.
>
> *Polyrhythm*: The simultaneous use of strikingly contrasted rhythms in different parts of the musical fabric.
>
> *Speech rhythm*: Rhythmic system of a musical composition wherein the rhythm is determined by the rhythm of the spoken text without reference to proportionality or other factors.
>
> *Free rhythm*: Notes of irregular lengths with no discernible pattern.

⚙ Activity: Determine and Describe the Tempo(s) of a Piece or Song

Tempo is the speed at which beats occur. It may play an important role in describing meter, and may convey meaning itself. It is usually indicated in beats per minute, marked as MM (short for Maelzel's metronome). Note also that performance genres specify ranges of allowable tempos for a piece or segment thereof, or their increase or decrease.

While listening to a recording of a piece or song, count the number of beats that occur during a period of 15 seconds. Multiply that number by four and you have the tempo. Note if the tempo changes at different points in the piece.

⚙ Activity: Determine and Describe the Dynamic(s) of a Piece or Song

Dynamics refer to the volume and changes of volume. Listen to a recording of the piece and describe any sections as loud, soft, or somewhere in between. Then note any changes in volume, which may correspond with contrasts in form, text, or dramatic elements.

⊛ Activity: Determine and Describe the Notes of a Piece or Song

Notes are minimal structural units of pitch or rhythm produced by a voice or instrument. If you transcribe the melody of a song, you can make note of its *pitch inventory, range,* and *contours* in the Community Arts Profile.

Pitch inventory: All the notes used in a musical piece or genre.

Range: The pitch difference between the lowest and highest notes used in a musical composition. This term is also used to describe the absolute highest and lowest notes normally sung by a certain voice (e.g., tenor, soprano) or normally played on an instrument.

Tonal center: The pitch around which the musical piece revolves. The tonal center is often the most frequent pitch in a piece and fills prominent structural roles, but further analysis is beyond the scope of this Guide.

Modulation: Change of tonal center or key within a composition.

Melody: A succession of musical notes; the horizontal aspect of pitches in music.

Contour: The characteristic (motion) shape of a melody within a musical composition. Figure 4.9 shows some possible shapes of a melody.

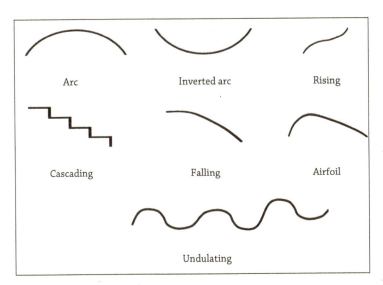

FIGURE 4.9. Melodic contour examples.

Content

Content refers to the subject matter in artistic activity.

Summary and Relationship to Other Lenses

Content associated with music relates primarily to song texts and speech surrogates.

⚙ Activity: Explore Relationships between Melody, Rhythm, and Other Features of Sung Text

A melody's shape and rhythm may be influenced by stress, linguistic tone, part of speech, discourse features, and the like (Richards 1972). To expose relationships between linguistic tone and melodic movement, do the following: (1) write down the text of the song, marking tone on each syllable; (2) transcribe the melody over the text, or draw the melodic shape with curved lines; (3) note the direction of melodic movement over each syllable, and compare with the direction of linguistic tone movement. Describe your findings in the Community Arts Profile according to the following kinds of relationships:

Parallel: Tone and melody move in parallel directions.
Contrary: Tone and melody move in opposite directions.
Oblique: Tone or melody moves, while the other remains level.

Note also the term *vocable*, which refers to a syllable without lexical meaning set to music.

⚙ Activity: Identify and Briefly Describe Speech Surrogates

Communities sometimes mimic elements of spoken language with instruments or whistling to communicate verbal content. When used this way, these sound producers are called *speech surrogates*. Common instruments acting as speech surrogates include pitched drums, xylophones, and harps. To learn more about speech surrogates, ask questions such as:

- Are there instruments that can communicate messages?
- What kinds of messages can these instruments convey? Give examples.
- Who knows how to communicate in this way?

Record examples of people communicating this way, with translation to spoken language.

Underlying Symbolic Systems

Underlying symbolic systems refer to the grammatical and social rules and structures that guide participants' actions in artistic activities. Systems like scale and meter provide grammatical structure for composing and understanding musical production. Although the analytical procedure to determine scale and meter are beyond the scope of this Guide, the following definitions may help you get started. It is important to note that *underlying symbolic systems* of music are not universal. Features that convey one emotion or purpose in one culture may convey entirely different emotions and purposes in another culture. Aesthetic features and valued features differ from culture to culture and genre to genre.

Scale

A *scale* consists of all the notes used in a genre and their functional relationships; it refers to a closed set of notes and the grammar that orders their production. Examples include the following:

> *Diatonic scale*: In Euro-American music theory, melody or harmony confined to the pitches within a major or minor key; it consists of five whole tones and two semitones, as it is produced on the white keys of a keyboard tuned to Western pitch conventions.
>
> *Tetratonic, pentatonic, hexatonic, heptatonic, octatonic scales*: These terms simply describe the number of notes a scale uses within an octave (i.e., 4, 5, 6, 7, or 8).
>
> *Raga*: A term used in East Indian musicology that includes the concept of scale but also implies much more, such as the relationship of the notes and melodic themes. Different ragas are associated with different concepts such as fire and the time of day.

Meter

Meter refers to the underlying pattern of beats, by which the time span of a piece of music or a section thereof is organized (Apel 1972:523).

Divisive meter: A basic unit of time (usually a measure) is subdivided into a number of equal notes, each of which may be subdivided. It is indicated by time signatures in Western notation (e.g., 2/2, 4/4, 6/8).

Additive meter: A pattern of beats subdivided into smaller, irregular groups. Larger periods of time are constructed from sequences of smaller rhythmic units added to the end of the previous unit (e.g., 2 + 2 + 3, or 3 + 2).

Isometer: The use of a repeated pulse without its organization into groups.

Mixed meter: The sequential use of two or more different meters in one piece.

Polymeter: The simultaneous sounding of two or more different meters.

Asymmetrical meter: A meter with beats of different lengths.

Non-metric: No sense of underlying pulse in the music.

Drama in an Event

This section will help you describe more completely the ways participants recreate actions, or create a world of possible actions, in a story event. We use the same seven lenses we introduced in "Look at an Event's Forms" (Part A), but introduce descriptive categories and terms particularly pertinent to drama. You will gather your discoveries about the dramatic characteristics of this event and others like it in the Community Arts Profile.

We learn about dramatic features of a tradition by observing rehearsals and performances, by participating in the activities of drama groups, and by analyzing scripts, transcripts, audio recordings, or videorecordings of performances.

When a drama contains dialogue in a language you do not speak well, or gestures in a culture whose nonverbal language you do not understand well, you can either take the time to learn these well, or look for bilingual, bicultural friends. Ask them to explain the meanings of verbal and nonverbal communication to you as understood from an insider's viewpoint through each of the seven lenses.

Space

Space is the location, demarcation, and physical characteristics of the areas used, which can affect the form of artistic communication.

Summary and Relationship to Other Lenses

Space has two senses in relation to drama. First, *performance space* is the place where actors relate to an audience. Second, the *dramatic setting* is the imagined location of the story conveyed by the performers' use of words, space, set pieces, and lighting or props to evoke an imagined place and time (see also the sections on *materials* and *content*). How people use their physical performance spaces to create imagined spaces is part of the *space* lens. The description of the imagined space itself belongs mainly under the *content* lens.

⊛ Activity: Describe How Participants Design Performance Spaces

Interview some performers when they are not performing. Ask them where they perform. It may be that they perform in places that are used for other purposes at other times, such as a clearing, under a tree, or someone's yard. A performance space like this is called an *arène trouvée* (found stage). Alternatively, performers may use a structured stage, such as a raised platform or floor designated for presentations. Ask whether performances always occur at a fixed location or at variable locations, and at what kinds of locations this genre's performances usually happen.

Ask where performers get ready before a performance. Backstage may be part of a structured stage that is not seen by the audience. Backstage may include a waiting room for actors (sometimes called a *green room*), a dressing room, prop storage, or costume storage areas. Space in view of the audience, beside the stage, may also serve as a de facto backstage, or waiting area, for the actors.

Write down the name of each preparation space and each performance space in the local language, and any other languages used in the area. Write down what performers do in each space. For example, in Japanese theater, a raised platform walkway leads out into the audience. The raised walkway is called a *hanamichi* (flower pathway). Actors may enter or exit on the *hanamichi* to perform nearer the audience than when on the main stage. Performers sometimes freeze in particular dramatic poses that are associated with particular emotions. The poses are called *mié*. *Mié* poses on the *hanamichi* particularly allow audiences to appreciate the poses and emotions at close range (Greenwald et al. 2001:588).

⊛ Activity: Describe the Performance Space Configuration and Directionality

Both an *arène trouvée* and a structured stage may have different configurations. The name of the configuration is determined by where the audience is located in relation to the performers. Write down how the audience is arranged in relation to the performers.

In *theater-in-the-round*, the audience is located on all sides of the performers, so the performers direct their performance in all directions. In a *thrust theater*, the audience is located on three sides of the performers, so the performers direct their performance in three directions. On a *three-quarter round stage*, the performance space has one wall and an audience is located in a partial circle around them, so similarly, performers act to an audience in a partial circle around them. On an *end-stage theater*, the audience is seated on only one side of the performers. The performers direct their performance in only one direction toward the audience. On a *proscenium stage*, an arch on the front of the stage frames the performers, the audience is located on one side of the stage like an end stage, the other sides are hidden, and the stage has many behind-the-scenes features and equipment for special effects.

After you have described the performance space configuration and performance directionality, also describe whether the performance space is all on one level or has multiple levels. Note if there are stairs, partitions, or other physical barriers. Ask performers how the shape of this space affects their performances.

Materials

Materials are all of the tangible things associated with an event.

Summary and Relationship to Other Lenses

Performers use materials to help them convey other places, times, people, and events. The dramatic setting is the imagined location of the story conveyed within the performance setting by performers' use of costumes, set pieces, props, instruments for sound and music, performing objects, lighting, and even words that cause the audience to imagine materials.

Costumes, props, scenery, and set pieces can be categorized as realistic, impressionistic, minimalistic, improvised, or mimed. The same performance may display more than one of these categories.

- Describe materials as *realistic* if they aim to reproduce real life as exactly as possible.
- Describe materials as *impressionistic* if they are prepared in advance and give an idea of an object without trying to reproduce it exactly as it occurs in real life.

- Describe materials as *minimalistic* when they are few and unassuming so that attention is placed on other aspects of a performance. Minimalistic costuming, for example, uses a few representative items to designate characters. Minimalistic sets use a few objects to represent a place.
- Describe materials as *improvised* if performers appear to find them on hand on the spot without preparing them in advance. They may be used by the performer's spontaneous ingenuity so as to function as things that they are not intrinsically.
- Props are *mimed* when the actors' actions cause the audience to imagine objects that are not physically present. (Mimed objects are actually an absence of materials, but it is worth noting this, so you do not influence participants to use more materials than they would normally.) Similarly, actors' words or actions may portray a setting in audience's minds using *a bare stage* with no set at all. Rather than preparing costumes, actors may perform in *street clothes*, meaning regular, unaltered clothing.

Use of any given prop may be *malleable* if the same object is used to represent more than one thing during a performance, or *stable* if the prop continues to represent the same object.

⭐ Activity: Explore How Participants Use Materials to Evoke an Imagined Story

Materials in the performance space may be used to evoke one or more dramatic settings, helping take the audience in their imaginations to another time and place, recreating a past world or imagining a possible world.

Attend a play and remember what you saw. If you obtain prior permission, record it. List and tentatively categorize types of props, set pieces, costumes, and performing objects (things used as characters, such as puppets). If these are numerous, you can list representative examples of each.

Talk about what you saw or watch your recording with one or more performers or audience members. Ask them where and when performed events occur, to whom, and why. Ask them what visual signals allow them to know these things. Make notes of characteristics you learn.

- Describe costuming: Describe the clothes and makeup the performers wear and what these signify. Clothes may indicate something about the character by color symbolism or by what type of character would wear that kind of clothing. How do the costumes make the audience think of a different place and time? Are masks used to change character? If so, which kind of character is evoked by which mask? In various Asian classical and folk theaters, makeup is very important to understanding the character, almost like a mask. Color in makeup can also be significant, as in Indian and other South Asian theater traditions.

- Describe lighting: Describe the quality of light. Is it natural, or how is light generated? How does the light make the audience think of a different place and time?
- Describe the set: Describe the arrangement of set pieces and objects within the performance space. Describe the set and scenery as realistic, impressionistic, minimalistic, or bare. Describe how scenery is created; for example, if there are painted flats, describe them. (A *flat* is a piece of wood, a hanging canvas, or a wooden frame covered by a sheet and painted to form scenery.)
- Describe performing objects: Describe any objects or puppets that are manipulated by a performer to give the impression that the object has a life of its own. Is the real performer hidden or visible?
- Describe props: Props are objects used by a performer that can change location in the course of acting. *Hand props* are carried by actors. *Set props* are pieces of the scene. Props may be realistic, as when a stick is a stick, or impressionistic, when one object suggests a different object to the audience's imagination, such as when a stick represents an arrow. Props are improvised if they are found on the spot.

Activity: Summarize How Costumes, Props, Set Pieces, and Lighting Combine to Show Dramatic Setting

Are they all realistic, impressionistic, improvised, or minimalistic? Are some in one category and others in another category?

Participant Organization

Participant organization highlights the people involved in an event, in terms of the roles they play, the ways they interact with each other through time, and how they use the space around them.

Summary and Relationship to Other Lenses

Participants who contribute to the representation of reality include one or more actors, and may also include a scriptwriter or scriptwriters, a director, set designers and builders, choreographers, light designers, and others. People who are observing a performance may also play important roles in the development or enactment of the story.

✪ Activity: Observe or Participate in a Rehearsal of a Performance

Performances may be based on a written document called a script, from which every word is memorized, or on an outline of events called a scenario. The scenario may be written, or may exist only in the performers' memories based on their prior oral discussions. They may memorize a few key lines and otherwise move their characters' actions in a generally agreed-upon direction, or they may memorize every word.

Discover who is responsible for the creation and execution of different aspects of the performance. Describe various participants' roles. Do performers create from a script, a written scenario, or an oral scenario? Describe how plot structure development happens. Who decides what happens in the story: a script, the director, or a collaborative effort among all actors? Who decides what the exact words will be: the actor, the director, or the scriptwriter? Are the words always the same, or do they vary from performance to performance? Who decides what gestures to use: the director, the actor, or the script? Who decides how actors position themselves in relation to one another: the script, the director, or the performer? How does characterization happen: entirely decided by the actor, the director, the script, or some combination of these? Is direction given by a single person or by consensus of the group?

✪ Activity: Describe the Members of the Performance Group and What Part Each Plays

The company or ensemble is the group performing a drama. Describe whether it is organized more collaboratively or more hierarchically. What are the different roles assigned to group members, or does everyone do everything? Is there a director giving instructions on how the actors should act (a hierarchical model), or do all the performers coach one another (a collaborative model)? Is there a prop manager or set designer, or does everyone create and set up the performance space? Is there an author, or do performers come to a group consensus about plot structure, theme, and characterization? Do they work from a memorized script, or from an outlined scenario?

An *actor* is a person who portrays a character.

A *playwright* is a person who creates scripts for plays. Many traditions do not write scripts and thus work without playwrights.

The *director* is the person who supervises the creative integration of all the elements of a drama and instructs the actors and crew as to their performance elements. There may be no single director in a performance, as when performers coach one another. Directing is to instruct the actors in the preparation of their performance. Some companies decide together what to do and have no director. Director William Ball (1984:81) advises:

> The only real reason a director is needed in rehearsal is to perform the following function: persistently to draw the actor to a more meaningful and appropriate choice of objectives, and then to persuade the actor to lend his full commitment to those objectives. This is the purpose of a director. He helps the actor choose an objective and then encourages him to play it with all his heart.

Ball describes directing as helping the actor find actionable verbs and then coaching the actors to strengthen the action verb they are playing.

The *crew* are the people who set up, take down, change scenes, manipulate the environment during performance (e.g., lighting, sound effects), advertise, and/or manage the set, costumes, and props. These may include set designers who create the scenes and stage; costume designers who create the clothes that performers wear; and a stage manager responsible for technical details during performance, costuming, setting, and prompting if an actor forgets a line. The *lighting designer* and *lighting operators* may deal with special lighting. In some companies the actors perform all the duties of a crew. A non-matrixed performer does not show character. Stagehands in Japanese *kabuki* theater, for example, move props, and the audience sees them but ignores them (Kirby 1972:3). A Foley artist specializes in creating sound effects. The group you observe may not have all of these.

The audience may participate passively or actively in the dramatic performance. Boal (1995:13) coined the term *spect-actors* to describe the participant role that blurs the line between spectator and actor. This occurs when the audience participates actively in the performance

⚙ Activity: Describe the Relationship between Performers and Audience

Watch a play. From the interaction between the audience and the actors, what expectations would you say actors have of the audience? What expectations does the audience have of the actors? Do actors and audience interact with one another during the performance, or do they assume that a wall separates them? Describe the play as presentational or representational.

A *representational* depiction of reality shapes stage action to appear as if it were happening in much the same way it would in real life. The onstage characters behave as if they are unaware of the audience's presence. Actors and audience suspend their disbelief and act as though everything in the play is happening for the first time. The onstage characters assume that an invisible fourth wall separates them from the audience. The audience members understand that they are not supposed to interact with the performers. A *presentational* play, on the other hand, knows it is a show. The characters break the fourth wall between actors and audience when they behave as if they are aware that the audience is watching. (We could call presentational theater in other performance spaces simply "breaking the wall.") The audience and the performers interact with one another or acknowledge each other's presence during the performance (McLaughlin 1997:166–167). This is a frequent occurrence in entertainment-education dramas, where actors may ask audience members to advise on particular situations in the play and audience members may join in singing, dancing, or recommending actions to actors.

Some mainly representational plays have presentational moments when an actor briefly addresses the audience directly and then returns to the world of the play: actors may make use of monologues (one actor talking at length to the audience) and asides (brief statements or questions to the audience).

Many plays contain one or two character(s) or a chorus that have a presentational relationship with the audience and speak to them, while all the other characters have a representational relationship with the audience and do not speak to them. That one character or group serves as a bridge between the two worlds.

There are different levels of presentational theater. In a small way, whenever a performer glances directly at the audience, he or she is being a bit presentational, because he or she is acknowledging the audience's existence; an interactional play from Ghana like "Orphan Do Not Glance" is presentational to a much greater extent since performers speak directly to the audience while in character, and audience members come on the stage to feed the actor playing a hungry child, breaking the fourth wall in both directions (Barber et al. 1997:92–116). These participants could well be described as *spect-actors*.

Activity: Describe How Participants Use Their Performance Space

Watch a dramatic event, or record it and watch it again later. While watching the video, or immediately after watching the play, note answers to these questions:

- Is there always an imaginary "fourth wall" between performers and audience? If there is, the audience does not interact with the performers, and performers pretend they are living their lives without the audience present.

- Is there *no wall* between performers and audience, so at any time performers may interact directly with the audience, or audience members may become performers?
- Is the *wall* between performers and audience sometimes present and at other times *broken*? If it is sometimes broken, is it broken by movement, by words, or by both? If by movement, is it movement of the audience into the actors' space, or movement of the actors into the audience's space, or both? If the wall is broken verbally, do audience members speak directly to performers, or performers to audience members, or both? Is the wall broken in both directions, or only in one direction? Is it broken occasionally or frequently? Is it broken only by some characters, or by all of them?

Shape of the Event through Time

Shape of an event refers to its segments, organized hierarchically.

Summary and Relationship to Other Lenses

Performances that include dramatic actions usually enact narratives, and so draw on cultural systems guiding the telling of stories, such as plot and character. Look for segment breaks. How do performed stories begin, develop, and end? What characteristics signal shifts in parts of a performance? These performances also frequently include features of other arts, such as song, dance, storytelling, and proverb telling.

Activity: Audio and/or Videorecord a Dramatic Performance in Preparation for Structure Analysis

Create a written transcription while listening to the recording of the performance. Make either a *summary transcription* providing a concise description of the key elements, or a *transcription* of every word, or a *complete transcription* of every word, gesture, and movement. Look for segment breaks and what characterizes each segment. If the work is in another language you do not know well, work with a bilingual person to translate the transcription into a language you know well. Note the date and place of the performance, because different performances will have different transcriptions.

Look for combinations of performance features that signal changes in parts. Your transcription may address some of the following components:

Line: One utterance. Do performers wait for one another to finish speaking? Are there times when performers speak at once? If the audience reacts or laughs, will performers wait to deliver the next line until the audience is quiet, or keep going?

Gesture: One bodily movement in the same place.

Cross: A performer changes positions from one part of the performance space to another part of the space. The combination of actors' changing positions in the performance space is called the performance's *blocking*.

Beat: One interaction between two performers. One does something or says something, and another reacts by doing something or saying something. Another meaning of the word "beat" is when a scriptwriter wants an actor to pause for a moment without saying anything. For example, a line may read, "All I have is (beat) now." This indicates the actor is thinking and adds emphasis to the word "now."

French scene: An event in the story with the same exact group of actors on stage. French scenes are shorter units than scenes, because the French scene number changes any time any actor enters or exits.

Scene: A series of events in one setting with the same approximate group of actors. When the imagined place changes, or the grouping of performers on stage changes significantly, the scene changes.

Act: A series of scenes. Often a first act situates the audience as to the place, situation, and characters; a second act develops a conflict; and a third act resolves the conflict. An act may be a single scene or a series of scenes.

Play: A full story enacted with a beginning, middle, and end. It can be a series of acts or a single act. Watch for what signals the beginning and the end, and any changes of structure in between.

Play series or play cycle: Several plays performed as one event.

Epic play cycle: A series of play cycles performed as a series of events.

Activity: Using a Play Script or Performance Transcription, Write a French Scene Analysis

Every time any character enters or exits, write what line is the first line spoken and the last line spoken. Number each segment as a new French scene. Go through the scene list and write down the setting (imagined place) for each French scene. Write down the names of all the characters onstage together during each French scene.

Summarize in one sentence what key action takes place in each scene. Directors may use this list to know what actors to call to rehearse which scenes.

⭐ **Activity: From Your French Scene Analysis, Create a Plot Summary**

A *plot summary* tells the main events of a play as a story. You can turn your French scene list into a plot summary. In *Story*, Robert McKee (1997:33) defines *structure* as "a selection of events from characters' life stories that is composed into a strategic sequence to arouse specific emotions and to express a specific view of life." Plot is the series of events in a play and their structured arrangement in time. The ordering of events helps express the worldview and meaning of the play (see the sections on *underlying symbolic systems* and *content* that follow)

⭐ **Activity: Using Your French Scene Analysis, Write a Dramatic Intensity Curve**

A dramatic intensity curve (McLaughlin 1997:131–134) shows the rise and fall of action across the time of the play. Make a line going left to right, denoting time passing from the beginning to the end of the play. Write the number of each French scene on this line as it occurs. Then make a vertical line on the left-hand side of your page, showing low intensity on the bottom and high intensity on the top. Plot an approximate point for the intensity of each numbered French scene. Note the names of story events that define major turning points in the story.

Performance Feature Categories

Performance features are observable characteristics of a performance that emerge from an event's unique combination of physical and social context and participants' actions.

Summary and Relationship to Other Lenses

Acting is to perform a role or roles by behaving in a manner suitable for a given character. Acting involves bringing to life or interpreting a character. Acting involves performing verbs. Speaking, moving, and appearance are the actor's three main observable tools. The actor's imagination is a fourth tool that is invisible.

⚫ **Activity: Describe to What Extent Actors Prepare Their Performances in Advance and to What Extent They Improvise**

Improvisation may refer either to making up an entire performance around a scenario without using a script, or may involve adding small elements that were not rehearsed before into a scripted performance. Different dramatic traditions accord varying importance to improvisation. Many classical Indian dramatic forms allow for very little improvisation because they value the precise reproduction of the performance tradition in the same way for every performance. Many African traditions value great amounts of improvisation for showing the versatility of the performers and for honoring interaction with the audience, so each performance is different.

⚫ **Activity: Describe the Acting in a Given Performance as Realistic, Brechtian, or Codified**

In *realistic acting*, the performer models behavior in life, giving the impression of actual events occurring, and emotion is not only displayed by the actors onstage, but also experienced. In *Brechtian acting*, the actor interprets a role but remains outside of the role and comments on the role or situation. The actor quotes the character rather than becoming the character (Schechner 2006:180–182). In this and other nonrealistic acting, emotion is displayed rather than experienced. In *codified acting*, a performer uses a symbol system of movements, gestures, costumes, makeup, or melodies whose meanings are set by tradition and passed down from generation to generation. Actors and audiences know the vocabulary and grammar of this symbolic system. Western mime, Chinese *jingju*, and Indian *Bharatanatyam* are codified acting systems. The actor does not need to feel emotions because the symbol system shows emotions. In Brechtian acting and codified acting, emotion is displayed rather than experienced (Schechner 2006:183–187). In *non-matrixed representation*, the performer does not take on the role of a character, such as the stagehands who move objects onstage in *kabuki* theater but do not become part of the story. They are ignored by the audience (Schechner 2006:174).

⚫ **Activity: Vocal Feature Analysis**

Speaking is verbal communication that has both lexical (dictionary) meaning and contextual (situational) meaning. How we understand what a character says depends on the context in which they say it.

Text is what a character says. We still call utterances text, whether they are scripted or improvised. *Subtext* is the implied meaning of how an actor performs the text when it is different from the plain meaning of the text. When discerning subtext, intonation carries more meaning than text. If an actor says the text, "I hate you," with the subtext "I love you," then "I love you" is what the audience understands. The audience believes the subtext more than the text. What makes intention and subtext difficult to interpret accurately cross-culturally is that different cultures convey emotions and intentions with different intonation and vocal features. The emotions we think we are picking up based on our culture's cues may actually be different in another culture until we learn the other culture's cues.

Interview a performer or audience member. Ask them to describe an instance where the text and the subtext are different. What signifies this? How does the actor or audience member know that the text and subtext differ?

Activity: Ask if Characters' Ways of Speaking Indicate Their Region

Accent is a way of speaking that is representative of a region. Are different characters from different regions, or are all characters from the same region?

Register is the level of vocabulary and grammar that indicates the speaker's level of formality or time period. Ask if different characters have different registers or if they all use the same register. How formal is it? Is the register different in different scenes? Is this the way people speak today, or when did people speak like this?

Activity: Describe General Sections of Speech

Dialogue is verbal interaction between characters. *Monologue* is a speech an actor gives directly to the audience. *Soliloquy* is a speech an actor gives to himself or herself, as though thinking aloud, usually with no one else on stage. An *aside* is a line an actor gives directly to the audience while other actors are on stage, but that the other actors pretend not to hear. See which of these you can find. Do characters generally give short lines alternating rapidly back and forth? Do characters often make long speeches?

Paralinguistic vocal features involve pitch, emphasis, volume, modulation, dialect, and timbre of a performer, and the emotions, intents, or other characteristics understood by combinations of these features.

Strength or *volume* refers to how loudly or softly a performer speaks. Performers generally try to speak loudly enough so everyone present can hear. We can speak more loudly by breathing more deeply before we begin to let out the air we use to speak. *Explosive volume* is used in shouts. *Expulsive volume* releases air from the lungs in a gradual way to prolong the sentence the way a singer holds a note (Frakes 2005:52).

Pitch refers to how high or low a performer's tone of voice is. *Quality* refers to how the performer's voice is perceived by the audience. With what adjective would someone describe the character's voice? Is it rough, scary, gentle, gravelly, squeaky, mellow, nasal, pleasing, guttural, hollow, or breathy? What kind of character speaks that way, or what does the quality of the voice say about the character? *Tempo, rate,* or *pace* refers to how fast or slowly a performer speaks. This can either be in regard to the duration of the words, or the length of the silences between words (Frakes 2005:48–51). What does the character's use of time say about the character?

✪ Activity: Perform a Line and Get Feedback on Emotion and Intent

Choose a line from the culture's play that you are analyzing. Use different volumes, pitches, qualities, and tempos to show different emotions and different intents in the style of drama you are analyzing. Verify with a native speaker that you are communicating the intention and emotion that you think you are.

✪ Activity: Identify Paralinguistic Features of Expressing Emotion

Listen to an audio recording of a performance and verify with a native speaker what emotions are conveyed by what paralinguistic features. Do not assume that the paralinguistic features that mean certain emotions in your culture indicate the same emotions in the local culture.

✪ Activity: Describe How Actors Modify Their Appearance to Convey Character

Describe the actors' *natural appearance* or inherent physique. Note how they craft their *artificial appearance*, making deliberate changes by use of masks, different hairstyles, wigs, makeup, or costumes to evoke a character (also see section on *materials*).

✪ Activity: Describe the Event's Blocking

Blocking is the arrangement of all actors' movements in space in relation to one another. Blocking may be designated by a director, by improvisation, or by prior group consensus. Emotion is conveyed mainly through the face, so most blocking patterns keep actors' faces fully or partially visible to the majority of the audience. To block the scene is to tell the story through movement of the actors on stage. *Stage business* is any activity that reveals character, often using a prop.

The audience's attention tends to go to the actor who is moving. Explore how participants use movement through activities such as the following:

- Ask participants to tell you terms they use to describe their movements in their local language. Note how actors' movements tell you about what their characters are like and reveal the action of the story sequence.
- How do performers keep the story action visible to their audience? Try performing the same scene with different sequences of movements, and ask participants which of the blocking options shows the story events more clearly.
- How are levels or differences in height used? How do groupings of performers place emphasis on the most important places they want their audience to focus their attention? How do actors' placements at key moments help convey their emotions and intents?

Content

Content refers to the subject matter in artistic activity. In drama's *content* lens, we describe the characters' identities and their character traits; the location and time of the story; the events of the story; the emotions conveyed by the story; and the main ideas conveyed by the performance.

Summary and Relationship to Other Lenses

Because drama is usually based on showing a story, its content relates integrally to almost everything else and may include elements of visual arts, music, dance, and verbal arts. The *content* lens describes characters who perform actions in a setting for a reason. Actions include movements, language, motivations, and emotions in interaction with one another, overlapping with the *performance features* lens. Describing *characters* and *setting* (time and place) overlaps with the *space* and *materials* lenses. The events that occur form part of the *content*, and the order in which events occur overlaps with the *shape through time* lens.

Content may originate from the person or people who write the scenario outline or the script; or it may originate from the performers, the director, or the audience. Different cultures may draw different boundaries around who may contribute what aspects of a performance's content to different people; this topic overlaps with the *participant organization* lens.

Text is verbal *content*, whether written or not. *Subtext* is the intended meaning conveyed when the actual meaning is different from the plain meaning of the text. The meaning of subtext is discerned from cultural knowledge of context, intonation, or veiled references. Both text and subtext are types of *content*, but the means of distinguishing them are best described under *performance features*.

✪ Activity: Complete an Overview of the Play's Characters, Actions, Setting, and Ideas

- Who are the characters?
- What are their actions and emotions? How do the characters' words, emotions, actions, and motivations contribute to their characterization?
- Where and when do the story's events happen?
- What are the main ideas expressed? What is the main idea or theme conveyed?
- At what points do text and subtext differ?

✪ Activity: Describe Each Character's Traits and His or Her Goals, Obstacles, and Tactics.

What characters want—called their *goal, motivation, objective,* or *intention*—determines what they do during a play. Goals, obstacles, and tactics motivate acting. What does each character want? That is his or her goal. What is hindering each character from getting what he or she wants? That is his or her obstacle. How is she or he going about getting what she or he wants? That is her or his tactic. How does she or he show this? How does the audience react to different characters trying to get what they want? Which characters and actions stand out most strongly? How does each character show what he or she is like? Is his or her characterization directly stated or indirectly inferred?

✪ Activity: Determine the Meaning of Any Verbal or Visual Metaphors or Image Systems

Ask a local person about the meaning of any symbols. A *metaphor* is an image comparing something concrete with an abstract idea. In *Fiddler on the Roof,* for example, the character of the fiddler may be a metaphor for the precariousness of the Jewish way of life in Russia.

An *image system* is a visual image repeated in various ways to convey an extended metaphor. In Peter Jackson's film *The Lord of the Rings*, for example, the white tree of Gondor may be a metaphor for the king's authority. The return of the king is foreshadowed or hinted at when Sam and Frodo see a toppled statue's head crowned in white flowers and Sam says, "Look, Mr. Frodo. The King has got his crown again." As the dead tree before the throne of Gondor begins to flower, this represents hope of the king's return, which ironically is right, as Lord Denethor, the Guardian of the throne, loses hope and commits suicide. Arwen sends Aragorn a banner with a white flowering tree as he goes to battle, and he stands behind a green banner with a white tree as he is crowned. The white tree is in full bloom at King Aragorn's coronation. The image of the white flowers is repeated in various ways and deepens its significance over time as an image system for hope and perseverance.

⊛ Activity: Identify and Describe a Play's Plot Elements

Plot elements are parts of the plot such as backstory, exposition, conflict, climax, and resolution (note that not all genres with dramatic features include all of these elements, especially in this order). From the transcription you made earlier, use the following definitions to describe the play's plot elements. Ask performers or other participants when your understandings are unclear.

> *Backstory* is what happened to the characters before the play began. The audience infers what events happened earlier, and what characters are like. This helps them understand the rest of the story. In Senegal, for example, when an audience sees a play with a rabbit character, they know from prior stories that the rabbit is a clever trickster.
>
> *Exposition* tells the audience the backstory and situates them through performers' conversations and actions, or through visual design that sets the scene.
>
> *Conflict* is created within a character or between characters, either by characters seeking opposing goals or by adverse circumstances a character seeks to overcome. *External conflict* is opposition to a character who does not doubt him- or herself. *Internal conflict* is struggle within a character to make a decision, control personal emotions, or determine values.
>
> The *climax* of the play occurs when the central character makes a decision that will lead to a resolution of the conflict.
>
> The play's *dénouement* or *resolution* shows how the conflict ends.

⚙ **Activity: Determine the Idea, Theme, or Dramatic Premise**

Idea, theme, and *dramatic premise* all refer to the message or main idea the play is seeking to communicate, which may be communicated by characters the audience approves or disapproves of, by their actions and those actions' results. What main action leads to what main, overall result? This is the dramatic premise of the play. Interview audience member(s), the director, or performer(s) to learn what they believe to be the main idea, theme, or dramatic premise of the play. The following descriptions may help you in your exploration. The theme may be overt, as when it is stated at the beginning or end by a narrator or character, or it may require effort on the audience's part to ascertain, as when it is shown rather than stated. Episodic plots in particular emphasize idea or theme, as this idea is what links the scenes into a coherent whole.

Dramatic premise is usually revealed through plot or the structured sequence of events. In climactic plots, dramatic premise is the idea or message that the play is seeking to communicate by the string of events that unfold. It is like a theme or idea, but it may be stated as an action that leads to a result. The dramatic premise determines how the play is put together structurally in terms of cause and effect, such as "greediness leads to loneliness" (McLaughlin 1997:31–41). A performance's theme, idea, or dramatic premise may choose to either support or call into question a culture's values, assumptions, and norms. Drama may change how audience members view their lives.

Underlying Symbolic Systems

Underlying symbolic systems refer to the grammatical and social rules and structures that guide participants' actions in artistic activity. What are a given genre's expectations for what must happen for a work to represent the genre? What makes a valued instantiation of the genre? *Underlying symbolic systems* describe knowledge critical for interpreting the other six lenses.

Summary and Relationship to Other Lenses

Systems like plot structure, idea, genre, character, and characterization provide grammatical structure for performing and understanding dramatic performances. The other six lenses (*space, materials, shape through time, participant organization, performance features*, and *content*) are transcribable. The *underlying symbolic systems* lens describes the rules by which the other six lenses function adequately or well in a genre. What features of each of the other six lenses create a good performance in this genre? The *content* lens describes what happens and who does what. *Underlying symbolic systems* related to the *content* lens describe genre expectations for what happens, and what kinds of characters are allowed and appreciated in the genre.

✪ Activity: Describe an Event's Expected Plot Structure and the Type of Action Appreciated in a Genre

Transcribe an audio- or videorecording of an event. If it is not in a language you know well, work with a bilingual speaker of the language to translate it for you. You may describe the plot structure as climactic, episodic, or cyclic:

> *Climactic* plots are the most common type of plot. They begin with exposition of a problem, build on a series of minor crises to a major climax or turning point, and lead to a resolution. Climactic plots may interweave subplots or secondary stories with their own smaller crises and resolutions. The basic structure is action-reaction or cause-effect (Greenwald et al. 2001:25). Climactic plots use cause and effect to arrange events in a story. The audience wants to find out what happens next. For this type of plot, "[t]he cornerstone of dramatic engagement is suspense" (Hatcher 1996:14).
>
> *Episodic* plots contain scenes linked by theme or idea more than by actions and reactions. The series of events is not necessarily linked by cause and effect. Many history plays, myths, and folk tales are episodic.
>
> *Cyclic* plots contain conflicts that are intentionally unresolved. The play ends with characters in the same situation as when the play began. Cyclic plots are the rarest type of plot in the world. They are found mostly in Bali and in some modern Western theater (Greenwald et al. 2001:25).

✪ Activity: Describe an Event's Temporal Structure

Temporal structure is the arrangement of events in time. It can also refer to the length of the event and what length is preferred. From the audience's point of view, how long do they expect the full performance to last? Time within the play may proceed linearly (chronologically) or cyclically (repetitively), or temporal structure may make use of flashbacks or other jumps in time.

✪ Activity: Identify and Describe Features of a Good Plot

As already discussed, plot elements are parts of the plot such as back story, exposition, conflict, climax, and resolution. Ask performers or other participants which elements of plot are absolutely necessary in this genre and which are optional.

⭐ **Activity: Identify Who Holds Creative Control in Determining the Play's Structure and Main Point**

Participate in or observe the creation of an event to determine who holds creative control, whether its plot is *malleable* or *fixed*. In dramatic traditions where performers memorize written scripts, the structure, plot, and meanings of the play come from *authorial intent*. They may also result from *directorial intent, performer intent*, or *audience intent*. Alternatively, they may be a collaborative effort by performers and audience. In *literary drama*, the outcome is decided in advance, and the audience has no input into the course of events. In participatory theater and often in *drama for development*, the audience participates in deciding the outcome of the play. The role of the audience operates along a continuum, and the audience may have greater or lesser input into the minor or major features of structure design.

To learn about creative control, ask participants questions such as:

- Who decided which idea would be the main point of the play? Was more than one person involved?
- How did you decide to show the main idea: through how the conflict resolves, through the idea that links the scenes, through images or symbols, or through some combination of these? Who determined it?

⭐ **Activity: Describe Types of Characters and Characterization Valued in a Genre**

A *character* is a make-believe person represented by an actor in a drama. Types of characters and their means of characterization vary according to their intended relationship to everyday reality. A play is usually about a main character who changes. A *character arc* is the progress or regress of a character as he or she changes throughout a story. Characters begin with certain viewpoints and characteristics and, through their actions and choices, their viewpoints and characteristics develop. List each character in the event and decide whether each is archetypal, individualized, stock, personified, or self-represented. Decide who the main characters are, and if they have a character arc showing change, what that change is, and what decisions signal it. Which types of characters and characterization are expected and allowed in a genre? Which are valued?

An *archetype* is the original pattern or model of a character on which later archetypal characters are based, like a cookie cutter from which the same shape of individual cookies may come. Example archetypes include the fairy godmother, the hero, the trickster, the witch, or the wise old man. Merlin is an archetypal wizard in the Anglo-Saxon tradition from a wizard archetype, but Merlin should not be described as the archetype for any other culture for their wizards.

An *individualized* or *developed character* reveals his or her individualized personality, life history, values, physical attributes, and family background. A developed character does not always do what the audience expects. The better the audience gets to know a character, the better developed that character is.

Stereotypical or *stock character* is a simplified or generalized, predictable representation of a character without subtlety. Stereotypical characters and stock characters do exactly what the audience expects them to do. Actors represent stereotypical characters by drawing on a smaller set of recognizable performance features than when representing individualized characters. Characters in a melodrama, for example, have exaggerated traits such as dastardliness and heroism, reducing the range of emotions and actions produced by the actor. In general, stock characters are stronger for creating humorous comedies than for creating serious dramas. "Stereotypical character" has a negative connotation if an individualized character was expected by the audience but not achieved by the actor, while "stock character" has a neutral connotation: while the actor does not give the character an individual personality, none is expected by the performance tradition. Chinese opera, for example, has expected stock characters such as the man, the woman, the white face representing an aggressive male such as a bandit or warrior, and the clown. Some would call these archetypes. In plays with developed characters, there is often not time to develop the personality of every character well, so less central characters are often stock characters. In the Western performance tradition, a good actor can make even a small stock character into an interesting individualized character.

Personifications are characters who represent abstract concepts, such as Good Deeds, Beauty, or Strength in the medieval English morality play *Everyman*.

A *self-represented character* is when the actor is playing himself or herself, but not in this moment. The actor shows himself or herself as he or she was or will be, as though that time could be brought into this moment. Storytellers telling about their day at work are self-representing their character.

⭐ Activity: Determine Broad Roles of the Character(s)

Reflect on each character, using the following discussion to decide whether it is a narrator, focal character, antagonist, or protagonist.

A *narrator* is a storyteller in a play. A narrator speaks directly to the audience to set the stage, provides transitional material between parts of a story, or gives the moral at the end. This person may be called different things in different drama traditions; in *Therukoothu* drama in India, the narrator role is served by the stage manager (through song) and the buffoon (who humorously comments on the action). Other traditions have no narrator.

A *focal character* is a character the audience pays attention to and with whom the audience is most emotionally concerned. It is usually the protagonist, but may sometimes be someone that the audience wants to fail.

Protagonists are characters the audience identifies with and wants to succeed. A play is usually about a main protagonist who changes in some way during the play.

Antagonists are characters whose desires or efforts conflict with the protagonist. The audience does not want them to succeed. A play is usually about a conflict opposing the objectives of the antagonist(s) and protagonist(s). If the antagonist is the focal character, his or her emotions and ambitions are not meant to be empathized with by the audience. Sometimes the antagonist may be an idea, a force, or an event rather than a person.

⭐ Activity: Explore the Actor's Relationships to His or Her Character and the Audience

Interview an actor, asking questions like these:

- Do you actually feel the character's emotions, or do you imitate what it looks like to feel the character's emotions?
- Do you like the character? Is he or she similar to you?

Performers' relationship to their own characters may be described as *representational* if the actor represents the character without necessarily needing to feel the emotions of the character in order to act as the tradition or genre requires. A representational actor-character relationship like this is most often accompanied by a *presentational actor-audience relationship*, in which performers acknowledge the presence of the audience. These relationships are likely to describe a more *codified* acting style.

Performers' relationships to their characters may be described as *presentational* if the actor is fully present with the character and feels what the character feels. Note that a presentational actor-character relationship is most often accompanied by a *representational actor-audience relationship*, in which the performers represent reality without acknowledging that they are present with an audience. These sets of relationships usually describe a realistic acting style.

Some literature on drama analysis is imprecise, calling theater "presentational" or "representational" without specifying whether this refers to the relationship between actor and character (the *performance feature* lens) or the relationship between actor and audience (the *participant organization* lens). We encourage you in your own descriptions to clarify which aspect you are describing to avoid further confusion in the literature.

Activity: Determine Whether Characterization Is Direct or Indirect

Characterization is the underlying model guiding the creation and representation of a character or set of characters. It is shown by dialogue, through action, by appearance, and by the choices the character makes. *Direct* or *explicit characterization* relies on the performers to tell the audience what the characters are like through statements a narrator makes about a character, statements another character makes about a character, and statements the character makes. *Indirect* or *implicit characterization* relies on the audience to deduce for themselves what the character's traits are through the character's actions, choice of words, clothing, appearance, and interaction with other characters.

Activity: Determine the Frame of the Play

Frame is the overall purpose of an event and lets the audience know how to interpret it (Tillis 1999:85). A performance frame is culturally accepted knowledge about how to receive communication in a genre. The audience needs to accept the frame to correctly understand the communication within the frame. Frame sets audience expectations: Is this to make us laugh, make us think, teach us, or reinforce or change societal values? Frame helps audience members know what kinds of content and features to expect. Clues early on must let the audience know in what ways they are expected to respond. The title of the performance or the first few interchanges usually let the audience know if the play is comedic or tragic, for education or for entertainment, for community change or to uphold established community values. Often, audiences are unhappy if the beginning of a performance does not give them a clear idea of what kind of performance it is and therefore how they should respond to the performance. That said, a play may have more than one frame, for instance, both to entertain and to educate. Differing frames include different expectations of what the audience should expect out of the story and how to interact appropriately with the performers. The audience has differing expectations if a story is about love, growing up, family problems, adventure, history, science fiction, or fantasy.

Interview a director or actor involved in the event, and ask, What elements does this type of play need to make it a good example of this genre? What kinds of standards are you aiming for? What kinds of things do audiences appreciate in this kind of performance?

Ask audience members or people who watch a recording questions such as, Why did you come to this event? What did you like about it? What may someone not have liked about it? How well did it meet your expectations? How was this play different from other plays? What did you get out of it?

Activity: Explore the Type of the Event Further

Type (often referred to as *genre* in discussions of drama) consists of a cluster of attributes that lead the audience to expect certain sets of performance features and respond in set ways. By performing any of the research activities in "Look at an Event's Forms" (Part A), you are already identifying this cluster of attributes. Here we provide a brief discussion on types with a large number of dramatic features.

The first major type of distinction is if the play is literary or oral. In *literary drama*, a scriptwriter or scriptwriters create a text to be brought to life through performance, and a director coaches performers on how to bring their performances to life. In *oral traditions*, a group creates collectively without using a written script.

Each of these broad types may be described by more specific terms. Stories in the same type share the same kinds of characters and plots. Types of a given culture need to be understood from an *emic* (insider's) perspective through researching the categories of performance in a community. For example, the two most popular kinds of Sanskrit drama in India are *nataka* (heroic) drama, drawing from history or mythology to portray stories of gods and kings, and *prakarana* (social) drama. Research the terms used to describe kinds of performances in your community.

Historical analysis of many plays will allow you to discover how traditions of drama have developed over time and have influenced one another, both within a given culture and cross-culturally.

Etic terms (terms from the researcher's own culture) may be used by way of comparison of cross-cultural performance to dramatists from the researcher's own community. In Western drama, some broad types are *comedy*, intended to cause the audience to laugh and ending happily; *drama*, in the more specific sense of a serious story; *tragedy*, evoking sadness and an unhappy ending; *tragicomedy*, involving both tragic and comedic aspects; and *morality plays*, intending to give an example of how to live or how not to live.

Aristotle described drama in terms of six parameters: character, action, idea, language, music, and spectacle (what is seen). Western theater is based on Aristotle, but Indian theater is based on the *Natyasastra*, which has its own definitions of what makes up a good plot—five stages (*avasthas*) that must be followed. If any are omitted, there are rules for what else must be omitted. Explore which rules apply in the culture in which you are working.

Interactions with Other Domains

Dramatic elements often interact closely with musical and other sound elements.

Activity: Explore the Relationship between Drama and Other Artistic Genres

Ask participants (actors, musicians, audience members, directors, etc.) what role(s) they see drama playing versus other artistic elements. For example:

- What makes this genre different from other genres? What is this genre particularly good at? Is drama more useful for some purposes, such as communicating a message or teaching new ideas or making people laugh, than other artistic genres?
- Is drama considered to be inseparable in performance from any other artistic genres? How was this performance strengthened by its use of music? Poetry? Storytelling? Visual arts? Dance?

Activity: Determine the Ways Musical Elements Interact with Dramatic Elements

Reflect on the dramatic and musical features of the event. Describe if any of the following occur:

- Songs or instrumental music may be used to attract audience members, but not as part of the main drama.
- Songs or instrumental music may comment on the plot, serve as an interlude, or provide a chance to involve the audience.
- Ambient music may be used to set a scene.
- Songs may form a feature of dialogue, allowing the plot to progress or showing what characters are like. A recognizable musical theme (*leitmotif*) may serve to refer to a certain character.

Sound effects produced deliberately by actors or other participants may be realistic to the action or representative of it.

⊛ **Activity: Determine the Ways Oral Arts Interact with Dramatic Elements**

Ask a performer, director, or audience member to reflect on:

- How was this performance strengthened by its use of poetry? Storytelling? Proverbs? Jokes? Song lyrics?
- Is the level of language modern/archaic/high/common/difficult to understand/easy to follow/funny/beautiful? What makes it funny/beautiful/difficult to understand?

⊛ **Activity: Determine the Ways Visual Arts Interact with Dramatic Elements**

Ask a performer, director, or audience member to respond to these questions:

- What did you especially like about the costumes? Setting? Special visual effects?
- How did the overall emotion of the play feel to you? How did visual features contribute to that?
- What did the colors or shapes that characters were wearing say about what their characters were like?

Dance in an Event

This section will help you to describe more completely how participants move in patterned ways in an event. To understand this section best, you should first work through some of the activities in "Look at an Event's Forms" (Part A). We use the same seven lenses here, but introduce descriptive categories that are particularly pertinent to dance. Gather your discoveries about the dance characteristics of this event and others like it in the Community Arts Profile.

Dance features are recognized visually and performed viscerally with auditory and visual awareness. An observer sees the performers, the environment in which they are moving, their relationship to other dancers, their relationship to any other participants and collaborators (such as singers or musicians), their relationship to props and costumes, the use of their bodies in the space surrounding them (kinesphere), and their use of storytelling or abstract ideas in movement. A performer feels her body moving in her personal kinesphere and the environment, hears the atmosphere (e.g., music, clapping, vocalizations, breathing, impact of feet on floor, etc.), and responds to it. She understands the purposes of the genre of the event in which she is dancing, and senses physical and spiritual changes in her own body and in the environment.

It is often very different to observe a dance versus participate in a dance. A dancer may recognize that the important thing about a step is its weight and contact with the ground (quality and dynamic), while an observer may believe that the important thing about a step is its direction in space (function and aesthetic). Watching, interviewing, and doing are all important aspects of movement analysis and documentation.

Some analysts transcribe movement using notation systems. Like musical notation does for sound, these systems use symbols to refer to elements of human movement through space. Rudolf Laban developed notation that serves as a foundation for dance analysis in many places around the world. Kinetography Laban ("Labanotation" in North America) is highly detailed, and used for choreography, composition, and documentation. It graphically illustrates continuity, time, and direction (Guest 2005). Motif Description reduces Labanotation to its essentials, allowing users to focus on the most significant aspects of movement (see Guest and Curran 2008). Irmgard Bartenieff studied with Rudolf Laban, extending his work to correct people's movement as a physical therapist (see Hackney 2000). Ohio State University's Department of Dance provides helpful resources on learning and teaching these and other systems (https://dance.osu.edu/research/dnb/resources, accessed March 24, 2018).

Space

Space refers to the location, demarcation, and physical characteristics of the area used, which can affect the form of artistic communication.

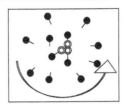

FIGURE 4.10. Sample floor plan.

Summary and Relationship to Other Lenses

The space allotted to human movement in an event may have profound effects on how participants move. A large space in proportion to the number of dancers, for example, allows larger movements covering more physical space. In addition, features of the space allow or restrict certain kinds of movement, as walls permit dancers to push off or climb upward.

Activity: Draw a Floor Plan of Part of the Dance

Choose a one-minute excerpt from a videorecording of the event that includes a representative movement pattern. Include the boundaries of the space, permanent objects, and "snapshots" of dancers beginning and ending a movement pattern and their pathway to get from point A to point B.

Figure 4.10 gives an example of a simple floor plan. It depicts eight men (shown as filled circles with a line pointing the way they are facing, e.g.,) in an outer circle facing inward, three men playing drums in the middle (drums shown as empty concentric circles), and one walking around within the circle. The large arrow shows that the outer circle of men are moving together in a counterclockwise direction.

Materials

Materials are all of the tangible things associated with an event.

Summary and Relationship to Other Lenses

Costumes and props are the most common objects associated with patterned movement. These interact primarily with dance performance features, allowing the dancer to accentuate, extend, or otherwise modify his or her movements. Floppy grass rings attached at the ankle, for example, emphasize a dancer's forceful stomps on the ground. In addition, a dancer with a cane can lean farther than one without.

⚫ **Activity: Identify All Movement-Related Objects and Their Functions**

Look at the list of objects you created in the section on *materials* in "Look at an Event's Forms" (Part A) or make one now. Watch a videorecording of the event with one of its dancers, answering questions such as:

- Which objects are in direct or indirect physical contact with a dancer? For each, describe the interaction between the dancer and object in terms of the parts of the body and object in contact, and motions of each.
- What visual effect(s) results from the dancer's interaction with each object? Does such interaction magnify, reduce, or otherwise modify the dancer's movement?

Participant Organization

Participant organization highlights the people involved in an event, in terms of the roles they play, the ways they interact with each other through time, and how they use the physical space around them.

Summary and Relationship to Other Lenses

Dancers are often set apart in some way from the rest of an event. In Western concert dance, the stage is clearly delineated from audience seating (e.g., proscenium stage, thrust stage, black box, etc.). Community ceremonial dancers may be in the center of a gathering, or the dancers may surround the community members. Recreational dancers may move in the whole space with observers surrounding them in scattered seating.

⚫ **Activity: Describe the Basic Organization of Dancers**

Watch a videorecording of an event, and note which of the three following categories describes the dancers:

Solo: One person is moving, whether truly alone or in the midst of a stationary group. This dance may be related to a rite of passage, exceptional virtuosity, social status, and so on.

Ensemble: A small group of people moving either in unison, counterpoint, or in contact with one another and/or a soloist.

Corps: A large group moving in unison, canon (dancers repeating exactly the movements of a first dancer, one after the other), or other large coordinated effort.

⚙ Activity: Describe How Dancers Relate to Each Other

Watch a videorecording of an event with one or more of the dancers, and observe and ask questions like these, when appropriate:

Group relationships: How do people express relationships as individuals and within groups? What does it mean for a single dancer to be broad and expansive versus minute and articulated? What similarities and contrasts exist within group movement and/or individual performances? What is the level of awareness and/or physical contact between performers, props, and/or an invisible/visible focal point of the performance?

Solo: Does the performer keep his body parts close or use the environment minimally (i.e., small extension/near-reach, such as working with a prop)? Is he purposefully aware of his surroundings, or is he internally focused?

Solo within an ensemble or corps: Are the performers aware of everyone, or just a few others? Are the kinesphere and environment used in medium extension/mid-reach (e.g., greeting one another or in a circle dance) or large extension/far-reach (e.g., a teacher addressing students or a performer addressing the audience)?

Ensemble within a corps: Is there a main group that has more complex movement than a secondary group that may use simpler movement?

Group agreement: When does the group's movement begin? Is it dictated by a planned sound or visual cue, perhaps from a lead speaker, singer, instrument player, dancer, or community member? Or is it open-ended and determined by the performers themselves in silent agreement and awareness?

The following concepts may help you discuss these relationships more clearly (Hutchinson Guest 2005:296–298):

Awareness: Knowing something/someone is somewhere, demonstrating conscious perception.

Addressing: Acknowledging something/someone is somewhere, demonstrating conscious interaction.

Transient relationships: Awareness and/or addressing that comes and goes throughout the performance.

Retained relationships: Awareness and/or addressing that is maintained and sustained throughout the performance.

Canceled relationships: Awareness and/or addressing that ends at a specific time during the performance.

Shape of the Event through Time

Shape of an event through time refers primarily to its constituent segments, organized hierarchically.

Summary and Relationship to Other Lenses

In "Look at an Event's Forms" (Part A), you may have described an event with dance content, such as a concert, festival, religious service, or ritual. In this section, we focus on any concentrated periods of dance in the event, which we define as follows:

Dance: A composition consisting minimally of patterned movement.

We describe the shape of a dance in terms of its total dance form and constituent segments. Note that there is commonly an intimate link between musical and movement features in performance, so that similar techniques for analyzing music will likely work with dance. This system of hierarchical segmentation is drawn from a more detailed expansion available in Giurchescu and Kröschlová (2007). Definitions of these segments from highest to lowest place in a hierarchy follow:

Total dance form: The highest structural level, resulting in an organic and autonomous entity through the summation of all the integrated structural units.

Part: The highest structural unit within the total dance form.

Strophe: A closed higher form that is composed of phrases and organized according to the grouping principle.

Section: An intermediate macro-structure consisting of a linking or grouping of phrases. A one-phrase section decomposes directly into motifs.

Phrase: The simplest compositional unit that has sense for the people and by which dances or dance genres are identified.

Motif: The smallest significant grammatical sequence of movements having meaning for both the dancers and their society and for the dance genre within a given dance system.

⚙ Activity: Determine the Form of a Dance

You must first identify a dance. You can do this by choosing a segment you have already elicited and recorded as part of a collection. Another method is to look at a time line of an event that you created following guidelines in "Look at an Event's Forms" (Part A), noting the beginning and ending times of a dance. Watch a recording of this segment many times, marking repeated sections and points of change. If you can, transcribe its major movement segments.

After becoming familiar with the dance, note in the Community Arts Profile whether its form follows any of the following common patterns (Giurchescu and Kröschlová 2007):

- *Chain forms*: Movement segments are lined up one after another, and their number and relationship are not important. Sub-categories include the following:
  - *Homogeneous chain form*: Unlimited repetition of one segment.
  - *Variation chain form*: Each repeated segment is a variation of the basic unit.
  - *Heterogeneous chain form*: Individual segments are different and without consistent organization.
  - *Rondo form*: Regular recurrence of one or more basic segments in a certain order.
- *Grouping forms*: Movement segments have a precise number of components set in a fixed and contrastive relationship. Sub-categories include the following:
  - *Two-segment form*: Two equally important and contrasting segments tightly bound together in a stable balance.
  - *Three-segment form*: Three equally important and contrasting segments with a fixed relation of interdependence.
  - *Multi-segment form*: A variable number of more or less equally important segments often framed by an introductory and closing segment.

Performance Feature Categories

Performance features are observable characteristics of a performance that emerge from an event's unique combination of physical and social context and participants' actions.

Summary and Relationship to Other Lenses

Actions that produce movement can be initiated by gravity (e.g., arm raised and then released to drop), outside forces (e.g., another dancer in contact, dancer holding part of her own body, body part in contact with a prop or architecture, etc.), and voluntary muscle directing the movement in specific styles (e.g., loose and free, bound and controlled, etc.).

⚙ Activity: Identify Parts of the Body Involved in Patterned Movement

Conceptualize the body as an instrument with different parts, perhaps six "limbs": the head, the tail, the two arms, and the two legs all connected to the "center," "core," or "trunk" of the torso. Observe a dance and identify the main initiators (gravity, outside forces, voluntary muscle) and how one or multiple initiators "divide" the different body parts. Bartenieff developed symbols to describe these different connections, using ⯄ to denote a whole body facing you with legs spread and arms raised out (see Hackney 2000:71–218). Use the following as a starting point:

Breath ⯄: All movements derive from breath, but some very small movements are initiated or guided by the breath, such as an ensemble taking a breath before commencing a particular movement phrase, then returning to still- ness, and then the breath initiating the next movement phrase.

Head-tail ⯄: A clear connection between the head and the pelvis; perhaps the head is weaving side to side, and the spine weaves as a result, culminating in a large pelvic sway.

Core-distal ✳: A clear connection between the "center" or "core" of the body and the limbs of the arms and legs, usually very three-dimensional and asymmetrical; often considered a "gathering," or drawing inward, mo- tion followed by a "scattering," or releasing outward, such as a performer hunching over a focal point and then throwing himself away from the focal point.

Homologous ⯄: A clear connection between the upper half of the body (head, arms) and the lower half of the body (pelvis, legs), usually very two- dimensional and symmetrical, such as a rhythmic, repeated bowing at the waist or a jump into the air that "scissors" the body with the legs and torso coming forward.

Homolateral ⯄: A clear connection between the right side and left side of the body, usually very two-dimensional and symmetrical, such as the right elbow coming toward the right knee and the same motion repeated on the left side.

Contralateral ⚛: A clear connection between the upper right (usually arm) and lower left (usually leg) of the body and vice versa, such as walking or exaggerated walking-like movements; for example, when the left arm extends upward and the right leg contracts or lifts off the ground.

⭐ **Activity: Describe Broad Characteristics of Patterned Movement**

When viewing a live performance or a video performance or imitating the movements, decide what the "big-picture" happenings are by observing the following (see Hutchinson Guest and Curran 2008:1–25, 133–152):

- Is the movement constant, or are there moments of stillness?
- Does the performer(s) travel or remain stationary? If traveling, is it in a straight path, curved or circling path, or a meandering/free-form path?
- Is the performer always facing a particular direction, or does the facing change? If facings change, does this affect the method of traveling or remaining in place?
- If there is turning, is there a pattern in how many revolutions (around a performer's own axis), or is there spiraling closer or farther away from a focal point, or does turning occur in degrees, or is the performer turning while traveling on a path?
- If there is jumping, are there gestures in the air or jumping while traveling? How many or how big are the jumps? Are they always one foot to the other, one foot to the same foot, two feet, one foot to two feet or vice versa, and so on?
- Does the whole body or do parts of the body flex or contract and/or extend or elongate and/or fold (such as the knee or other hinge joint)?
- Are there rotations of the whole body or parts of the body? Does the body revolve around a vertical axis (like a spin while standing), a horizontal axis (like a cartwheel), a sagittal axis (moving through a vertical plane, like a somersault), or are there revolutions that occur when the body is on the floor (rolling, spinning, etc.)?
- How is the dancer supported or connected to the ground—feet, hands, torso, stilts or other props, knees, forearms? How is the sense of weight/gravity and balance treated—"on" center, "off" center, tilting, falling?
- Do the parts of the body seem to have relationships to other body parts or other performers, such as grasping, sliding, enclosing nearness, approaching, retreating, supporting?

- Are gestures (non-weight bearing) making designs or shapes in the air (or elsewhere), making paths, occurring symmetrically or asymmetrically?
- Do the performers seem to operate in an axis of physical space (e.g., "forward" is toward an audience, "backward" is away from the audience, "up" is toward the heavens, "down" is toward the ground), or do the performers operate in an axis of personal space—especially if the body has moments of being on the ground (not supported by the feet)—(e.g., "forward" is always in front of the face/chest, "backward" is always toward the back, "up" is above the head, "down" is toward the feet)?
- Check to see if the performer moves in ways relating to her personal space or kinesphere primarily (or secondarily) in one or several of the following ways:
  - One-dimensional or one directional "pull": ◈ : forward/backward, side/side, up/down (often a pin-like posture), as if standing within a life-size octahedron and touching the connecting points.
  - Two-dimensional or two directional "pull": ◉ forward and up/down, backward and up/down, side and up/down, forward and side/side, backward and side/side (often a wall-like posture in the vertical "door," sagittal "wheel," and horizontal "table" planes), as if standing within a life-size icosahedron (i.e., with 20 plane faces) and touching the connecting points.
  - Three-dimensional or three directions "pull" forward/side/up or down, backward/side/up or down, as if standing within a life-size cube and touching the connecting points. This can include ball-like or screw-like postures. ▱

✪ Activity: Identify Characteristic Types of Movement Phrasing

Movements are performed with a particular quality of energy or intensity that may vary from performer to performer and which can make the same movement performed with a different phrasing both look and feel different. Identifying phrasing involves subjective interpretation but can assist in understanding phrase types that are valued, commonly used, or rarely used within a culture or performer's movement style (Maletic 2004:57–95). Phrasing types may be used consecutively (one at a time) or simultaneously (multiples or overlaps).

> *Even*: Maintaining the same level of intensity—most easily identified with slow, steady movement, but quick movements can also be even if the intensity remains the same.

Increasing: Energy starting at one level and going to a more intense level, which can also end with an *impact* or sudden stop (either of strong or light accent), such as an inhale that leads to a shout or a stomp (increasing, impact), or a spin that starts slow and gets faster and faster (increasing).

Decreasing: Intensity starting at a high energy level and becoming less, which can also begin with an *impulse* or outburst (either of strong or light accent), such as a sharp gasp followed by an exhale (impulse, decreasing), or a flaying arm that gradually becomes still.

Increasing-decreasing: Builds energy up and then diminishes; the building and diminishing can be of equal time (symmetrical intensity; e.g., jogging into a run in one minute and then returning to a jog in one minute), or one may take longer or shorter than the other (asymmetrical intensity; e.g., breathing in quickly and breathing out slowly). Can also include impacts or impulses.

Decreasing-increasing: Diminishes intensity and then builds intensity; the diminishing and building can be of equal time (symmetrical intensity; e.g., kicks starting very "loose" for 10 seconds and then becoming very "tight" for 10 seconds), or one may take longer or shorter than the other (asymmetrical intensity; e.g., a flippant gesture goes on for several measures and becomes a very firm gesture within one measure). Can also include impulses or impacts.

Accented: Spurts of intensity or energy that can be repeated with pauses or stillness between each spurt, which can be strong, such as flamenco dancing, or light, such as typing on a keyboard.

Vibratory: A series of quick and repetitive movements that can be repeated at various "wavelengths," which can be strong, such as whole-body convulsions, or light, such as a shoulder shimmy.

Resilient: Energy that plays with gravity, emphasizing the strength or heaviness and/or the lightness or "weightlessness" of a movement. There are three possible variations:

- *Elasticity*: Equal balance between strength and light, like bouncing a basketball down the length of a court.
- *Buoyancy*: Demonstrates the lightness more clearly and has a rebounding quality, like jumping in the air and "hovering" for a moment.
- *Weight*: Demonstrates the strength of gravity and releases into the ground, like jumping in the air and spending more energy on the ground than in the air.

✪ Activity: Identify Characteristic Types of Movement Dynamics or Efforts

While *phrasing* can be used to identify movement energy or intensity, *dynamics* are used to identify movement quality or engagement of effort. It is the nature of individual performers to use multiple variations of movement quality, but it is possible for particular qualities to be highlighted and to become more prominent than others, and these prominent dynamics can be used to identify existing movements and to assist in creating new movements. *Dynamics* or *efforts* deal primarily with *space, time*, and *weight* (*flow* will not be emphasized here, as it is easy to confuse with *phrasing*; see Maletic 2004:57–95).

Dynamics can be categorized broadly as *efforts* (*space, time, weight*) that are *fighting* (i.e., resisting gravity, momentum, etc.) or *indulging* (i.e., giving in to gravity, momentum, etc.). Certain *efforts* have affinities to other *efforts*, but all *efforts* can be combined in a variety of ways. The pelvis is a good indicator of *dynamic* or *effort* because it is often the core or base of the majority of movement.

Space: Deals primarily with how the performer thinks of and uses traveling through the physical space, either *directly* (particular, planned, thought out) or *indirectly* (meandering, allowing other factors to guide). For example, *direct space* controls ("fights"), such as crossing a room or going around an object to reach another object or person, and *indirect space* allows ("indulges") other things to occur while en route to a particular object or person. Space-related movements tend to be (but are not always) horizontally oriented movements.

Time: Works with a performer's intuition or decision-making while moving, either *suddenly* (alert, immediate) or *sustained* (calm, lingering). For example, *sudden time* may mean a quick change in direction in response to a music shift, and *sustained time* may mean a change in direction in a more casual manner to the same music shift. Time-related movements tend to be (but are not always) sagittally oriented movements.

Weight: How a performer senses and uses gravity, either in a *strong* sense (firm, concentrated, grounded) or a *light* sense (delicate, refined, tender). For example, *strong weight* appears to be carrying a heavy burden and "fighting" it, while *light weight* appears to be unhindered ("indulging") by any effect of gravity. Weight-related movements tend to be but are not always vertically oriented movements.

Content

Content refers to the subject matter in artistic activity.

Summary and Relationship to Other Lenses

Dance is a highly interdisciplinary art form. It often overlaps with music and drama, but can also include vocal arts (spoken song or text is part of the dance) and visual arts (costumes, props, scenery). Since collaboration is crucial to its creation and performance, it is often difficult to dissect or separate a "pure" dance from other art forms. Dances can range in content and elaboration from telling stories or parables, giving didactic lessons, or reliving/remembering histories, to symbolizing and portraying abstract ideas or spiritual happenings.

Content can dictate how the other lenses function. For example, a mourning dance will use space, participant organization, and so on, differently from a celebration dance; mourning dances may be respectful movements in a confined space, while a celebration dance may feature exuberant movements in an elaborate space.

⭐ Activity: Identify Effects of Different Content on Movement

Using multiple live performances or videorecordings of multiple performances, observe and describe all of the lenses, especially *participant organization*. Notice how *phrasing, dynamics*, and so on, vary depending on the content or subject matter, and articulate what are the clearest variations.

Underlying Symbolic Systems

Underlying symbolic systems refer to the grammatical and social rules and structures that guide participants' actions in artistic activity.

Summary and Relationship to Other Lenses

The conceptual systems that performers interact with when performing these actions construct time and relationship with the music (movement phrasing sharing or counterpointing musical phrasing), weight or relation to gravity, space or relation to kinesphere and environment, and flow or relationship to performative focus and body control. Dance systems interact with music, song, text, and costume/prop systems.

Questions related to underlying systems include the following: What prescribed moves and movement combinations are allowed or disallowed? What are improvisation etiquette and dancer/audience interaction etiquette? What rules are followed in composition? How are movements controlled by the music being played, or how do the movements control the music? How does the text affect the movement? What are dance-related lexical items or moves that must be memorized to be culturally functional? What kinds of moves are clearly outsiders' moves, and why?

⊛ Activity: Perform Embodied Interviews

Understanding another culture's symbolic systems requires multiple in-depth interviews with local performers to understand the movement language and its complexities. You may use symbolic systems such as Laban's Motif, or Labanotation, to make a written and visual record of a particular dance or particular movements. While this can help an observer understand the intellectual information about a dance performance, dance can often only be truly understood by actual doing and moving. Work with a local performer to learn the movement language (which may raise more questions than answers) in order to understand viscerally (and sometimes spiritually) the nuances of the symbolic system.

Oral Verbal Arts in an Event

This section will help you describe more completely the ways participants use words in the event you began to explore in "Look at an Event's Forms" (Part A). We use the same seven lenses, but introduce descriptive categories particularly pertinent to oral verbal arts. Gather your discoveries about the verbal characteristics of this event and others like it in the Community Arts Profile.

We use the term *oral verbal arts* to refer to special kinds of oral communication that use words. There are countless varieties of and names given to oral verbal genres of communication: anecdotes, anthems, ballads, bedtime stories, boastings, complaints, curing chants, curses, diatribes, divinations, epics, exhortations, fables, fairy tales, folk tales, funeral dirges, ghost stories, greetings, heroic tales, hunting songs, hymns, jokes, jousts, legends, love songs, lullabies, magical chants, mourning songs, myths, odes, origin narratives, parables, personal narratives, poems, praises, prayers, protest songs, proverbs, puns, return songs, riddles, scatting, slam poetry, tall tales, taunting songs, tongue twisters, war songs, weeping rites, work songs, and more (see the Oral Tradition website: http://www.oraltradition.org). In this chapter we will limit our exploration to characteristics common to oral verbal arts, and offer advice on researching song texts, stories, proverbs, and oratory.

Common to oral verbal arts are poetically modified words, and vocal modifications and gestures. These communication forms are primarily experienced through auditory channels, though deaf communities attend to verbal communication visually. The essentially verbal nature of these art forms requires the hearer to understand the semantic content of what is being communicated. However, oral verbal arts draw on artistically formulated words, and add additional levels of communication. They use not only everyday language and patterns of speech, but also special patterns of speech and manners of speaking. This specialness allows verbal arts to communicate both expressive and semantic meaning. Expressive meaning includes attitudes, feelings, sentiments, and tone. Artistic forms are also particularly apt at clarifying semantic meaning, as when particular words, phrases, themes, and actions are highlighted or brought into focus by extraordinary grammatical constructions, intonational patterns, rhythmic segmentations, or speech registers. Their oral manner of production not only intensifies expression, but can also clarify thought.

An adequate understanding of people's oral verbal art forms cannot, of course, be limited to these generalizations. We begin with such generalizations, but must gradually come to recognize and interpret them on their own local terms: similar form and use do not necessarily mean similar meaning and function. The activities that we have included in this section are intended to help you begin such a process of recognition and interpretation.

Although we have stated that oral verbal arts are primarily experienced through auditory channels, visual channels play important roles in helping the experiencer understand auditory information. Hand, face, and body gestures, for example, typically complement auditory signs. The activities we propose in this section focus on auditory phenomena, but we encourage you to expand these to include some of the complementary visual activities proposed in this Guide's sections on dance and drama. Furthermore, you can extend your analyses of the sonic dimensions of oral arts—like speaking, chanting, and singing—to include many of the complementary sonic dimensions treated in the music sections of this Guide. Finally, although we are focusing on oral verbal production, written arts play important roles in working toward a better life for communities. Consult the activity "Turn Orature into Literature" (*Step 5*), and explore the relationship between existing oral and written verbal arts.

Groundwork

As with many of the other artistic domains, the most helpful research activities in understanding the artistic aspects of verbal performance include audiovisual recording, ethnographic interview, and participant observation. The activities we describe next are fundamental for the research of all oral verbal art forms. Most of the subsequent activities depend on the initial two activities.

✪ Activity: Isolate Verbal Elements of an Audiovisual Recording of an Event

You cannot adequately research the features of an oral verbal performance without the aid of audiovisual technologies, particularly if you are researching performance in a culture that is not your own. While some cultures have experts in oral verbal performance, such as the *jali* in Mande areas of West/Sudanic Africa, most of us have difficulty keeping up with and retaining a stream of oral communication. Audiovisual recordings typically serve as the basis for many other research activities: text transcriptions, music transcriptions, ethnographic interviews, ethnographic analyses, discourse analyses, and so on. Watch or listen to a recording that you have made of an event and identify the time segments that include verbal content. Verbally intensive genres such as narrative, song, proverb, and oratory may consist of words from beginning to end. In other forms, verbal content may be less frequent. In this latter case, it may help you logistically to create new files that contain just the verbal segments.

✪ Activity: Transcribe the Verbal Texts of a Recorded Event

The first step in understanding the verbal elements of an event is text transcription. Transcribed representations of orally performed texts afford the analyst multiple alternative perspectives on complex real-time performances; these perspectives would otherwise be impossible for any individual to perceive in real-time performances. Your transcriptions should minimally include the following interlinearized fields of data:

- *Vernacular language*: The full text in its original form and language.
- *Word-for-word gloss*: A literal translation into a language of wider communication (as needed).
- *Free translation*: A translation that is natural in the language of wider communication.

- Optional: Gestural indications.
- Optional: Recording time line.
- Optional: Brief description of the linguistic and external event context.

Figure 4.11 presents such a transcription of one line of a song lyric in the Mono language (Democratic Republic of Congo). Eventually you would edit this transcription to indicate larger sections of the discourse's structure.

Space

Space is the location, demarcation, and physical characteristics of the area used, which can affect the form of artistic communication.

Summary and Relationship to Other Lenses

There are many potential correlations between where an oral performance takes place, what is verbalized, and in what manner it is verbalized. For example, national and regional specifications can help explain the use and meaning of borrowed words in the performance's text; urban and rural specifications can help to explain the decline or vitality of traditional oral performance types; and indoor and outdoor specifications may correlate with the relative loudness or softness of the oral delivery, the relative distance between speakers and hearers, or the relative casual or formal tone of the performance.

Activity: Locate Each Recorded Verbal Element Nationally, Regionally, Macro-Locally, and Micro-Locally

For every recording or transcription that you make of oral verbal elements in an event, perform activities such as the following:

- Describe in varying degrees of specificity (from national to local) the location of the performance. This can include multiple degrees of space; for example, neighborhoods, courtyards and areas of courtyards, buildings

Vernacular language	'bœ mbœrœ anda nœ zœ-a
Word-for-word gloss	You are child wisdom you make house of you (question marker)
Free translation	If you are wise, how will you build your house?

FIGURE 4.11. Sample text transcription.

and areas of buildings, indoors and outdoors, open and enclosed, stages and areas of stages, bodily movement into and out of any of the above, relative spatial relationship of verbalizers and hearers, and so on.

- Describe how participants change the content or manner of their oral performance in response to their physical space. Do certain genres only take place in certain places? When performers move to a different location, does some aspect of their verbal performance change?
- Interview participants to explore if and how participants choose, design, or use that performance space to achieve particular performance goals.

Activity: Explore How Participants Modify Their Verbal Actions in Response to Their Physical Space

Perform activities such as these:

- Ask performers of verbal arts about different contexts in which they have performed. How did they change what they did in response to characteristics of each space?
- Observe a single performer of verbal arts in more than one context. Note his or her volume, distance to other participants, and other characteristics in each context. Compare.

Materials

Materials are all of the tangible things associated with an event.

Summary and Relationship to Other Lenses

Participants in oral verbal arts use objects to emphasize points (e.g., an item referenced by a storyteller), evoke characters and places (e.g., costumes or props), or amplify or modify sound (e.g., microphones or acoustic shells). There may be close relationships between a participant's role and the objects he or she interacts with.

Activity: List Objects and Describe How Participants Use Them to Emphasize or Otherwise Modify Verbal Content

Watch a videorecording of an event, list all of the objects with which performers of verbal content interact, and discuss questions like these with a knowledgeable friend:

- How does this object affect the hearers' understanding and experience of the performers' words?
- What symbolic meaning does this object evoke?

Participant Organization

Participant organization highlights the people involved in an event, in terms of the roles they play, the ways they interact with each other through time, and how they use the space around them.

Summary and Relationship to Other Lenses

Participants in oral verbal arts fall broadly into roles of those who perform words and those who hear them.

✳ Activity: Identify the Roles of Participants Producing Verbal Content

Certain genres of oral verbal art may only be performed by people with very particular roles in a community. The association of such performance genres with specific social roles may be explicit or implicit. An interview may be necessary to determine the case.

The voice of the oral verbal performance may change. Your transcription should reflect this. Further analysis may indicate a correlation between shifts in voice (who is speaking or singing) and the content, form, and delivery of the text. These correlations may be socially malleable or stable. They may follow social convention, or they may be due to individual style. The patterns of multiple recordings and transcriptions will do much to clarify the nature of these correlations between the identity of the performers and the resulting form of the performance.

Note each person who produces verbal content in the event, and perform activities such as the following:

- Ask knowledgeable friends if there are local names for various roles people play in the event that include verbal production. If there are, ask them to describe what these roles entail.
- Decide if any participants in the event fill roles sometimes associated with the kinds of verbal arts listed here:
  - Roles sometimes associated with narratives: crafter, contributor, teller, listener, affirmer, heckler;

- ◦ Roles sometimes associated with oratory: speaker, orator, preacher, listener, crafter, affirmer, audience;
- ◦ Roles sometimes associated with proverbs: speaker, listener;
- ◦ Roles sometimes associated with poetry: speaker, crafter, listener;
- ◦ Roles sometimes associated with songs: crafter, singer, listener, improviser.

Shape of the Event through Time

Shape of an event refers primarily to its constituent segments, organized hierarchically.

Summary and Relationship to Other Lenses

Performance of a verbal form can happen very quickly—as with a proverb or curse—or move through a complex, long progression—as in a story or oration. Narrative forms relate closely to dramatic forms.

Activity: Explore Associations between the Temporal Occurrence of a Recorded Oral Verbal Element and Broader Cultural Factors

Write down the month, day, hour, season, and occurrence of a verbal performance in its overall social event. Many genres are socioculturally associated with particular seasons, months, days, hours of the day, and past historical events. The reasons for these associations are many, and are often taken for granted. To learn about these associations, ask a knowledgeable friend questions such as:

- When have you experienced someone producing a verbal event like this? List every time you can remember.
- Are there particular times, seasons, or events when this kind of verbal performance is more likely to occur? Why?

Activity: Identify and Describe the Length of Each Verbal Element in the Event

Write down the time in the event that every new set of words begins and ends. Use the Hierarchical Segmentation Time Line you began in "Look at an Event's Forms" (Part A).

⚙ **Activity: Determine the Temporal Form of the Artistic Verbal Performance**

Oral verbal performances unfold in real time. Traditional genres are *expected* (though often subconsciously) to progress according to basic local time patterns. Exceptions to these patterns yield new effects—some desired, some undesired. Progress in neo- or nontraditional events may be determined by other factors, for example the format of an event (competition, CD recording) or the organizer's or funder's guidelines. In any case, all verbal discourse genres are in one way or another based on socially received formal templates.

Temporal Form of Narrative

If the recorded and transcribed oral discourse under investigation has narrative, or story components, describe its temporal shape in terms of the following developmental template (see Longacre 1996:33–50):

- the stage,
- the inciting incident,
- the mounting tension,
- the climax of tension, and
- the release of tension.

You may be able to identify these elements by noting the

- introduction and actions of characters;
- increase or decrease of rates of events in the narrative (a quicker succession of events often implies a climax);
- introduction of special words to mark a climax; and
- change in a performer's vocal timbre, volume, and pitch.

Temporal Form of Poetry

If the recorded and transcribed oral discourse under investigation is organized poetically, such as in a song or oral poem, describe its temporal shape in terms of the following:

- *Repeated units*: For example, lines, verses, verse segments, stanzas, strophes, refrains. You may represent these as "A, A, A, etc." or "a, a, a, etc."

- *Contrastive units*: You may represent these as "A, B, C, etc." or "a, b, c, etc."
- *Varied units*: You may represent these as "A^1, A^2, A^3, etc." or "a^1, a^2, a^3, etc."
- *Derivative units*: You may represent these as "A, B, B^a, C, C^b, etc."

You may describe these same phenomena in conventional Western literary terminologies (e.g., poem, stanza, and line) or local terms.

Temporal Form of Narrative Poetry

Many artistic verbal forms are constituted at multiple formal levels, as in the case of narrative poetry. Mark Doty's narrative poem, "The Embrace" (1998), illustrates elements of both poetry and story, as depicted in Figure 4.12.

Temporal Form of Proverbs

Proverbs, riddles, and other short verbal forms have little internal shape over time. They are more often woven or inserted into larger discourses, like court proceedings, games, or communal reconciliation events. Make note of how people use and respond to proverbs in their temporal context.

Strophe 1, The Stage	You weren't well or really ill yet either; just a little tired, your handsomeness tinged by grief or anticipation, which brought to your face a thoughtful, deepening grace
Strophe 2, Crisis	I didn't for a moment doubt you were dead. I knew that to be true still, even in the dream. You'd been out—at work maybe?— having a good day, almost energetic.
Strophe 3, Mounting tension	We seemed to be moving from some old house where we'd lived, boxes everywhere, things in disarray: that was the story of my dream, but even asleep I was shocked out of the narrative
Strophe 4, Climax	by your face, the physical fact of your face: inches from mine, smooth-shaven, loving, alert. Why so difficult, remembering the actual look of you? Without a photograph, without strain?
Strophe 5, Dénouement	So when I saw your unguarded, reliable face, your unmistakable gaze opening all the warmth and clarity of you—warm brown tea—we held each other for the time the dream allowed.
Strophe 6, Resolution	Bless you. You came back so I could see you once more, plainly, so I could rest against you without thinking this happiness lessened anything, without thinking you were alive again.

FIGURE 4.12. Strophic analysis of "The Embrace."

Temporal Form of Oratory

Verbal production with oratorical characteristics often is used to persuade and educate, and may be relatively long. Elements of oratory often include

- connection to listeners,
- explanation of a problem and its importance, and
- a call to action.

Performance Feature Categories

Performance features are observable characteristics of a performance that emerge from an event's unique combination of physical and social context and participants' actions.

Summary and Relationship to Other Lenses

Performers of verbal arts make their words special through unique combinations of poetic features, gestures, and vocal modulation.

⚙ Activity: Identify the Poetic Features of Verbal Content

Most artistically rendered verbal communication will have poetic features that influence its overall feel. Study a transcription of a short section of an event while listening to or watching the recording from which it was produced. Then, using the following list of features, note which features the event exhibits. This is just a small sample of possible poetic features, so remain open to others.

Overall Characteristics

- *Verbal play*: A highly creative act that overlaps with other features. It is often found in storytelling by means of various semantic devices, including metaphor, allegory, metonymy, puns, humor, and so on.
- *Rhythm or pulse*: This often is structured by syllables. These syllables come together in a certain number of beats or a certain pattern.
- *Text density*: Number of lines per verse, number of verses per poem or song, number of syllables per line, number of notes per syllable (in song).

Poetic Devices

You may find these devices in short verbal forms like proverbs and riddles, and longer forms like song lyrics, speeches, and poems. In poems, they may be distributed between lines, within lines, or between verses.

Word-Level Poetic Devices

- *Lexical repetition*: Use of the same word in more than one context.
- *Homonyms*: Two or more words that share the same pronunciation and spelling but that have different meanings.
- *Archaic language*: Words, phrases, or grammatical structures no longer used in normal speech.
- *Borrowed words*: Words adopted from another language.

Phrase-Level Poetic Devices

- *Phrase repetition.*
- *Subphrase repetition.*
- *Acrostic*: Arrangement in which the first letter of a phrase or line combines with other first letters to spell a word or other meaningful sequence.

Poetic Devices Related to Sound

- *Assonance*: Rhyme referring to the same or similar vowel sounds in neighboring words.
- *Rhyme*: The same or similar vowel sounds at the end, beginning, or middle of lines.
- *Vocables*: Words without propositional meaning.
- *Ideophones*: A vivid representation of sensory imagery.
- *Consonance*: Close correspondence of sounds.
- *Alliteration*: Repetition of the same or similar sounds at the beginning of words.
- *Rhythmic speech.*

Poetic Devices Related to Meaning

- *Semantic categories*: Examples include similes, metonymy (where a word or expression stands for another one; e.g., sweat = hard work), synecdoche (when part of something refers to the whole; e.g., set of wheels = car), personification, hyperbole, euphemism (describing something socially unpleasant in indirect terms), and symbols.
- *Rhetorical questions*: Meant to persuade rather than elicit information.
- *Ideophones*: Words that sound like the thing they refer to.

- *Loan word synonymy*: A word in a language other than that of the verbal event.
- *Metaphors*: Figures of speech in which a word or phrase corresponds to an object or action that is not literally applicable.
- *Ellipsis*: The omission of words that one expects to be there.
- *Semantic parallelism*: Similarity of structure in the meanings of two or more words or phrases.

Activity: Identify How Participants Use Physical Gestures to Modify Their Verbal Production

Watch a videorecording of part of an event with a friend who knows the genre and language(s) of the event, with a transcription and translation of the words. Whenever a speaker or singer moves a part of his or her body, stop the recording and discuss questions such as the following with your friend:

- Does the gesture emphasize, contradict, add to, or otherwise modify the words being produced?
- Do participants use the same gesture in other parts of the event? If so, is the effect on meaning the same or different?
- Is this gesture codified (i.e., with a set meaning agreed upon by the group and tradition) or unique to an individual?

Activity: Identify How Participants Modify Their Voices in Their Verbal Production

Performers use combinations of words, gestures, and vocal modulation together to communicate in verbal arts. *Vocal modulation* refers primarily to changes in pitch, volume, and timbre. To explore how participants in an event enlist vocal modulation, watch a videorecording of part of an event with a transcription and translation of the words in front of you. Perform activities like these:

- Along the top of each line of words, draw a line representing the pitch of what's coming out of the performer's mouth. When the pitch rises, let the line rise. When the pitch falls, let the line fall. When there are abrupt changes in pitch, write a note to that effect.
- Note significant changes in volume at points in the transcription. You may use words (e.g., "abrupt volume drop") or symbols (e.g., ">" for a drop in volume).

- Note changes in vocal timbre (also known as vocal color or voice quality) when they occur. These could include qualities like nasal, open, muffled, thin, and so on.
- Discuss how these vocal modifications affect the meaning and impact of a performer's words with a friend who knows the genre and language(s) of the event.

Content

Content refers to the subject matter in artistic activity.

Summary and Relationship to Other Lenses

Oral verbal arts features almost always have to do with words. Since words commonly carry semantic content, you can expect the *content* lens to reveal especially important data for genres with poetic, plot, and related features.

⊛ Activity: Identify the Range of Content Expected in a Verbal Performance

Watch a videorecording of part of an event with a friend who knows the genre and language(s) of the event. Ask questions such as:

- What is this *verbal item* (e.g., story) about?
- Think of another performance of this kind of verbal event. What was it about? Repeat as long as possible.
- Then suggest other topics as possible content in the same kind of verbal event, asking, "Would this fit?"

Underlying Symbolic Systems

Underlying symbolic systems refer to the grammatical and social rules and structures that guide participants' actions in artistic activity.

Summary and Relationship to Other Lenses

Underlying symbolic systems relate to verbal arts in complex relationships between the linguistic rules that govern everyday speech and those associated with heightened verbal communication. Because of this, most of the research activities we have included require familiarity with linguistic analysis.

Activity: Identify Basic Elements of a Story's Plot

The characters and their actions in a story form its central series of events, or plot. The plot may flow in a form that contains the following major sections:

- *Introduction*: The way that a story begins.
- *Body*: The body of a story reveals the plot (if there is one), characters, events, and main point or peak of the story.
- *Closure*: The ending of a story may draw some lesson or invite questions or speculation on the purpose of the story.

How the plot develops depends upon genre expectations and the central theme or purpose of the story. Its structure will determine how best to use the grammatical, syntactical, and semantic features inherent in the language. The structure of the language and its context will affect how and when characters are introduced, how they are described, and what actions will follow. For further discussion of plot, see activities related to plot in the section "Drama in an Event."

Activity: Analyze an Oral (Monologue) Narrative

There are numerous kinds of narrative discourse analyses, not to mention numerous degrees of detail to which they are carried out (see Schiffrin et al. 2003). However, we strongly suggest that you initially *describe at least four fundamental dimensions of your chosen narrative*, even if only modestly. These dimensions include (1) type of content, (2) means of production, (3) manner of production, and (4) medium of production. The type of content (genre) and manner of production (style and register) are particularly complex dimensions of analysis. Because of this complexity, seek the assistance of someone trained in discourse analysis when analyzing these two dimensions of any discourse. We recommend Dooley and Levinsohn's *Analyzing Discourse* (2001) as a basic introductory methodological text.

There are two prerequisites to carrying out this research activity adequately: (1) access to a basic grammatical analysis of the language at hand; and (2) a complete text transcription of the verbal performance, including vernacular text, a word-for-word gloss, and a free translation. We recommend that you also learn the facts of the discourse; for example, who did what to whom in the immediate context, and the relationships between their actions (Longacre and Levinsohn 1978). This means that you should have a fairly complete picture of the text world, and of the external contextualization as well (Dooley and Levinsohn 2001:22).

For the narrative discourse genre in particular, we recommend that you also try to address two additional, fundamental domains of analysis: (1) narrative discourse cohesion, and (2) narrative discourse development.

Narrative Discourse Cohesion

Describe some of the more common grammatical devices affecting narrative discourse cohesion. These include *substitution* (of nouns, verbs, clauses; e.g., anaphora), *ellipsis, reference, conjunction* (by addition, causality, temporality), *lexical cohesion* (through reiteration, as accomplished through repetition, synonymy, hyponymy, metonymy, antonymy, etc.), and *collocation* (Renkema 1993:37).

Narrative Discourse Development

Narrative development may take place on a number of levels. Your description of narrative development should account for the organization of various *thematic, grammatical,* and *schematic* phenomena.

- Describe some of the narrative's *thematic development*. For example, you may mark whether the narrative's "continuities and discontinuities" are according to one or more of the following domains: time, place, action, and/or participants (Dooley and Levinsohn 2001:18–21).
- Describe some of the narrative's *grammatical development*. First, distinguish and describe the characteristic features of the narrative's *foreground* (mainline) and *background* (supportive) material. Second, describe the marks of its *climactic development*.
  - Identify the *mainline material*; it is most often marked by "a characteristic constellation of verb forms" (i.e., tenses, aspects, and/or moods) (Dooley and Levinsohn 2001:39–48).
  - Once the marks of the mainline material are determined, identify *supportive material*. Supportive material is commonly categorized according to *participant information, setting information, explanatory information, collateral information,* and *evaluative information* (Grimes 1975).
  - The *expressive qualities* of oral verbal arts encode evaluative information— attitudes, feelings, opinions, beliefs—in countless ways. Artistic verbal acts may range from heightened speech forms to poetic devices to explicitly musical phenomena. More specifically, *expressive grammatical markers* may include *obligative mood, imperative mood, exclamatives,*

interjectives, ideophones, intensifiers, rhetorical questions, and *vocatives*. *Expressive poetic devices* may include specially formalized *rhythms*, *syntaxes*, *phonologies*, and *semantics. Expressive musical formalizations* commonly include particular configurations of *melodic, harmonic, rhythmic, timbric, dynamic, formal*, and *performative features* (see "Music in an Event," Part B).

o Describe some of the narrative's *climactic development*. It is most commonly signaled by (1) *particular verb forms*, (2) *rhetorical underlining* (e.g., repetition), (3) *heightened vividness*, (4) *change of pace*, and (5) *incidence of ideophones*. All of these marks are extraordinarily expressive and often are achieved by the peculiar qualities of oral verbal arts. The special musico-poetic devices of oral verbal arts—whether rhythmic, syntactic, phonological (including timbre, dynamics, melody, and harmony), or semantic—are kindred marks of climactic development.

• Describe the narrative's overall (or episodic) *schematic development*, which typically reflects—though not simplistically—the following develop-mental template: the narrative's *stage, inciting incident, mounting tension, climax of tension*, and *release of tension* (Longacre 1996:33–50).

⭐ Activity: Make a Preliminary Musico-poetic Analysis of a Song

Describe some of the distinctive musico-poetic features of a single song. The analysis assumes the availability of a text transcription of the complete performance of an audio recording of the selected song. The transcription should minimally represent the vernacular text, a word-for-word gloss, and a free translation. Like the narrative activity outlined earlier, the transcription should include notes indicating a fairly complete picture of the text world, and of the external contextualization as well.

Your analysis should describe five basic domains of musico-poetic phenomena: rhythm, syntax, phonology, morphology, and semantics.

• *Rhythm*: Describe the rhythmic nature of the song's poetic *line*. A song's *line* is its most fundamental poetic feature. Most *song* lines are measured *periodically* (as patterned groups of beats, or pulses). Often, but by no means always, these periodically measured lines also pattern with phonological and/or semantic patterns, or combinations thereof. Search, then, for patterns of vowel sounds, consonant sounds, accents, vowel stresses, syllable stresses, word stresses, phrase stresses, tones, and combinations of these. Simple quantifications, like typical words and/or syllables per line, should not be discounted, for whether strictly repeated or approximately repeated, their quantitative patterning affects the performance.

- *Syntax*: Describe the corresponding syntactic formalizations of a song's poetic line. Multiple distinctive characteristics may constitute the syntactic nature of a song's poetic line. The syntactic ordering (versification) of morphemes, words, phrases, and clauses is segmented according to the constitutive rhythms of the song's musico-poetic line. The subsequent segmentation and ordering of these morphemes, words, phrases, and clauses give rise to a variety of syntactic poetic units conventionally identified as *verses, verse segments, stanzas*, and *repeated, contrastive*, or *varied refrains*, and so on. The boundaries of lines and verses often coincide, but by no means always. This play between line (a rhythmical unit) and syntax (a grammatical unit) is yet another effect of the song's poetic function. Your present analysis need not determine the exact affective function of this play (though you could speculate); your job, for now, is to simply identify such phenomena as further potential poetic resources.
- *Phonology*: Describe a variety of distinctive phonological poetic devices. Identify, for example, the use of particular *vocables, ideophones, assonance, rhyme, consonance, alliteration*, and so on. You may observe that certain phonological patterns appear to function rhythmically, though not exclusively so. There may be other functions, but an in-depth functional analysis is probably beyond the scope of this project. Your job, again, is to simply identify these phenomena, and thereby highlight many potential poetic resources.
- *Morphology*: Describe some of the lexical poetic devices exhibited. Identify, for example, any use of homonyms, or any number of repeated, reiterated, or reduplicated phonemes, ideophones, or words.
- *Semantics*: Describe various semantic poetic devices. Identify, for example, various uses of ideophones, similes, metaphors, metonyms, personification, meronymy, semantic parallelism, syntactic-semantic parallelism, syntagmatic-paradigmatic substitution, rhetorical questions, archaic language, loan word synonymy, ellipsis, etc. Any of these devices may be subject to repetitive processes as well.

Activity: Compare the Rhythmic Devices of Three or More Songs

For this activity, first you will need to record and transcribe the texts (and if you are able, the music) of three or more songs. It is best to sample songs performed by different performers and different social occasions.

Second, for each song, carry out the *rhythm* step: "Describe the rhythmic nature of the song's poetic *line*." Third, compare your descriptions of the rhythmic devices used in the performance of all the songs. Which rhythmic devices were exhibited in every song? Which were performed in most songs? Which were unique to each song? Those devices common to every song may turn out to be *systemic*; that is, they are culturally expected—consciously or unconsciously—to be in most if not all songs. We assume that every song will exhibit the general rhythmic phenomenon conventionally called a *line*. The length or meter of that line, however, may vary significantly. For example, some may be measured by particular patterns of vowel sounds, consonant sounds, accents, vowel stresses, syllable stresses, word stresses, phrase stresses, tones, or combinations of these. Some may only be described in terms of words and/or syllables per line. Whatever the case, such devices are typical indicators of underlying symbolic systems that guide what and how sung poetic discourse is *competently* performed.

Visual Arts in an Event

This section will help you describe more completely the ways in which participants produce and experience visual symbols in a work or event. To understand this section best, you should first work through some of the activities in "Look at an Event's Forms" (Part A). We use the same seven lenses here, but introduce descriptive categories particularly pertinent to visual arts. Gather your discoveries about the visual characteristics of this event and others like it in the Community Arts Profile.

Visual communication, like any other kind of communication, uses symbols to convey or create meaning. Each culture agrees upon relationships between *signifier* (symbol) and the *signified* (the meaning that the symbol represents: a person, a story, or a concept). The study of visual symbolism looks for the meaning behind visible signifiers. This meaning is often contained in shapes or colors whose meanings are culturally defined. *Visual vocabulary* is a shared knowledge of the meaning of visual symbols, such as being able to recognize a West African *kanaga* (see Figure 4.13 and following section on "Interactions with Other Domains")

FIGURE 4.13. *Kanaga* symbol.

as both a representation of a lizard and a symbol of peace between heaven and earth.

Meanings can also be combined in specific ways through a visual grammar. A *visual grammar* is the set of rules governing composition and interpretation in a visual system. *Visual rhetoric* describes the tools artists use for reaching a communication goal such as persuasion, education or entertainment (Hart 2007:36–38).

Interactions with Other Domains

Visual messages may stand alone, as in functional design such as architecture, material cultural objects, or objects created purely for their aesthetic value. They may also be part of other expressive arts, such as reminding people of important stories. They may summarize large amounts of information originally conveyed through oral verbal arts. Researching the story that goes along with a work of visual art allows us to understand the people, events or concepts that are signified.

Among the Dogon people in Mali, for example, when people have a quarrel, they go to the *togouna*, or "the place of words," to make peace. This is a low roof supported by pillars on a raised platform. By sitting under a low roof, the Dogon say people are unable to fight. The symbols on the pillars of the peacemaking place are important to the Dogon people's identity and their understanding of peace. The *kanaga* symbol (Figure 4.13) can symbolize the peaceful intersection of heaven and earth, or a lizard, or a myth in which a man became a lizard to make peace between heaven and earth (Michelle Petersen, personal communication, June 20, 2016). Visual features are primarily experienced through the eyes, initially at a subconscious level. Most art forms have a visual component— paintings and sculptures, the movements of the body or hands in dance, the colors and costumes in drama, or the visual composition of musical instruments. Some visual features also may be experienced through touch: people can feel textures and shapes. This may be especially important for visually impaired experiencers or other participants involved in an event where there is little or no light.

Visual arts may include accessories for rituals (costumes, masks, garments), and the design and appearance of musical instruments. Some visual messages are created for use at specific times or events, such as invitations, birthday cards, or skull-shaped pastries for the *Día de los Difuntos*.

We apply the following lenses on artistic objects as both independently meaningful and meaningful as part of a larger event.

Space

Space is the location, demarcation, and physical characteristics of the area used, which can affect the form of artistic communication.

Summary and Relationship to Other Lenses

Space relates to visual artistic communication both in how it is used in an event, and how visual features are arranged in and on an object.

Activity: Describe Spatial Relationships between an Object's Visual Features

Examine an object. In the Community Arts Profile, describe how its features express the following spatial concepts:

- *Visual unity*: An integrated message in which the various parts of the message are in harmony with the other parts: *proximity*, in which objects are spatially related; *repetition*, in which objects are quantitatively related; *continuation*, based on psychological principles of closure; and *controlled chaos*, to name a few (Lauer and Pentak 2015).
- *Balance*: The way some elements in an image relate to other elements in that same image. This can be *symmetrical*, in which the parts are subjectively mirrored; *asymmetrical*, in which the elements have a distributed weight that is not symmetrical; or *radial*, in which the parts appear to balance outward from a point of origin.
- *Rhythm*: The process of directing eye movement through an image, based on repetition.
- *Proportion*: The relationships between visual elements, particularly with reference to relative size.

Materials

Materials are all of the tangible things associated with an event.

Summary and Relationship to Other Lenses

Creators of art objects choose materials that will allow them to produce the visual features they desire. Characteristics of materials that can inform these choices include strength, plasticity, smoothness, texture, color, shape, and the like. An artist may also choose a material simply because it is available, along with the necessary tools to work it.

 Activity: Identify and Describe the Materials Used in an Object

Obtain an example of an object that friends think is representative and of good quality. For each material it contains, ask the creator of the object questions like these:

- What is this material? What names do you know to describe it in different languages? Why did you choose it?
- Where did this material come from? How did you get it?
- How did you manipulate it to make this object?

Activity: Document the Creation of an Object

Arrange with someone who is recognized as a skilled creator of an art form to document his or her creation process. This may include payment or other forms of compensation. Video record a representative portion of each step, photograph the object in different stages of completion, and ask the creator what he or she is doing in each step. You might decide to edit a video of the process to give to the creator and for the community to use to pass on these skills. You could also create a short, illustrated document of the process.

Participant Organization

Participant organization highlights the people involved in an event, in terms of the roles they play, the ways they interact with each other through time, and how they use the space around them.

Summary and Relationship to Other Lenses

Common roles of participants in visual artistic activity are the message creators, manipulators, and experiencers.

✪ Activity: Identify the Role(s) in Visual Art Creation

One or more people will be involved in the production of objects with artistic features. *Creator* roles could include painters, sculptors, weavers, dye makers, carvers, potters, and the like. Ask friends questions such as the following:

- Who made this?
- Who makes similar creations?
- Who is recognized as being especially skilled at doing it?
- What is the local name for a person who fills this role?
- Who is part of the creative process?
- Does the artist rely on traditions of prior artists who influence his or her work?
- Does the artist ask representative members of the intended audience to check the work, and perhaps make changes in response before presenting it to a larger audience? If so, who participates?
- Whom does the artist intend to experience the work?

✪ Activity: Describe How People Manipulate Art Objects

Art objects often function within larger events, as instruments, set pieces, costumes, props, and the like. In these cases, manipulators play, place, wear, hold, or otherwise use them. Watch a videorecording of an event with people who participated. For each object you are interested in, ask questions such as:

- What is that person doing with the object? Are there restrictions on who can do it?
- How does what they are doing with the object affect how people experience it?

✪ Activity: Describe How People Experience Art Objects

Experiencers are people who receive the meanings encoded in the objects intended by their creators and manipulators. The key activity of the experiencers is *perception*—the process of decoding the visual message. The perception process is influenced by one's culture, previous experience, the expectations created by enculturation through experience, and physiological processes in the human brain.

Watch a videorecording of people experiencing an object. This could include someone interacting with a sculpture in a museum, watching actors wearing costumes, walking into a specially designed building, or other event. Write down where their eyes are directed at different times, and describe any other visible responses (such as crying). You can also watch the video with the experiencer and ask him or her to describe what they saw, felt, and thought of. (See also "Emotions" in Part C of *Step 4*.)

Shape of the Event through Time

Shape of an event refers primarily to its constituent segments, organized hierarchically.

Summary and Relationship to Other Lenses

Shape here refers primarily to change through time, which relates to visual artistic action in four important ways. First, we consider the artist's process for creating the work over time. What is the order of events? Animation artists, for example, begin with one or more drafts or thumbnail sketches: "small, quick drawings that provide a blueprint" (Polson 2013:81). Artists may work as a creative team choosing from among various possible designs, revising, and refining over time, as with storyboarding a film; or they may work largely independently, like a weaver creating a design on cloth in Burkina Faso, West Africa, although he may rely on traditions of color combinations and patterns learned from weavers before him. Artists may ask their intended audience for advice or ideas to improve drafts, as UNICEF checks draft illustrations by asking members of the intended audience what they understand so as to improve the final version (Haaland 1984). *Participant organization* thus overlaps with *shape through time*.

Second, we describe how long the work lasts. Objects generally retain their form for long periods of time, in contrast to other kinds of artistic communication that are dynamic. That said, some works are more durable than others: Navajo sand paintings are only intended to last for the length of a specific occasion or ceremony, and ice sculptures melt when the weather warms.

Third, as we discuss in the following section on *participant organization*, an experiencer's interaction with an object is structured through time. We see this as a person experiences architectural features while walking through a cathedral, or when someone spends 30 minutes examining a painting in a museum.

Finally, at given moments in a performance event, the participants, objects, and other elements of the performance may create a series of visual snapshots, each with its own set of features which may be described.

⭐ Activity: Describe the Process for Creating Art over Time

Watch a work being created, or interview an artist about the process involved in creating his or her work. Describe the steps.

⭐ Activity: Compare Two Visual Snapshots of an Event

Watch a videorecording of an event. Pause the recording at two moments that seem visually contrastive to you, save freeze-frame images of the moments, and describe them through *performance features* and *space* lenses. Look at the two images with a participant in the event, noting what stands out to him or her visually in each.

⭐ Activity: Write the History of an Object

Identify the oldest example that you can find of an object with artistic features, perhaps one that is well known in a community. Ask several people questions such as:

- Who created it and when?
- Would the artist be willing to send you any drafts or thumbnail sketches that led to the creation of the final work?
- On what occasions and how often do you remember it being used? How has it changed over time? What events have happened to it, like being broken, repaired, lost, or stolen?
- How often and for how long is the work viewable, by whom, where, and when?

Performance Feature Categories

Performance features are observable characteristics of a performance that emerge from an event's unique combination of physical and social context and participants' actions.

Summary and Relationship to Other Lenses

Although visual artistry is not always performed by participants in real time, its features are the building blocks of visual communication. We define several features that creators manipulate to create meaning and aesthetic pleasure.

Activity: Describe the Visual Features of a Static Object

Look at an object and write down its use of the following kinds of features:

Line: "The path made by a pointed instrument: a pen, a pencil, a crayon, a stick. A line implies action because work was required to make it" (Feldman 1992:207).

Shape: A two- or three-dimensional area, often formed by lines, usually with defined edges or colors.

Color: The visual response to the wavelengths of light reflected from something, identified as red, blue, green, and so on. Communities may assign meanings to particular colors. For example, in a graduation ceremony, the colors of the gowns and hoods have a particular meaning. The color of the front of the hood identifies the discipline in which the degree was earned, while the colors of the trim and back represent the school colors of the granting institution.

A *dominant color* is the color that occupies the greatest area in a work or demands the most of the experiencers' attention.

Supporting colors occupy less space or demand less of the experiencers' attention.

Accent colors occupy small amounts of space but emphasize design elements.

A *color scheme* is an arrangement or combination of colors in a work.

Analogous color schemes contain colors next to one another on a color wheel.

Complementary color schemes contain colors opposite one another on a color wheel.

Split complementary color schemes use an analogous color scheme as their base, with a complementary accent color (Polson 2013:110).

Saturation is the intensity of a color, whether bright or dull. Two colors of similar saturation tend to compete for the viewers' attention, whereas one more saturated than another tends to focus viewer's attention (Polson 2013:124).

Value: The lightness or darkness of a color that forms part of an image compared to other parts of the image. Value can be based on a gray scale, from black to white, or in tints and shades of colors.

Hue or *middle value*: The prototypical color definition in a culture.

Shades: Darker variants of a color formed by adding varying amounts of black to the hue or base color.

Tints: Lighter variants of a color formed by adding varying amounts of white to the hue or base color.

Tones: Added gray or a color complement to a hue, describing its lightness or darkness.

Texture: The sense of feeling that a visual message evokes, such as roughness or softness; the message creator substitutes an imagined sense of touch by a visual representation.

Contrast: A difference between light and dark or other opposing design elements such as sharp and rounded lines, or warm colors and soft colors.

Focus: The area of a work where the experiencers' attention is drawn. The eye usually focuses on "the area of highest contrast, the area of darkest dark against lightest light, in a composition" (Polson 2013:88).

No focus: The eye is not attracted to any part of a work more than to any other.

Split focus: More than one part of the work competes for the eyes' attention.

Strong focus: High contrast creates a focal point that draws the experiencers' attention; no other part of the work competes for attention (Polson 2013:88).

Content

Content refers to the subject matter in artistic activity.

Summary and Relationship to Other Lenses

Visual art forms relate directly to content when they use symbolic symbols like language, and when they evoke ideas through other means. A work of visual art may convey a concept or a story. If there is a story, research the characters, settings and events portrayed. If it is a concept, research what concepts are conveyed.

⭐ Activity: Elicit a Visual Symbol's Story or Concept

Research any story that goes with a given symbol or work of art in your community, such as the story and symbol that accompany the Dogon *kanaga* pictured earlier (Figure 4.13). Many works of visual art cannot be understood without hearing an accompanying story. Ask a local storyteller what story or concept each visual symbol or image conveys. Some works may convey both stories and concepts. Always interpret a visual image with its oral story if there is a story associated with it. Who are the characters portrayed? How do visual features help us know what these characters are like? What places and events are portrayed? What concepts or themes are conveyed?

Underlying Symbolic Systems

Underlying symbolic systems refer to the grammatical and social rules and structures that guide participants' actions in artistic activity.

Summary and Relationship to Other Lenses

The symbolic systems underlying a community's visual communication contribute to its *visual literacy*: the understanding that people have of the various components and elements of visual messages; the learned ability to understand and create visual images to communicate messages. Visual communication skills allow message creators to create and manipulate mental images. Every community has different rules of visual literacy that rely on a shared knowledge of visual grammar, vocabulary, and rhetoric.

✪ Activity: Analyze the Message of an Image

Begin by identifying the content elements of the message:

1. Create an inventory of the content elements.
2. Notice the composition of the image—which elements are visually centered and which are marginal (at the edges).
3. List "the visual cues of color, form, depth, and movement within the image" (Lester 2003:112).
4. Attempt to place the image in a geographical and temporal setting, and identify its purposes.

Lester (2003) suggests the following perspectives for critical analysis of visual messages:

Personal: Refers to the subjective viewer response.

Historical: Attempts to place the message in a historical context.

Technical: Attempts to understand specific techniques, quality, expertise, and budget for the production of the message.

Ethical: Attempts to understand moral implications of the message for the producer, the subject, and the viewer.

Cultural: Attempts to understand cultural symbols that affect the meaning of the message by applying insights from historical, technical, and ethical perspectives in a specific context and time. It is closely related to semiotic theory. The cultural perspective analyzes cultural values and worldviews.

Critical: Expands the viewer's perspective beyond the specific image to include medium, culture, and audience. This helps the viewer (1) understand how this message makes a broader statement about human nature, and (2) better understand why some cultures find messages like this one acceptable or unacceptable. As the final perspective, it incorporates the results of all the other analytical perspectives.

Part C: Relate the Event's Genre(s) to Its Broader Cultural Context

Nothing you encounter in a community exists in isolation. Words, clothes, houses, food, movements, facial expressions, family—everything is interwoven, like threads in fabric. Likewise, events with artistic communication exist in relationship to other parts of a society and interact with local, regional, national, and global realities. Understanding how an event connects to its broader context allows you to enter more accurately into its creation, evaluation, integration, and celebration.

We have chosen some categories of cultural investigation that have helped other people gain insights into the workings of artistic activity. Each topic consists of the following sections: the central question or questions that should guide your investigation of the topic; and a discussion of the aspects of the topic that have proven to be relevant for others, with research activities to help you begin. Note that there may be other topics particularly appropriate to your context; working with indigenous minorities, for example, often leads to questions about origins, land rights, sovereignty, nation, blood, colonialism, and indigenous knowledges.

A common way that communities connect an event to the rest of their lives is through *genre*. Continuing our usage throughout the Guide, genre simply refers to a type or category of artistic production. People usually perform something that connects strongly to an event they have experienced before, such as a wedding, concert, or particular ceremony. In many places, communities have names for these types of events or kinds of communication. Never does someone create a new bit of artistic communication without any connection to something they have experienced before. Nothing comes from nothing. The explorations we guide you through here are centered on a particular event containing the enactment of a particular genre, but relate to broader realities. The Community Arts Profile contains a section for you to compile summaries of your discoveries about how genres in an event relate to the following themes.

Also note that you cannot be sure of the reality of broader cultural themes unless you have had a detailed familiarity with actual artistic communication. Keep investigating genres in events, guided by activities in this step. For each topic ask, how does this relate to the lenses and artistic domains? In addition, listen to what people are talking about, and choose related subjects. For example, if the community is feeling excluded from or stereotyped by a group or nation, research *identity and power*.[2]

Artists

People are at the core of artistic communication. They learn, perform, and pass on the skills and knowledge that make such communication effective. They add their individual skills, interests, and goals to existing traditions. They are the keepers of artistic treasure. So any plan a community makes to draw on its arts for their goals must have understanding of and interaction with artists at its core. Other people will play strategic roles in encouraging, limiting, and accepting a type of artistic communication. But without the artist to create and perform, plans will never succeed. We need to learn from, welcome, and encourage them.

The exploratory activities that will help you answer the questions in this section have to do with getting to know people: interviews, participation, and observation. In addition to the particular tasks noted in the following, you may decide to study formally or informally with a skilled artist, join artists in their personal and artistic worlds, sit with a composer and see how he or she creates, ask to watch an artist teach someone else, or share your own life and artistic gifts with him or her.

Who Are the Artists Related to This Kind of Event?

Everyone in a community is likely to be involved in artistic communication in some way—by listening, watching, singing, dancing, composing, admiring, critiquing, and so on. Some people, however, have more knowledge and skills related to creation, performance, and transmission; our focus is on these people. Every community categorizes and defines artists in different ways, and not all use broad categories like "musician" or "artist." Sometimes, an artist is given a role and identity in his or her language of singer, player of a particular instrument, mask maker, or other such designation. Other times, artists emphasize the interlinking of arts. Several performers with whom Kathleen worked in Nairobi, Kenya, preferred to call themselves artists rather than drummers, dancers, singers, actors, and so on. Abil Ochango was one of them. His choice to call himself an artist reflected in part his skills in multiple art forms. However, this choice also revealed a way of thinking about the arts. "You have art as an element, just one element," Ochango explained to Kathleen in an interview. "And when you divide it, then it's not strong" (Kathleen Van Buren interview with Ochango, Nairobi, September 1, 2004).

To find artists involved in a type of event you have experienced, perform activities such as these:

- Through interviews, list the roles of participants in an event. "Look at an Event's Forms" (Part A) will help you in this.
- Choose one of these roles and ask friends and other community members to list some of the most respected fillers of that role. Repeat this for other roles.
- Over time, ask, listen, watch, and confirm the skills and reputations of artists you get to know. Everyone will have different combinations of skills and attributes, and so will play different roles in artistic activities. You may find, for example, an older man who knows the most songs in a genre, but is not recognized as the best singer. The community may decide to have the older man lead the choice of which songs to record on an audio product they create for wide distribution, but have someone else sing.

How Do Artists in This Genre Relate to Their Community?

A community may ascribe high, neutral, or low status to an artist associated with a particular genre. Although the status level may be determined by the individual character of an artist, respect or disrespect is often associated with a particular artistic role. People who play drums associated with royalty, for example, may enjoy high levels of respect and honor. Artists who perform for activities a society deems less respectable—for example, lewd dramatic entertainment in a brothel—may be merely tolerated. Artists also may be feared due to their ability to publicize personal or community faults through their arts. We need to be aware of community attitudes when encouraging artists to create for particular purposes, because these feelings will have a strong effect on how others respond to their activities.

It also may be useful to investigate how a community compensates an artist, either monetarily or through some other means. In Daasanech society in northern Kenya and southern Ethiopia, a man pays a woman *gaaro* specialist to compose songs relating important events of his life (Schrag, unpublished research). Most Daasanech mothers compose songs for their babies, but are not paid.

To find out how artists involved in a type of event you have experienced relate to their society, perform activities such as these:

- Through sensitive interviews, ask people their opinions of people who fill particular roles in an artistic event.
- As you get to know an artist, ask how she is treated by different segments of society, and if and how she gets paid for her work.

⚙ How Do People Become Artists in This Genre?

Becoming an artist in a particular genre may be largely determined by societal patterns, achieved by individual effort and skill, or—most often—through a combination of the two. In parts of West Africa, for example, members of certain castes are expected to work as professional singers and storytellers. Because of this societal expectation, children in these castes are taught musical skills and performance practices from a young age. In other cultures, people are encouraged primarily to follow individual interests and skills.

To find out how artists become involved in a particular genre, perform activities such as these:

- Do a biographical study of an artist's life, using common journalists' questions: Where have you lived? How did you learn the skills associated with this role? Who has influenced you in your art? Why did you follow this path? Describe some important events in your life that have impacted your artistry.
- Similarly, ask people knowledgeable in a genre to describe its history: Where did it originate? Who were important figures in its development? When did important steps in the genre's development take place? Who can become an artist in the genre?

Creativity

We define *artistic creativity* as occurring when one or more people draw on their personal competencies, symbolic systems, and social patterns of their community to produce an event of heightened communication that has not previously existed in its exact form (see also Csikszentmihalyi's concepts of person, symbolic domain, and field; 1996:23–31). To find out how it works in the community you are working with, you will need to get inside what is a very dynamic process. You can do this through asking questions, participating in creative acts, and commissioning new works and watching what happens.

⭐ Who Are the Creators of New Works?

Creation can be performed by an individual specialist—someone who is recognized for his or her abilities, or a casual "one-shot" composer who produces a work for a particular occasion—or a collaboration of several individuals. To find out who the creators of the artistic elements of an event are, watch a live performance or a video of a performance, or look at an artistic object with a friend and ask questions such as these:

- Who made this, and when?
- Who made each element of this event, and when? Examples of elements might include a dance move, a song, a play, a poem, or a woven cloth.

⭐ How Do New Examples of This Form Come into Being?

Composition can take place through deliberate and conscious effort, or may be received through dreams or visions. If through conscious effort, an individual may make it happen, a group may work on it together, or it could be a combined effort (several composers working on different parts or at different times).

Techniques for composition include the following: conscious creation of an element of a genre, like a song, poem, dance, or mask; taking parts of old creations and putting them together in a new way; improvisation; communal re-creation; creating out of emotional stress after a particularly meaningful or traumatic situation; and composition-in-performance.[3] To find out how people compose new works, perform activities such as these:

- Watch a live performance or a video of a performance, or look at an artistic object with a friend and ask questions like this: What did people do to make this? Who was involved?
- Commission a new work in a genre, then ask the creator(s) what steps they will follow. You can also ask if you could document the process by written notes, photographs, and video.

⚙ What Does "New" Mean in This Art Form?

Creativity is about making something new. But each community values and defines newness in different ways. If a group values tradition and continuity more than innovation, then they may discourage changes in a tradition. If they have the opposite view, they may reward creators who depart significantly from tradition.

To find out how people involved in the creation of this art form think about newness, perform activities such as these:

- Interact with a creator while he or she is making something. Ask what aspects of the new creation are different from existing creations, and which are the same. Ask if they can list any principles, wisdom, or proverbs that guide their creativity.
- Ask a group of people if they can remember an example of a work that jarred them because it was too new. Ask if they can isolate an element that displeased them.

⚙ Where Do the Components of Creativity for This Genre Lie?

Each community performs arts that draw on a unique combination of its components of creativity—creators, language and other symbolic systems, and audience and gatekeepers. Each component, in turn, can vary in its nearness to the community, measured geographically, conceptually, and in communal identity. According to this rubric, then, a community may have composers and performers who draw on symbolic systems residing in local traditions, in traditions from another community, in a regional or national artistic genre, or in the artistic traditions of a distant culture.

Applying the following questions to this event, fill out a rubric like that in Figure 4.14.

		Creativity Components		
	Location	**Creators**	**Conceptual Systems & Skills**	**Social Structures**
Distant – Near	Community			
	Region or Nation			
	World			

FIGURE 4.14. Rubric to identify locations of a genre's components of creativity.

- *Creators*: Where are the creators, the individuals and groups who compose and perform each element of this event? This may refer to singers, instrument players, lyricists, composers, playwrights, sculptors, and others.
- *Conceptual systems and skills*: In what communities do the systems and skills underlying their artistic production reside? This speaks to systems of language, melody, scale, rhythm, timbre, poetic devices, dramatic characterization, movement, repertoire, and the like. Also included are competencies such as instrument building, and means of learning artistic skills, such as formal and informal educational structures.
- *Social structures*: Where are the individuals and groups who influence artistic production most in this context? This comprises knowledgeable audiences; highly and widely regarded artists; commercial, social, political, religious, or aesthetic gatekeepers; and others.

This analysis can help uncover historical development of existing genres. For example, when European and American missions began significant work in Africa in the early nineteenth century, they encountered musical and social contexts supporting enormous creative capacity. However, they generally translated their own musical repertoires into local languages, thereby initially retaining foreign sources of creativity. Protestant churches initiated in northwestern Democratic Republic of Congo (DRC) by the Scandinavian-rooted, American Evangelical Free and Evangelical Covenant denominations exemplify this pattern. These churches have sung from the hymn book *Nzembo na Nzambe* (*Songs of God*) since the late 1940s. This book consists of texts of American and European hymns translated into Lingala, a regional language that ties multiple ethnic groups together through business and government. As shown in Figure 4.15, local performers of these songs drew on geographically and conceptually

Location		Creativity Components		
		Creators	Conceptual Systems & Skills	Social Structures
Distant - Near	Community	*performers*		*song choices in performance*
	Region or Nation		*language(s) of lyrics*	*songbook publishers*
	World	*composers*	*musical, rhythmic, conceptual systems*	

FIGURE 4.15. Loci of creativity components of young Congolese ethnolinguistically centered churches.

distant melodic and rhythmic systems, and slightly nearer systems of language (Schrag 2016).

Ownership and Rights

Communities approach who can do what with each element of an art form in a wide variety of ways. They may give an individual the right to experiment within a genre and take credit for everything he or she produces. Or a community might claim ownership of any artistic work produced by one or more of its members, highlighting the traditions that give birth to artistry. DAKASTUM, a Cameroonian dance association, required each of its 40 members to give written authorization to Brian to publish articles about them. In fact, each community handles ownership and rights related to its artistry through a unique combination of several interrelated factors.

To find out a community's approach to ownership and rights related to artistry, observe a current contested case, or ask about a previous one, exploring answers to questions like these:

- What feature(s) or items of artistry are under consideration? These could include a dance movement, lyric, song, sketch, melody, plot, two-dimensional shape, production technique, photograph, audio- or videorecording, an idea, a particular enactment, and so on.
- What act related to artistry is being considered? Acts include disseminating, enacting, describing authoritatively, giving or trading, profiting financially from, modifying, claiming ownership, and so on.
- What social or conceptual systems does someone need to follow to make a claim to rights or ownership? Such systems could include social protocols, laws, informal agreements, oral traditions, and so on.
- Who has the right to decide what happens to artistry? This could be an individual, a performance group, an ethnolinguistic community, a leader or spokesperson, a legal representative, every single member of a community, a mentor, a family, a clan, a museum, an archive, a government, an institution, a company, and so on.
- What criteria are used to evaluate questions of rights and ownership? Formal systems sometimes quantify such questions, requiring a particular percentage of new features to constitute individual ownership of a work. Other systems might appeal to the lineage of an artist to determine his or her rights.

- What degree of importance does a community place on questions of ownership and rights? They may care deeply about how their artistry is disseminated and changed, and enforce their standards strictly and consistently. Or a community may not care much about these issues.
- How and to what degree are a community's approach to ownership and rights experiencing change? Rapid global social change makes change highly likely.

Language

The language(s) and types of language used in an artistic event can reveal much about its relationship to its broader cultural context. Song lyrics in a regional or national language support regional or national identity. A woven tapestry with words in a minority language, using that language's unique alphabet, accentuates identity with a minority community. It is also common in artistic communication to use archaic or special registers, forms not used in everyday speech. This may reflect a sense of mystery or fear associated with the genre, or it may simply have been frozen in that form for other reasons.

⊛ What Language(s), Dialect(s), and Register(s) Are Appropriate for This Form?

Watch or listen to a recording of an event, or look at an object with someone knowledgeable about it. List every component containing language, and write down answers to questions such as these:

- What language or dialect is this in? Are there some words in other languages?
- Can you imagine someone saying this in normal speech, or is it a special kind of language?

⊛ What Status and Identity Are Associated with Each Language Choice?

With the same list of language types used, ask questions such as these:

- When you hear this type of language, who does it make you think of?
- Why do you think the creator(s) used this type of language?

Transmission and Change

The participants in an artistic event learned its associated skills and knowledge somehow. This transmission may have happened in a socially structured way, through schools, lessons, or formal apprenticeships. It could also have happened informally, through learning by watching, or individual exploration. Methods could include aural activities like imitation of an expert's singing, playing, or acting. The process could also include written helps, like music notation or a dance score. This human-to-human transfer always includes some measure of change: the teaching process is not perfect, people remember inaccurately or forget completely, and each individual has different interests and levels of skills that affect what they learn.

How Are Competencies Associated with This Form Passed on to Others?

To find out how people learn this type of event, perform activities such as these:

- Ask participants in the event to tell how they learned to do what they did. Ask if you can participate in or watch that process sometime. As you watch, note the interactions between people, how more knowledgeable people are treated, and what objects are part of the process.
- If this event is part of a long tradition, ask an older person how and when people used to learn it. Then ask if they still learn it this way, and if not, what has changed to make the difference.

How Has This Form Changed Historically?

To find out how this type of event has changed over time, perform activities such as this:

- Find old and newer recordings or examples of an art form. Watch or listen to them with a knowledgeable person, and ask how the two differ. Ask what might have caused differences.

Cultural Dynamism

Communities maintain a mix of continuity and change. Artistic genres can feed into this vitality through interactions between their stable and malleable elements.

	Performance Organization	Song Structure	Rhythm
Malleable	Occasional performances	Changing vocal call	Improvising drum
Stable	Rehearsals	Unchanging vocal response	Unchanging percussion

FIGURE 4.16. Example of malleable | stable pairs.

Stable elements occur regularly in time and place, and are tightly organized. More malleable elements are less predictable (perhaps marked by improvisation) and more loosely organized. Cultural dynamism happens when artists masterfully use the most malleable elements of their arts to invigorate the most stable. Figure 4.16 gives an example of malleable/stable pairs in a song genre with percussion instruments:

Without creative, malleable structures to infuse new energy into the stable structures, the stable structures may decay and dissipate. And without stable undergirdings, the creators in malleable forms will have no dependable reference points to anchor their creativity.

Discuss these questions with artists to begin to understand the interplay between stable and malleable elements:

- *To identify stable artistic elements*: Which art forms or aspects of art forms occur most regularly, with the least amount of variability and tight organization?
- *To identify malleable artistic elements*: Which art forms or aspects of art forms occur with less predictability and are more loosely organized?
- *To identify interactions between stable and malleable elements*: See if you can find any artistic elements in the domains of rhythm, performance organization, or shape of the event through time that interact in pairs. For example, does the rhythmic structure of a performance have some parts that never change, allowing a master percussionist to improvise?

For more resources on artistic vitality, see *Closing 7*.

Identity and Power

People express who they are or who they want to be by choosing what, how, and where to communicate, including artistically. This means that every dance step, song, story, proverb, and woven cloth is an act of identity affirmation. These affirmations relate to social power structures in different ways, which can cause controversy. It is important, then, to know how an art form fits into its local and wider communities, so that members of these communities can make informed decisions about how to improve their future. Be cautious and humble in addressing issues of power.

⚙ What Kinds of People Identify with This Form, and What Characterizes Their Identification?

To explore participants' identification with this type of event, perform activities such as these:

- Make a list of elements associated with the event: language, dress, colors, instruments, and so on. Ask a friend which people each of these is associated with.
- Interview participants in the event to find out demographic information: age, gender, education, occupation, geographic origin, ethnic self-identification, language(s) spoken, and religion. Avoid discussing categories that may cause contention or invite danger.
- Ask participants why they are involved in this event.

⚙ How Does This Form Relate to Social Stratification, Gender, or Other Distinctions Within Culture?

Artistic communication can affirm power structures, as with national anthems or royal pageantry. People can also use it to oppose power, as in early African-American rap and Rastafarian reggae. In terms of visibility, art forms can be expressed publicly or in hidden ways. Public expressions affirming power include national anthems and West African praise songs. Less direct and visible comments on power occurred when slaves in the United States embedded anti-slavery messages in spirituals. To research this type of event's relationship to power, perform activities such as these:

- Transcribe any texts associated with this event, like song lyrics or story content. Examine them to see if there are overt messages affirming or opposing a person, activity, institution, or other entity. Discrete discussion with a friend may help you find out if there are any hidden messages.
- Observe the event. Did people communicate messages that challenged authority in the event that you have not seen them do elsewhere? Artistic

action can provide a safe place for contestation or resolving conflict. It might also invite negative repercussions, so be careful.

Aesthetics and Evaluation

People find pleasure in their experience of artistic communication for many reasons: the group solidarity it may engender, the association of the experience with an enjoyable memory, or satisfaction in the attributes of an art form. This last possibility has to do with aesthetics, the study of the criteria people use to judge an artifact with respect to attributes perceived to be intrinsic to it (Margolis 1965). Though there may be overlap between different communities, every society has a unique set of criteria they use to judge the intrinsic value of works of art they experience. In other words, there is no formal characteristic of artistic communication that is intrinsically pleasing, beautiful, or good.

Humans are quick to judge others' arts by their own aesthetic standards, but we must help ourselves and others not fall into this trap. Here are a few activities you can perform to find out how the community you are working with approaches correction and evaluation in general:

- Ask a friend how (or if) he or she would correct someone older or younger, and in roles of higher or lower status. The community might value direct correction in some contexts, and require indirection in others.
- Ask the same friend how the kinds of people he or she just described would correct him or her.

Here are ways to explore evaluation specifically of the form of artistic objects:

- Ask people to discuss what they view as critical aspects of an artwork; that is, would the art be effective (for aesthetic/practical/other purposes) without certain components (related arts, particular colors, particular timing, etc.)? This may help point to elements that are perceived as critical to genres.
- Observe experts teaching an art form to someone else—perhaps you— and write down what advice they give or mistakes they correct. These may point to an ideal.
- Notice items that are put in a place of prominence, spoken of with reverence, or that take special expertise and time to create. These may have ideal characteristics. Ask people what makes them good or pleasing.

- Gather a small group of people to watch and listen to a recording of an event or look at an artistic object. Ask them to describe what they liked or did not like about it.

⊙ Time

Artistic communication intersects with time in two important ways. First, because most arts provide some sort of rhythmic structure, people often experience time during performance differently than they do in other parts of life. Goodridge (1999:43) describes movement rhythm in performance as "a patterned energy flow of action, marked in the body by varied stress and directional change; also marked by changes in level of intensity, speed and duration." Time may flow more quickly, more slowly, or in unpredictably complex ways to the experiencer of a performance. Second, the structure, flow, and timing of a performance may intersect with broader cultural temporal patterns. In many communities, certain events only occur at particular points in agricultural, religious, or other calendrical cycles.

To find out more about the intersection of artistic and community time, perform activities such as these:

- Soon after an event, ask participants questions like these: How did you know when to do certain things? How did you experience time? Was it linear, cyclical, or flowing in waves? When else do you experience time this way?
- Ask a small group of people to list all of the times an event of this type occurred in the last two years. Do you notice any temporal patterns? Ask why they happened when they did.
- Ask experts in a genre to describe the passage of time during performance. Do they explicitly connect this description to broader calendrical cycles?

⊙ Emotion

In the 1970s, K. N. Bame (1973) conducted focused interviews of approximately one thousand audience members from different regions of Ghana to assess the effects of dramatic performance. Among the questions he asked were the following: (1) Have audience members seen others shed tears, or have they themselves shed tears, while watching a play, and what do they think was the cause of the weeping?

(2) Did audience members receive anything other than entertainment from the plays, and if so, what did they receive or learn? (3) Did viewers feel that the plays benefited their communities? And (4) did the moral advice offered by the actors aid them in their lives? His findings suggest that artistic events can have multiple influences on audiences: immediate emotional effect on at least some audience members (yielding tears); effect on the thoughts of audience members (in making them recall real life situations while watching performances, and remember moral lessons from the performances during real-life situations); and effect on the behavior of audience members.

One of the most celebrated characteristics of artistic communication is its capacity to express and evoke emotion. The arts have a way of connecting a sound, sight, movement, scent, or taste directly to potent, emotionally charged memories. They also often provide a socially accepted release for intense feelings, as lamentations and wailing do for grief. In addition, artistic communication can envelop a person's whole being, allowing gifted performers to magnify emotions in others by playing with their expectations of the art form. Finally, the arts are often associated with trance, ecstasy, and other states of overwhelming emotion.

To research an event's connections to emotion, perform activities like these:

- Watch a recording of an event and write down what emotions participants—including audience members—appear to express. Ask someone who was there if they agree with your interpretations.
- Watch a videorecording of an artistic event with people who were there. Watch the observers, and when they exhibit any emotion—joy, surprise, sadness, anger, disdain, etc.—stop the recording and ask about what they are responding to. Make a list of the words they use to describe their emotions and what was going on in the performance that sparked them. Record their comments.
- Ask friends if they remember an artistic event that evoked strong emotion in them. Have them describe the event and their reactions.

 Subject Matter

The verbal content of songs, proverbs, plays, tapestries, and other arts flows from the minds, experiences, and histories of the participating individuals and communities. Sometimes artistic communication reveals information about subjects available almost nowhere else, such as historical events. Other times, it communicates the values of the community in memorable form; proverbs are a strong example of this. The references of textual content may be metaphorical or cryptic, so your first understanding may not be the only one, or the deepest. To explore patterns in the subject matter addressed by artistic communication, perform activities such as these:

- Make a list of the elements in an event that have verbal content, like songs, proverbs, or stories. Ask an expert to describe the messages in each. Ask: What is this about? What are they trying to communicate? Is there a lesson? If so, who is the lesson for? You may want to consult the Human Relations Area Files (2018) for examples of themes that are common to many cultures.
- As you watch a recording or read a transcription of an event, ask a small group of participants to list all of the references to people, objects, places, events, or spiritual beings. Ask them to describe each. Record or write down their answers.

 ## Community Values

Artistic communication often provides a place to challenge community authorities. However, how it is organized and performed may also reflect a community's values and social structures in important ways. Reflecting on the physical and social organization of participants may provide clues to broader community values. To research these relationships, observe an event and afterward ask participants questions like these:

- How do participants interact with representatives of authority within the event? How does this differ from such interactions in other contexts?
- Does the physical organization of participants show a hierarchical structure, as in the first, second, and third seats of performers in a symphony orchestra? Or are participants organized on the same physical level? Answers to these questions may reflect values of hierarchical versus egalitarian social structures elsewhere in the community.
- In what ways, if any, are participants encouraged to express themselves individually? What signs of free versus rigid atmosphere are there? Answers to these questions may reflect values of conformity versus nonconformity elsewhere in the community.

⭐ Communal Investment

The amount of energy a community invests in different kinds of artistic activity varies widely. A grandfather speaking a proverb to his granddaughter involves only two people, requires no preparation, costs no money, and lasts for only a few seconds. A funeral for a king in western Cameroon, on the other hand, may last a month, includes hundreds of people, and requires significant finances to pay for food, transportation, and gifts. An assessment of the social, material, financial, and spiritual resources a community invests in an event provides important clues to its importance and influence.

To research a community's investment in an event, observe, ask, and write down information about the following parameters:

- length of time of event;
- status of scheduling: high-status time, low-status time (e.g., some communities believe particular times of day, week, or year to be more auspicious than others, and so compete to secure those times for their events);
- amount of preparation;
- cost of the event;
- location of the event: high status, low status;
- event space: status, size, expense, exclusivity;
- participants: number, status, exclusivity, level of skill or professionalism;
- complexity: number of relevant features.

Notes

1. For further study on communication channels, see Finnegan (2014).

2. To guide your research, you may also find it useful to answer questions at SustainableMusic.org (Schippers and Grant 2016).

3. "Composition-in-Performance" is a particular kind of improvisation formulated by Milman Parry and Albert Lord to describe oral poetry (Lord 1960). See Duffy (2014) for further discussion and applications.

Step
5

SPARK CREATIVITY

WE HAVE FINALLY reached the climactic moment in the creation process. You might think of it as the point in a pregnancy when the baby is born. In *Steps 1–4*, you and the community have prepared for and nurtured the mother and the infant in the womb, and you are about to see the fruit of this preparation. New artistry is about to enter the world.

Steps 6 and 7 will address how this new creation will grow in quality and influence. In *Step 5*, however, our goal is to help you

- design an activity
- that will result in new artistry in a genre
- which, when performed in a community event,
- will likely produce particular kinds of effects in those who experience it
- and thereby provide a chance for the community to move toward a better life.

We have already worked through all of these elements except the first. Here is the process for designing a sparking activity:

- Keep the benefits of scientific rigor in mind.
- Think about what a sparking activity is.
- Prepare to draw on familiar methods of composition.
- Think carefully about the meristem.

- Identify opportunities to capitalize on and barriers to overcome.
- Decide on the type of activity.
- Design a new activity or modify an existing activity.
- Perform the activity and describe the results.

Some activities might build on others you have completed. You will also see that many activities we describe may contribute to multiple goals. For example, you may commission an artist to create a new work in a traditional genre about how globalization is affecting his or her community. From this, people will begin to discuss how they can respond wisely to changes around them, which feeds into our *health and well-being* category discussed in *Step 2*. But the social status of the genre will also increase, which ties into the affirmation of creativity we discuss in relation to our *identity and sustainability* category.

Keep the Benefits of Scientific Rigor in Mind

To increase the likelihood that planned projects will occur and be effective, try to follow criteria that local and other gatekeepers (including funders) trust. If you have access to institutions with resources for rigorous research, consider whether you can make projects have impact beyond the local context. You may be able to partner with a scholar or group that can help design a project that follows accepted scientific standards of validity, thereby increasing understandings of causal links between arts-based interventions and holistic outcomes.

In one such study, Shanahan et al (2017) administered a randomized controlled feasibility trial comparing Irish set dancing with usual care in people with Parkinson disease. Researchers integrated ethnochoreological insights about Irish identity and social life into health measures, such as motor function, quality of life, functional endurance, and balance. Results show that the dance group avoided normal deterioration in endurance, and gained in quality of life (though statistically insignificant). This study provides a foundation for future studies designed to identify the kinds of ethnographic and dance elements that will maximize the benefits of dance therapy in non-Irish communities.

In another first-of-its-kind study, Monique van Bruggen-Rufi (2018) conducted a multi-center randomized controlled trial to compare the effectiveness of group music therapy with group exercise therapy for 63 patients with late stage Huntington's Disease. Unfortunately for people seeking immediate help in this population, quality of life measurements did not significantly improve in the music therapy group. Results, however, point to therapy designs that are more likely to succeed, and which can be tested; rigorous research provides reliable data that can lead to more effective interventions. Sadler and Joseph (2008), Staricoff (2006), and Clift and Camic (2016) provide additional examples of plans and progress in connecting arts to increased well-being in rigorous and fundable ways.

The American Dance Therapy Association states its need in this way: "Trials of high methodological quality, large sample sizes and clarity in the way the intervention is put together and delivered are needed to assess whether dance movement therapy is an effective intervention for dementia" (Malher-Moran 2016). The more that arts advocates can contribute to efforts like these, the more people will experience improvement in their lives, and the stronger will be our case when developing proposals and applying for funding for future programs.

Think about What a Sparking Activity Is

A sparking activity is anything anybody does that results in the creation of new artistry. It will require different amounts of community investment, from low to high. For example, the act could be as casual as suggesting to a friend that she respond with painting during an oration at a meeting that afternoon, or it could entail the enormous complexity of planning a festival involving scores of artists and government officials. Also, a sparking activity may lead to immediate products or may provide a structure where future creativity can happen. Finally, such an activity may involve many or all of the seven *Make Arts* steps (*meet, specify, connect, analyze, spark, improve, celebrate*) or focus on just one. For example, workshops often include times to identify goals, perform initial analysis of a genre, and create and improve works. Other kinds of activities may focus solely on the act of creating. In any case, the community needs to see the sparking activity in the context of the whole creation process.

With this backdrop, here are the components you need to describe in the Community Arts Profile when you design a sparking activity:

- *Title and summary*: A brief overview of the activity and its main purposes. Include its overall type—commissioning, workshop, showcase event, mentoring, apprenticeship, publication, creators' club, or something you make up (not more than a paragraph).
- *Participants*: All of the types of people who need to be involved for the activity to succeed. This may include creators and gatekeepers of various kinds. Identify actual people when possible.

- *Information you will need from the Community Arts Profile*: Information someone needs to learn about the community or genre for the activity to succeed. Note which information is already in the Community Arts Profile, and that which still needs exploration. You can draw upon research activities in *Step 4*.
- *Resources needed*: Financial, technical, logistical, formal, and other requirements to make the activity happen.
- *Tasks*: The items that someone needs to perform to carry out the activity. You may make these as detailed or as broad as you like, depending on your context. The sample activities we provide are somewhere in the middle.
- *Indicators of success*: Results of the activity that will show whether or not it does what you hoped it would.
- *Big-picture analysis*: In order to identify which of the seven steps are present in this activity, make three lists following Figure 5.1.

Big Picture		Steps included in activity
		Steps already taken outside the activity
		Plans for future steps

FIGURE 5.1. Big-picture analysis.

Fill in the graphic with (1) *Make Arts* steps included in the activity; (2) steps already taken outside the activity, such as someone else's analysis of an event (*Step 4*); and (3) plans for future steps to address anything that is missing.

Prepare to Draw on Familiar Methods of Composition

Every community and all creative individuals have patterns they follow to make art, and you want to draw on those as much as possible. Community members may compose individually, in a pair or group, with pencil and paper, in dreams or visions, on paid commission, with spontaneous improvisation, or through any number of methods.

As part of the preparation for the activity, perform some of the research in the section "Creativity" in Part C of *Step 4*. Ideally, you will be able to integrate some of these dynamics into the sparking activity; the familiarity will smooth the creation process and likely increase the quality of its products. On the other hand, people are usually agile in adopting new methods. The activity you and the community design will likely include both familiar and new kinds of invention.

Think Carefully about the Meristem

A meristem is the region in a plant in which new cells are created—the growth point. Likewise, the growth point in artistic production usually consists of one person (or a few key people), the person from whose mind and body the art actually emerges (see also "Artists" in Part C of *Step 4*). In our sparking activities, she is the crux of creativity. Her skill and reputation may also exert the most influence on how others respond to her new art.

Thus when the community chooses the composers (we include everyone who creates something, including painters, weavers, and the like), they should look for people who are already recognized as having experience and skill in creating within a genre. There may be many such qualified people to choose from, or only a few. The choice of certain artistic genres may automatically determine the gender or age of the composer and performer. Local people will be able to make a list of potential experienced composers.

In some cultures, there is already an established role for composers who create arts for other people. There may be a local praise singer, for instance a *jali* in Mande-speaking areas of West Africa, or there may be royal court musicians. Find out if an institutionalized form of composing for patrons is already in place. Note that these professional composers are used to working for some form of compensation.

Identify Opportunities to Maximize and Barriers to Overcome

In a discussion about music developments in Nairobi, Kenya, staff members from the street rehabilitation project Daraja identified divisions between the following types of listeners: older listeners who reside in rural areas or maintain ties (emotional or physical) with these areas and who listen to music in local languages; youth, many of whom listen to hip-hop; and those who can afford cars, who often purchase foreign music (modified from Van Buren 2007). These types of divisions may explain the choice of potential audience members to attend or dismiss events.

In developing arts initiatives, it is important to identify barriers and opportunities in the community associated with a particular genre. The following lists provide a few common examples of each.

Opportunities include the following:

- talented artists eager to use their gifts in new contexts;
- government interest in promoting local art forms;
- growing recognition of the value of local arts and fear for their loss in the wider community;
- a respected champion of local arts in the community who could lead innovation.

Barriers include the following:

- negative attitudes toward use of certain languages and art forms in some domains, either due to urbanization and globalization or for other reasons;
- lack of knowledge and skills associated with a genre;
- lack of finances for artistic productions;
- apathy toward change in the community.

After discussing these examples with members of the community, ask:

- What might help us spark a flowering of new works in this genre? How could we draw on these opportunities when designing a sparking activity?
- What might stop us from achieving this flowering? How could we overcome these barriers when designing a sparking activity?

Include the results of this conversation in the Community Arts Profile.

Decide on the Type of Activity

In this section, we present overviews and help for several different types of activities that spark creativity. We also point you to more resources when available. *Closing* 7 contains additional resources that may point you to helpful activities.

Commissioning

We define *commission* as follows: to charge an artist or group of artists with the task of creating a new instance of an artistic genre for an agreed-upon purpose.

Commissioning commonly consists of these steps:

1. With the community, identify the following:

   - the event for which the item will be created;
   - the purpose(s) for the created item (e.g., literacy or community development);
   - the genre(s) of creation (e.g., *haiku, olonkho,* or Broadway musical);
   - the content;
   - the creator(s); and
   - sources of funding or other necessary resources.

2. Then

   - work with the maker(s) in the creative process, including evaluation and revision of the work(s);
   - prepare the rest of the community and the event organizers for a public presentation;
   - explore other distribution means, including recordings; and
   - explore ways that this work, and others like it, can enter into other domains of the community's life.

Respect and trust in your relationship with the creators are crucial to the commissioning process. Ask confidants what sort of compensation is appropriate for the artist, genre, and event. Compensation may be in the form of money, services, goods, social capital, or goodwill borne of friendship.

It is also important to think through the commissioner's roles during the composition process. Who will decide what aspects of the artwork are effective for the intended purpose, and what needs to be changed? How much freedom will the artist have to innovate? As much as possible, the commissioner and artist should agree on these issues before the composition process begins.

One other curious case arises: Can you commission yourself to create something? Spark yourself? Certainly people decide to compose new things on their own. We encourage this, but argue that you should always act in relationship to a community. It is much better to include gatekeepers early in the making of new works so that everyone has a stake in its success.

Workshops

Workshops are short events—typically one or two weeks—that gather people to make progress together on a particular task. Workshops produce a ferment of productivity when participants interact with each other in a concentrated way. Consider a workshop when there is an organization in a community that can provide logistics and goals that will motivate participants to set aside the rest of their lives for a while; examples of such organizations include cultural associations, schools, churches, and nongovernmental organizations (NGOs). Listen carefully to views within the community and, guided by community members, choose the organization wisely.

There are many potential goals for workshops that draw on artistic communication: to compose songs for a particular cultural or community event, to create and record works with dramatic content to be distributed through radio or other media, to weave cloths communicating health messages—the possibilities are endless.

Planning an Arts Workshop

An arts workshop gathers a community's artists, social and political leaders, and content experts to (1) reflect on their local artistic resources; (2) specify community needs; (3) imagine how they can use their artistic resources to help respond to some of these needs; (4) produce samples of artistic enactments that may meet these needs; and (5) plan for the integration of these creations into community life, and contexts for continued artistic creativity.

Long-Term Impact

Ideally, this workshop would help spark the emergence or enhancement (i.e., solidification, deepening, broadening) of a sustainable tradition of artistic composition and enactment that responds to a community's spiritual, social, and physical needs.

People to Invite

- *Community leaders and gatekeepers*: Participation of community leaders makes it more likely that innovations resulting from the workshop will be accepted. In addition, participation of these leaders helps ensure that they grow in understanding and respect for people with artistic gifts, and makes it more likely that these leaders will encourage continued creativity.

- *Artistic experts*: Participation of composers, performers, and other gifted people helps ensure artistic excellence.
- *Content experts*: Participation of people knowledgeable in whatever content is going to be communicated helps ensure the trustworthiness of artistic messages produced. These might include linguists, medical professionals, agriculturalists, and others. It may also be valuable to include these experts in any final events. For example, an artistic performance may be followed by a question-and-answer session in which audience members can ask the performers and content experts about issues that were raised in the performance.

Notes on Invitees

1. One person may play more than one of these roles, though it is usually better to include more people.
2. Not everyone needs to participate in every aspect of the workshop. It may be appropriate, for example, to invite a government leader just to opening and closing ceremonies.
3. When possible, it is important to incorporate appropriate diversity, for example in gender, dialect, age, denomination, and region.
4. It also may be appropriate to invite other types of people for all or parts of the workshop: media people, recordists, NGO representatives, government representatives, cooks, and note-takers.

Outcomes

At the end of this workshop, participants should have

- written descriptions of the various artistic genres in their community;
- audio, video, or photographic recordings of at least one new artistic work that draws directly on their local artistic systems;
- an example of any new object that was produced, such as a painting, mask, or tapestry; and
- written plans for expanded and sustained artistic creativity that responds to community needs.

Methodologies

Whenever possible, workshop leaders should use teaching methods that require high engagement by participants—such as those found in the Learning that Lasts approach (http://learningthatlasts.org).

Elements

Workshop Group Cohesion

We want to create a context of conviviality, mutual aid and support, and common vision and mission, in accordance with local social norms.

Research Artistic Resources

- Refer to or add to the Community Arts Profile, helping participants find this kind of information about events: settings, occasions, participants, material culture, social meanings, and formal features.
- Photograph, audio-, or videorecord examples of the relevant genre(s) to use as a references.

Specify Goal

If the exact purpose of the workshop has not already been determined, perform the participatory activity in *Step 2: Specify Goals*.

Spark Creativity

1. Help participants evaluate the list of artistic genres according to their capacity to communicate the desired content clearly, memorably, and reproducibly, and in terms of the existence, location, and availability of experts (composers, performers, knowledgeable audiences, etc.) in the genre. Choose one genre to communicate the desired message.
2. Describe this genre more deeply using "Take a First Glance at an Event" (*Step 4*, Part A).
3. Discuss and identify content that speaks to the community need identified.
4. Compose an event (or series of events) that contains all of the elements of the genre you have described most fully in "Take a First Glance at an Event." State the goals of this event clearly. This composition will contain some new and modified elements to accomplish its goals.

5. Photograph, audio-, or videorecord elements of the event that can be isolated for memory and evaluation.
6. Describe the composed event.

Improve Creations

As recorded, described, and/or performed for workshop participants, compare enactments to a researched description of local enactments in the same or similar genres. Is the enactment done well? Is the message clear? Is the message true? Refer to *Step 6*.

Integrate

Plan for the dissemination of works created in the workshop. Then plan for continued creativity, perhaps through the formation of composition groups.

Celebrate

If possible and appropriate, present the composed event for a local occasion at the end of the workshop.

Sample Workshop Schedule

Figure 5.2 shows a week-long workshop schedule that integrates each of the seven *Make Arts* steps. This approach has the instructors describing and demonstrating each step, then letting participants perform that step in smaller groups. It is also possible to devote the first half of the week to a demonstration of the whole process and the second half to participants applying the steps to small group contexts.

Notes on the Workshop

- Staff meeting every day at 14:00
- "Arts Together" session every morning consists of participants teaching others an example of an art form they identify with and value.

Possible Additional Topics for a Two-Week Workshop

- How to help your people make more arts
- Further notes on evaluating your artistic creations and how to improve them
- How to record your artistic creations.

	Sunday	Monday	Tuesday	Wednesday	Thursday	Friday	Saturday
08:00		Arts together	Arts together	Arts together	Arts together	Arts together	Arts together
08:30		01 Intro to the workshop	05 Select goals	09 Analyze an event	13 In groups : Create works for the goal	16 Plan for integration	19 Final recording, workshop evaluations
10:00		Break	Break	Break	Break	Break	Collect evaluations, distribute travel money (per diem)
10:30		02 Meet a community and its arts	06 In groups : select community goals	10 In groups : Analyze an event	14 Improve new works	17 In groups: Plan for integration	
12:30		Meal	Meal	Meal	Meal	Meal	
14:00		Staff meeting	Staff meeting	Staff meeting	Staff meeting	Staff meeting	Staff meeting
14:30	Opening ceremony	03 In groups : describe community and arts	07 Select effects, content, genre, and events	11 Spark creativity	15 In groups: Improve new works ; record drafts	18 Final recording/ evaluation	Closing ceremony Performance and celebration of new works
15:30		04 In groups : describe community and arts	08 In groups: Select effects, content, genre, and events	12 In groups : Create works for the goal			
16:30	Meal	Meal	Meal	Meal	Meal	Meal	

FIGURE 5.2. Sample workshop schedule.

Showcase Events

You may help a community plan or run a festival or competition that highlights creativity in local artistic genres.[1] Festivals are events designed to showcase a community's cultural identity and creative output. Many ethnic groups already have celebratory gatherings that may be open to including new works of art. It also may be possible to start a new festival tradition fueled by a newfound celebration of artistic gifts. Prizes for the best new works, selected by community members, can add energy and excitement to such events. Festivals also provide great opportunities for cooperation between different government, cultural, religious, and other groups within a community.

Showcase events normally emerge from a five-phase process:

1. *Imagining and planning*: How will we get from here to there? The larger the event, the more planning it requires—theoretically. Some communities excel in creating detailed schedules and goals. Other communities excel in pulling together fabulous celebrations through organic social dynamics. Contribute ideas, but do not impose a system.
2. *Promotion and networking*: How can we ensure the participation of key artists and a wide public? Festivals sometimes incorporate contests or prizes to motivate artists. Make sure to clearly communicate the types of arts that will be rewarded and how they will be evaluated.
3. *Composition and preparation*: Will artists have time and resources to create and practice their performance?
4. *Running the event.*
5. *Evaluation and planning*: A big event requires a dedicated time afterward to graciously evaluate with key people how it went. It is also an excellent moment to see how the event relates to all of the seven *Make Arts* steps and to discuss the possibility of similar future events.

Mentoring

Sometimes mentoring relationships can occur between arts advocates and artists or groups of artists. Such relationships often develop over time from personal rapport and common goals. Mentoring relationships can develop in two directions: (1) because of your age, education, or social position, you may be able to open doors to new opportunities or to share stories from your own experiences that can benefit an artist or group of artists; and (2) local artists can do all the same things for *you*, as well as teach you artistic skills and cultural insights.

Apprenticeship

Apprenticeship consists of providing a structure consistent with existing cultural forms where artistic experts can transfer their skills and knowledge to other members of their community. Structured apprenticeship makes sense when experts in the genre exist, contexts for transfer of competencies in the genre are declining, and community members value the genre.

A community may institute such a program in this way:

1. Choose the genre to be taught.
2. Choose a master of the genre.
3. Choose the apprentices.
4. Design a training context that (a) draws on familiar educational forms; (b) includes a place, time, and frequency that the master and apprentices can commit to; (c) covers the knowledge, skills, and attitudes crucial to the genre; and (d) lasts long enough for apprentices to reach a sustainable level of competency.
5. Implement the program.
6. During the program, explore how participants can continue to develop their skills and create in various contexts.

Publications

Almost any activity will have more long-term success if it turns thoughts and artistic production into media other than live performance. Paper, recordings, and electronic data of all kinds allow ideas and artistry to live beyond a single moment and to reach people beyond a single place. Periodicals and websites make it possible to disseminate information and inspire discussion on a wide range of topics. Audio and video products can be used to provide content for training programs and entertainment. Publications become repositories of history and biography when people begin to forget what came before them.

General aspects to planning a publication include the following:

1. Determine the target audience.
2. Identify editors, advisors, and contributors.
3. Solicit, select, and prepare the materials to be published.
4. Determine a scheme for the distribution of the publication.
5. Determine a schedule for ongoing publication.

6. Carry out the publication and distribution.
7. Develop and use feedback tools (e.g., electronic comments, letters to the editor, surveys, etc.) to help determine past effectiveness and plan for future developments.

In the early 2000s, Ferdinand Doumtsop, Hubert Sob Lontsi, and several friends in their teens and twenties saw that they and their age-mates growing up in their rural Ngiemboon kingdom (West Cameroon, Africa) were moving to large cities. This urban move took them out of the context where they would have learned the knowledge and skills that had been essential to being a Ngiemboon person for many generations. Thus they formed PROMOCUL (Group for the Promotion of Ngiemboon Culture) and launched a periodical news and culture journal focused on their ethnolinguistic community, Ngiemboon. Its name, *Mûɔ lá'*, means "child of our village." *Mûɔ lá'* (see Figure 5.3) contains articles describing Ngiemboon traditions, proverbs, specialty foods, interviews with older tradition-bearers, charts connecting calendars based on the traditional eight-day Ngiemboon week with those representing the international seven-day week, descriptions of musical instruments and carved masks, articles in both French and Ngiemboon, news of cultural events, and many other topics. Hubert Sob Lontsi says this in an editorial (*Mûɔ lá'* 1:8; Brian Schrag's translation from French):

In other times, knowing our own customs and traditions was the least of our concerns. Young people mostly grew up in the village around their parents, accompanying them to many ceremonies where they discovered—through discussions and events—the true face of their culture. Four centuries since the Ngiemboon people settled on the south east of the Bamboutos mountains, the situation has reversed and many people are vigorously pleading for the cultural library open to all to learn Ngiemboon knowledge and wisdom. This entreaty has become extremely important because of the rural exodus of youth from the countryside to the cities. For proof, let's climb to where traditional ceremonies take place and see the people who are in a mess because they don't have enough information to avoid scandal and deception. Listen to these complaints: "I haven't done things yet," "I don't understand anything," "people tricked me." . . . The PROMOCUL group, composed mostly of Ngiemboon youth, offer a stopgap measure by giving everything they've got to teaching the Ngiemboon language, promoting traditional arts and music. . . .

The journal is supported primarily by donations and advertising.

FIGURE 5.3. Front page of *Mûɔ lá'* journal.

Creators' Clubs

Artists form associations, clubs, and fellowships to encourage each other, critique each others' work, share resources and ideas, perform, and collaborate on products. Groups like these meet regularly in certain places and times, have expectations—however modest—of each other, and often center on a particular art form and purpose. In Western Cameroon, scores of Ngiemboon associations meet each week to practice and improve songs in one of a dozen traditional dance genres.

Each group will look different, but you should consider the following subjects when starting or assisting with a new group:

- A meeting place and time that accommodates the members and allows for artistic activity;
- A discussion of the goals for the group and expectations of its members. This could vary from fluid and informal to strict and explicit, depending on the group's wishes.

Design a New or Modify an Existing Activity

In this section, we describe a number of sparking activities that you can use as models, organized according to the goals in *Step 2*. They are all distilled from actual experience but leave most of the details for you to complete for your context; in particular, we seldom include resources you need, since they are so often dependent on the local context. You may also choose to design a new activity, making sure to address each of the components we have described in the preceding: title and summary, participants, information you will need from the Community Arts Profile, resources needed, tasks, indicators of success, and big-picture analysis.

Refer often to the Big Picture graphic (Figure 5.1) to help you note the place of the activity in the seven-step *Make Arts* process. Finally, we plan to post reports of implemented sparking activities on the Guide's website ().

Identity and Sustainability

Communities can promote positive cultural identity through local arts by organizing cultural celebrations (such as concerts, festivals, contests, etc.), documenting (through written descriptions, audio recordings, photography, and video), and publishing (on locally distributable media, websites, etc.). These activities should always be done with the leading and input of key community members and artists, and always in a way that will be accessible and appreciated by the community.

Activity: Meet a Community and Its Arts, Again

Your activities in gathering information about a community's arts that we have described in *Step 1* may in themselves increase a positive sense of identity. Go back and fill in some gaps.

Activity: Help Organize a Festival Celebrating Community Art Forms

The purpose of this activity is to encourage and invigorate the use of local arts in a community. A festival can raise the status of local arts, aid in their preservation, encourage innovation, and bring about positive changes.

Participants

Invite individuals from as many different social, age, and economic groups as possible, including community leaders, religious leaders, skilled artists, members of older generations, and younger people with a passion for their culture. By including all of these groups, the festival will more likely bring about lasting artistic change, particularly if younger people are engaged.

Information You Will Need from the Community Arts Profile

A list of artistic genres ("Take a First Glance at a Community's Arts," *Step 1*) and event descriptions ("Take a First Glance at an Event," *Step 4*, Part A) that include as many genres as possible.

Resources Needed

Dependent on the local context.

Tasks

1. *Initial community meeting*: Meet with community representatives to discuss the list of artistic genres, to ask and offer reasons why they are valuable, and to discuss the benefits that a festival celebrating these arts could provide.
2. *Logistics*: After initial commitment to a festival, discuss goals and plans through questions such as:
   a. Who will organize the festival? Work toward broad inclusion and unity.
   b. What items need to be in the budget and how much will it be? Who will underwrite the budget?
   c. Which arts will be promoted? Who are the influential and respected artists who should be included? Who is in charge of inviting them?
   d. Shall the festival include competitions for new works?
   e. When should the festival take place? Should it be included as part of another regular cultural event, ritual, or festival?
   f. How do participants wish to use photographs, audio-, and videorecordings? The organizing group should plan to obtain any necessary government or local permissions from authorities, and permissions from artists for the future use of recordings (see "Sample Permission Form," *Closing 3*).
3. *Implement the plans.*
4. *Evaluate*: After the festival, meet with the organizers or a larger community forum.
   a. Evaluate community involvement, quality of the artistic works, and overall successful and unsuccessful aspects of the event. What parts of the festival are the community excited about? Did anything catch their attention?
   b. Decide whether the festival should become a regular event.

c. Explore how the community can draw on the excitement and new works for other purposes. Did new purposes for traditional arts emerge? For example, it might be more possible after the festival to promote local arts for use in health education. Plan for more activities that feed into community goals.

d. Plan to create products from recordings of aspects of the festival, such as DVDs, a website, storybook, collection of poetry, or song books. There also might be interest in developing a Community Arts Archive housed locally or in a government or educational organization (see the activity "Help Develop Multimedia Collections of Local Arts" later in *Step 5*). Ensure that community members offer their perspectives on these activities; in some cases, community members may be interested in a local archive but may be wary of public distribution of their works.

Your roles as an arts advocate will vary according to the skills and needs of the community. You may be able to contribute through making and organizing audio and videorecordings, obtaining authorizations for use, and in providing international perspective on the value of the community's arts. You could also publish an article about the festival, an artist, or a particular tradition. If you are an outsider to an artistic tradition, you might lend prestige by learning to perform one of the showcased genres. Approach this humbly, though, to ensure that your efforts to learn and perform are viewed positively.

Big Picture		Steps included in activity
		Steps already taken outside the activity
		Plans for future steps

⊛ Activity: Commission a New Work in an Older Genre for an Existing Showcase Event

Older artistic traditions lose value in communities in part because social changes make them less common, and thus less visible. One way to counteract this is by commissioning new works that are shown or performed in contexts like festivals, religious events, radio and TV programs, or concerts. It is important to ensure that the new work is of high quality, and that people are able to connect practically and emotionally with it.

Participants

Expert(s) in an older artistic genre, and organizers of a community event.

Information You Will Need from the Community Arts Profile

Description of an event in the commissioning genre using "Take a First Glance at an Event" (*Step 4*, Part A). You can follow other research paths that seem relevant in "Look at an Event's Forms" (*Step 4*, Part A) and "Explore the Event's Genre(s) through Artistic Domain Categories" (*Step 4*, Part B). You will also want to explore a few subsections such as "Artists," "Creativity," "Aesthetics and Evaluation," "Emotions," and "Community Values" shown in "Relate the Event's Genre(s) to Its Broader Cultural Context" (*Step 4*, Part C).

Resources Needed

Dependent on the local context.

Tasks

1. With friends and colleagues, identify an influential community event that would provide an appropriate setting for new types of arts. Then explore what artistic genre and artist(s) would be most likely to result in positive responses and excitement within the community.
2. Conversely, you might know an artist well and decide to look for an event where a work in his or her genre could be showcased.
3. Work with the artist(s) in the creation of a prototype of something new.
4. Communicate with the event organizer(s) in locally appropriate ways. Explain that you and others hope to increase the profile and positive identity associated with the community's heritage. Bring an audio, video, or photographic recording of what the artist created. Invite the organizer(s) to help shape the content or form to better meet community goals. (Be aware that organizers and artists may have different ideas about content and form, so this process may require diplomatic negotiation and/or prior agreement on how conflicts will be managed.)
5. Follow procedures associated with the event in preparations, rehearsal, payment, and other logistics.
6. After the event, meet with the artist(s) and organizer(s). Review how everything went and discuss whether this type of commissioning could become integrated into future events.

Big Picture		**Steps included in activity**
		Steps already taken outside the activity
		Plans for future steps

✦ Activity: Help Develop Multimedia Collections of Local Arts

This activity is intended to raise the status and visibility of a community's arts by showcasing them in a multimedia collection. This collection will allow the community access to past performances, help them teach new artists, innovate for the future, and encourage the continued use of their arts (see ARSC 2016; Boerger et al. 2017; Seeger and Chaduri 2004).

Participants

Recordists, administrative help, artists, and people with technical expertise and access to technical resources.

Information You Will Need from the Community Arts Profile

A list of artistic genres ("Take a First Glance at a Community's Arts," *Step 1*), event descriptions ("Take a First Glance at an Event," *Step 4*, Part A) that include as many genres as possible, and a list of key artists associated with each genre.

Resources Needed

Multimedia collections are often expensive and require technical skills and equipment. Before beginning a project like this, consider whether

- there is already someone with the needed skills and equipment (computer training, recording training, etc.)—otherwise someone will need to be trained in how to create and maintain the collection;
- there is equipment available, such as computers, speakers, projectors, and recording devices;
- there are partners (individuals or organizations) with access to technical resources and training;
- there is ongoing funding and availability of personnel for maintaining and developing the collection.

You will also need to consider where the collection will be kept. Is there an existing building or organization in the area, or will a building and/or infrastructure need to be created? These items are essential to plan for because this is not a cheap or easy project to create and maintain; many archives have disintegrated due to lack of continued funding and training resources. However, this activity can be incredibly beneficial to a community; even a very limited collection is better than no collection at all.

Many examples of multimedia collections exist. Well-known archives featuring sound recordings and images from around the world are housed, for example, at the British Library (see http://sounds.bl.uk/), Indiana University (see http://www.indiana.edu/~libarchm/), and the University of California, Los Angeles (see https://archive.org/details/uclaethnomusicologyarchive).

Tasks

1. Identify the purpose(s). Before beginning, the collection needs to have a purpose. Is this going to be a collection of local genres of stories, songs, stools, or rite of passage dances created by community members? Is this an archive for audio- and videorecordings of ceremonies? If we are going to include physical items such as clothing or sculptures or musical instruments, do we need a large space to store and/or display them? Are the items in the collection loanable or shareable?

The community's needs and desires are crucial to the creation of a multimedia collection. For example, they may want digital audio files to put on their mobile devices. Or they may be interested in having a place where groups of people could come watch videos of ceremonies being performed by experts. They may prefer a paper-based library, with photographs and local-language books, stories, folk tales, and poetry. Community members may want a place to store and display important items while they are not being used—instead of the community's special attire and ceremonial musical instruments sitting packed away in between uses, why not have them on display?

This is a critical item because if the final product (collection) does not meet community members' desires and needs, the community will not have much use for it. The community *must* see value in this project for it to be anything more than an unused, dusty archive.

2. Identify the users. If this collection is to benefit the community, it needs to be easily accessible and usable. The audience needs to be identified.
3. Identify who will maintain the collection. Multimedia devices and formats are constantly changing, and the collection will always need

someone who is informed about technology and can keep the files available in the latest formats. The collection will quickly become useless to the community otherwise. Before beginning, either a person or an organization (government, library, NGO, etc.) needs to be identified that will become a partner in keeping this collection running and up to date.

4. Identify a location for the collection. Even in the digital age, a physical location is still needed. There is the possibility of housing the entire collection on a website, but that may require much funding and expertise. In addition, a web-only collection may not be very accessible to a community in a region with limited or inconsistent Internet access. The location could be something as simple as a desktop computer in a room.

5. Identify the media. Identify what devices people use to listen to audio, to watch videos, and to look at pictures. Do they own computers? Do they know how to use a computer? Do they have mobile devices that can play audio and video files? Do they use CDs or cassette tapes? DVDs or VCDs? Do they have their own tape, CD, and DVD players, or do these need to be available so people have a place to watch and listen? Would it be better to have a projector set up so that many people can watch a video at the same time, or is a computer monitor enough? Once the media are known, it is possible to set up the collection in the most accessible way possible.

6. Acquire recordings. Plan for and record or collect the artistry of key artists in the community.

Throughout research, constantly provide the community with products of research (audio- and videorecordings, photographs, etc.). If you have the technical skills needed, providing the community with small "products" throughout your work can really help them to understand the benefits of the process, and to see how a central collection for such material could be a great benefit to them. For instance, as you make field recordings, burn a CD and give it to the person you just recorded. If you record a formal event or ceremony, burn a DVD/VCD and give it to the community leaders as a gift. Sometimes these sorts of gifts can create a powerful motivation from within the community itself.

Big Picture		Steps included in activity
		Steps already taken outside the activity
		Plans for future steps

⭐ Activity: Publish Recordings and Research in Various Forms and Contexts

Publishing helps people identify and promote what they value to local, regional, national, and international communities. Although here we discuss presentations through booklets, websites, and academic articles, media could also include books, CDs, DVDs, concerts, social media, and so on. This activity dovetails well with the preceding "Help Develop Multimedia Collections of Local Arts" activity.

Participants

Depending on the publishing format, you may need to include a web designer, recordist, photographer, printer, editor, or others. Involve community leaders and artists.

Information You Will Need from the Community Arts Profile

A list of artistic genres ("Take a First Glance at a Community's Arts," *Step 1*), event descriptions ("Take a First Glance at an Event," *Step 4*, Part A) that include as many genres as possible, and a list of key artists associated with each genre.

Resources Needed

Dependent on the local context.

Tasks

Website
With artists and community leaders:

1. Create a prototype site with these sections: Meet *Name* Communities; Contexts for *Name* Artistic Communication; Cultural Initiatives Using *Name* Arts; Conversations about *Name* Arts; Other Resources Related to *Name* Arts.
2. Discuss the site and its social context with community stakeholders. Show prototype to a small group of primary stakeholders, discussing issues such as these:
   a. Should the community's arts be shown to a wider group through a website like this? If so, who are target audiences and purposes?
   b. Who should control the website's content? Process of publishing? Management of the site? Technical implementation?
   c. What personal and legal permissions are needed to publish the website?

    d. How should the presentation change?

3. Create a plan in which the community takes control of the website.

Booklet

With artists and community leaders:

1. List the art forms that they would most like to share with others.
2. Identify the target audience(s).
3. Choose overall booklet design, visual representations of each art form
    (e.g., sketch or photograph), and writers of texts explaining each
    art form.
4. Identity publisher, funding, number to print, and distribution plan.

Academic Article

1. Identify audience as regional, national, or international.
2. Identify several organizations likely to publish information about the
    community's arts.
3. Identify one or two people who are capable of writing an article satisfying
    the standards of the organization's publication. If no one within the com-
    munity has these skills, a trusted outside researcher may fill this role. It
    may be appropriate to co-write the article with a community expert.
4. Write the article, modifying it according to the suggestions of important
    community stakeholders.
5. Submit the article according to the organization's and publication's
    requirements.

		Steps included in activity
		Steps already taken outside the activity
		Plans for future steps

Activity: Identify and Mend Ruptures in Transmission from Older
to Younger People

Participants

Include people from as many segments of the community as possible, such as older
and younger community members, urban and rural community members, leaders,
local artists of many kinds, and teachers.

Information You Will Need from the Community Arts Profile

A list of artistic genres ("Take a First Glance at a Community's Arts," *Step 1*), and an understanding of transmission (see "Transmission and Change," *Step 4*, Part C).

Resources Needed

Dependent on the local context.

Tasks

1. Using participatory methods, mediate a discussion of topics like these (see "Steps to Specifying Goals" in *Step 2*; for further discussion, also see Saurman and Saurman 2004):
   a. What kinds of local wisdom and arts do you have in your communities?
   b. What is still strong? Why?
   c. What is being lost? Why?
   d. Is there anything you want to protect from being lost?
   e. How have wisdom and arts been passed on in the past? Does this process continue? If not, what caused the process to stop?
2. With this discussion as background, explore actions the community might take to help pass on this information to the youth and children of the community. These could include modifying older education systems (such as initiation schools), or tying into newer community channels (like government schools). Community members also may establish new systems like community groups or public opportunities where older adults teach younger adults and children about playing instruments, storytelling styles, dances, poetry creation, and so on.
3. Make an action plan and discuss who will take responsibility for carrying it out.

Big Picture		Steps included in activity
		Steps already taken outside the activity
		Plans for future steps

Health and Well-Being

The *Make Arts* approach dovetails well with therapeutic disciplines using arts to increase individual and community well-being. For example, community music is "a musical practice that is an active intervention between a music leader or

facilitator and participants" (Higgins 2012:21), fostering inclusive musical participation as an "expression of cultural democracy" (Higgins and Willingham 2017:1).
Related disciplines include music therapy (Borczon 2004), dance therapy (Chaiklin
and Wengrower 2015), expressive arts therapy (Levine and Levine 2011), art therapy
(Kaplan 2006; Rubin 2016), drama therapy, and community arts. You will find the literature by practitioners in these fields rich in additional examples of activities related
to healing. Two resources are especially helpful because they are available for free online: *Art Became the Oxygen* (Goldbard 2017), which provides guidance in using arts in
response to disasters and other crises; and *The National Endowment for the Arts Guide
to Community-Engaged Research in Arts and Health* (Chapline and Johnson 2016).

Therapeutic approaches can benefit from integrating ethnographic and research
activities from the *Make Arts* process. Delving more completely into clients' lives
and arts allows therapists to spark more deeply rooted creativity that can result in
more enduring healing. At the 2017 World Congress of the International Council
for Traditional Music, a small group of scholars working in both ethnomusicology
and arts therapies formed a group with this purpose (Vrekalić et al. 2017):

> We want to develop and disseminate ethnomusicology and health-based
> concepts and methods that will increase the effectiveness of the work of
> music, dance, and expressive arts therapists. By "ethnomusicology-based,"
> we refer to therapies with two primary characteristics. First, their methods
> need to flow fundamentally from a posture of learning. This is borne out in
> therapists performing ethnography with clients, asking questions informed
> by cultural anthropology about how families work, how music takes on sym-
> bolic meanings, how arts can both reflect and transform lives, how creativity
> happens, and so on. Second, such therapies intentionally engage with the
> forms and features of the arts in a person's life. This may include exploring an
> artistic genre's normal performance practices, relationship to events, struc-
> ture, capacity to include different types of improvisation, and instruments
> and other materials involved.

⊛ Activity: Organize a Trauma Healing Workshop

First a word of caution: Where wounds are deep within an individual or a community, we must tread extremely carefully. Arts can "help us find our ability to make
a new world together" and arts can actually help make that new world (Levine and
Levine 2011:29). In other words, the arts can be a powerful means to help people
acknowledge and express the hurt they have experienced, and to help people move
past this hurt as individuals and as parts of a larger community. We may be eager to

be part of this process, but we need to think carefully about our skills and our limitations. Where we are trained in arts but not in therapy or counseling, we may need to acquire additional training or partner with others trained in these areas. Consult the resources listed in the following and think ahead before launching into an activity.

Participants

Include local leaders (thinking carefully about implications if leaders have been involved in the trauma), victims of any kind of trauma, and experienced facilitators where possible. In some cases, with careful planning, perpetrators of trauma may also be included to help facilitate communication and healing between victims and perpetrators; this has been the case, for example, in northern Uganda (see Harada's case study in Foundations).

Information You Will Need from the Community Arts Profile

A list of artistic genres ("Take a First Glance at a Community's Arts," *Step 1*), and an understanding of emotional connections to artistry (see "Emotions," *Step 4*, Part C). Explore in more depth how people in the community mourn, express strong emotions through various arts, use rituals to pass through difficult times, and use rituals to promote a sense of solidarity.

Resources Needed

A variety of resources provide further discussion and case studies from around the world. Examples include *Art in Action* (Levine and Levine 2011), *Mass Trauma and Violence* (Webb 2004), and *Healing the Wounds of Trauma* (Hill et al. 2016).

Tasks

These are broad kinds of tasks. Consult the preceding resources for specific examples of how the arts can be used in trauma healing.

1. Gather people traumatized by war, disease, fears, or anything else.
2. Consider the needs within the community. These might include rebuilding a sense of community and celebration, or helping individuals mourn, or both. As Stephen K. Levine reminds us, "Both our tears and our laughter hold us together" (Levine and Levine 2011:29).
3. Consider whether there are any existing arts-based healing rituals in the community that might be useful or whether new healing rituals should be created.

4. Lead participants through arts-based healing exercises.
5. Help leaders translate lessons into their community's language, if necessary.
6. Ensure post-workshop support (e.g., counseling) is available to community members.
7. Train community members to facilitate trauma healing workshops for others.

Big Picture		Steps included in activity
		Steps already taken outside the activity
		Plans for future steps

Activity: Commission Local Artists to Address Community Health Problems

In 2004, Kathleen witnessed one of a series of collaborations in Nairobi, Kenya, between members of the Family Programmes Promotion Services puppetry program and Médecins sans Frontières (MSF)/Doctors without Borders. The puppeteers explained that organizations such as MSF would identify a theme, then the puppeteers would develop skits about this theme, and finally the puppeteers would present the skits to the organization for approval before they finalized a contract.

Held near a market area in the low-income community of Kibera, the event that Kathleen attended included puppetry skits about HIV and AIDS, recorded and live music, a talk and condom demonstration and distribution by two doctors representing MSF, and a question-and-answer session. The skits raised a variety of issues related to HIV and AIDS, and the doctors assisted the puppeteers in answering audience questions. The puppeteers and doctors directed audience members to a local MSF clinic for further resources. The puppeteers explained that each event is different, but in this case a large crowd gathered and audience members were highly engaged and not afraid to ask potentially sensitive questions.

Here are some suggestions for developing programs that, like the previous example from Kenya, involve artists in addressing health issues within communities:

Participants

When possible, partner with existing NGOs and local groups and artists already addressing health needs in their communities. Include expert creators of artistic genres chosen and experts in the health information they wish to communicate.

Information You Will Need from the Community Arts Profile

A list of artistic genres ("Take a First Glance at a Community's Arts," *Step 1*) and how people create in the chosen genre ("Creativity," *Step 4*, Part C). Explore in more depth how people in the community use art forms to pass on trustworthy and important information and types of content associated with a genre ("Subject Matter," *Step 4*, Part C).

Resources Needed

Dependent on the local context.

Tasks

1. Gather artists, community leaders, and health experts who are concerned about the health problem.
2. Decide together who should create the new artistry, what the content should be, and how it should be disseminated.
3. The creator(s) makes a prototype of the new artistry in a comfortable setting and time frame, and presents it to the advocacy group. Evaluate and improve the artistry (see *Step 6*).
4. Ensure that material and emotional support is available to community members post-performance (e.g., health centers, doctors and counselors, medical supplies).
5. Implement the events in which the artistry will be expressed.
6. Plan for continued methods of creating arts to address physical and social needs.

Big Picture		Steps included in activity
		Steps already taken outside the activity
		Plans for future steps

⭐ Activity: Organize a Special Event to Play Traditional Games

Although the focus of this activity is on play and recreation, games and sporting events also feed into increasing a community's sense of well-being; valuing of their identity; developing solidarity; and transmitting language, values, and history to more people.

Participants

Include experts in the game genre, children, parents, community leaders, and good organizers.

Information You Will Need from the Community Arts Profile

The community has chosen an artistic genre that includes competition or communal play. Analyze an entire event to identify its artistry. This may exist in the form itself, in costumes or equipment, or in special artistic communication that participants and others perform before, during, or after an event. Also ask friends about how they view play, leisure, and competition.

Resources Needed

Dependent on the local context.

Tasks

1. Gather a small group to organize the special event.
2. Decide the date, time, location, order of events, and celebration of those who excel (if appropriate).
3. Decide who to invite and how to spread the word. If this is a new kind of event, start with a smaller group. If it catches on, such events could become bigger.
4. If many people who attend are unfamiliar with the game, explain its history and rules.

Big Picture		Steps included in activity
		Steps already taken outside the activity
		Plans for future steps

⊗ Activity: Hold an Alternatives to Violence Workshop

A key element of avoiding violence where there is hurt is preemptive conflict resolution. The aim is to creatively transform unhealthy relationships through sharing, caring, improved communication skills, and sometimes even surprise and humor.

Participants

People who live in communities where conflict is strong, but who want to avoid violence. A trained Alternatives to Violence facilitator could organize such a workshop. Alternatives to Violence is a network of volunteers who run workshops to teach people how to keep conflict from turning into violence (https://avp.international.org, accessed May 17, 2018).

Information You Will Need from the Community Arts Profile

Information on genres containing storytelling and dramatic elements.

Resources Needed

Alternatives to Violence volunteers.

Tasks

Role plays and other forms of drama allow persons to explore possible approaches to different forms of conflict. Important insights are gained through the role plays, which are flexibly adapted and include debriefing as they run, helping those involved to assess and digest whatever is learned.

Big Picture		Steps included in activity
		Steps already taken outside the activity
		Plans for future steps

Human Rights

 Activity: Hold Workshops That Allow Marginalized People to Be Heard

Questioning power relationships can be dangerous. This activity should be carried out with much patience and as widespread community involvement as possible.

Participants

A group of people in a community who suffer from being outside social power structures. Common categories include women, members of minority ethnic groups, children, handicapped, or poor people. If possible, also include members of the community who are not marginalized. This breaks down "othering" and promotes respect between groups.

Information You Will Need from the Community Arts Profile

A list of artistic genres ("Take a First Glance at a Community's Arts," *Step 1*), a general understanding of power relationships between different community subgroups, and a specific understanding of how certain artistic genres are used to promote or circumvent power relationships ("Identity and Power," *Step 4*, Part C).

Resources Needed

Dependent on the local context.

Tasks

1. Talk individually to people who represent marginalized groups in the community, exploring what they think of themselves and how they are treated by others. Evaluate needs within the groups (e.g., whether these include increasing the self-confidence of group members or communicating grievances to other members of the community). Decide together how, when, and where to meet for a workshop.
2. Review the artistic genres that exist in the wider community and within their own sub-community(ies).
3. Evaluate each genre in terms of its potential to provide a sense of solidarity among people in the group.
4. Evaluate each genre in terms of its potential to uplift members of the marginalized groups and to safely communicate grievances to those in power. For example, during church services, women in the African Apostolic Church in southern Africa are allowed to admonish men for abusing them, without fear of retaliation (Jules-Rosette 1985). If such forms exist, discuss what messages the group wishes to communicate, and when they could communicate it.
5. As a group, or by identifying or commissioning an individual within the group, develop new artwork.
6. Plan for continued creativity and community-building activities.

Big Picture		Steps included in activity
		Steps already taken outside the activity
		Plans for future steps

⬡ Activity: Commission an Alphabet Song

Michelle Petersen and Pat Kelley (personal communication, June 30, 2016, and October 25, 2017) describe how song has been used in various parts of the world to help teach literacy:

> Among the Waodäni of Ecuador, some jungle animals make sounds that seem to simulate vowel sounds. The Waodäni used that feature in composing a call-and-response song to help teach the reading of the ten vowels in their language. The song gives questions and answers like: "What does the *odœ*/peccary/wild pig say? The wild pig says 'æ, æ, æ.'" "The young *iwä*/howler monkey says 'i, i, i.'" And so on.
>
> Other people, like the Quechua Ambo-Pasco of Peru, taught each letter of the alphabet with a word that begins with that letter. Their song says, "What are we going to learn today? We're going to learn our letters today. With A we say *algu* [dog]. With B we say *bandera* [flag]. With C we say *cuchi* [pig]." After every four letters, they repeat the question, "What are we going to learn today?"
>
> Others, like the Sango in Central Africa, created an alliterative poem associating each letter with a sentence that uses that letter many times. Each line of the poem repeats a new letter many times. The poem became the words to "The Sango Alphabet Song."

This activity shows you how to help a local composer create a new song in a familiar style that lists the building blocks of literacy skills—language sounds and letters.

Participants

Work with one or several teachers, songwriters, and/or poets who know a local style appropriate for teaching. At least one of these people needs to know how to write the language well, to write the composition down for others to learn.

Information You Will Need from the Community Arts Profile

Look at artistic genres of song that can have lots of repetition. Also consider the types of songs, riddles, or poems people use to teach children or adults.

Resources Needed

You need a recording device and means to distribute copies in the format you choose to help people learn the new song.

Tasks

1. Decide who your intended audience is. You may choose to make one alphabet song for everyone, or one for adults and another for children.

2. List all of the symbols in the alphabet on a sheet of paper. Choose words that begin with each of these sounds.

3. Discuss what kind of a song would best help people learn these symbols. If there is a call-and-response form, you may want to imitate that to ask questions and give answers that teach the letters with words or sentences. You could associate a word with each sound, or a sentence with each sound.

4. Ask someone talented in the song genre to compose a song that matches the words or sentences with a melody. The tune must be an appropriate kind of song for teaching your intended audience.

5. Discuss any potential problems; for example, words or sentences may be modified for musical reasons.

6. Test the new song with a few literacy students and literacy program leaders to make sure it is easy to remember, fun, and accepted. Revise it if you think of ways to make it better.

7. Plan how to teach teachers the new song so that they in turn can teach it to their students. Ask students to teach it to friends or family.

Big Picture		Steps included in activity
		Steps already taken outside the activity
		Plans for future steps

Activity: Commission Local Visual Art for Books and Literacy Materials

Participants

Local illustrators and book makers.

Information You Will Need from the Community Arts Profile

Since each culture follows unique visual rules, perform the activity "Analyze the Message of an Image" in *Step 4*, Part B. For example, in some cultures "big" means "near" and "small" means "far," but in other cultures "big" means "important" and "small" means "less important." The more you can learn about local visual rules and how people show stories, the better. Do people portray one event per image, or do they portray many events in the same image? Maybe people find a key moment to illustrate instead of a series of events like a comic strip, or maybe they put many events all in one picture. How does their art reflect how they depict events in life? That helps determine content in literacy materials and illustrations.

Resources Needed

Talented local illustrators to work with, the texts to be illustrated, people from the community to check the illustrations with, and respected leaders.

Tasks

1. Gather a group of literacy specialists, visual artists, and respected leaders. Decide the goals of what you would like to illustrate. Illustrations may be needed for local language calendars, wall hangings, educational materials, and religious studies.
2. Find local artists. Agree to pay normal local wages as appropriate for similar work.
3. Tell the local artist the story you would like illustrated. He or she needs to understand it well enough to tell it back to you before he or she can draw it well. Talk together about the main characters, actions, emotions, and main point of each illustration before the artist begins to draw. You may want to ask the artist to put a member of the intended audience somewhere in the picture to help with audience identification so the audience will learn well from the illustration. Women tend to identify with women, men with men, and children with children. Agree about the actions the illustrator will show, who needs to be shown participating in the actions, and the emotions the participants should show.
4. Ask the artist to create three or four rough drafts. Ask him or her not to put too much time into rough drafts; these are just to give ideas.
5. Look at the rough drafts together. For each illustration ask questions such as, "Why is the jaguar so big and the man so little?" The artist may tell you that the jaguar is more important to the story, or more dangerous, so you should not impose your rule, for example, that relative size indicates relative distance. Make sure all the people or animals and objects needed to understand the story well are in the picture and no key people are left out. Make sure that the correct action is

shown happening, and that characters' emotions are what the story calls for. If you find changes are needed so that complete information is communicated, then ask the artist to revise the rough draft. Be aware that the local culture may portray things in ways you do not expect, and emotion may be shown differently than you expect. Rather than telling the artist to change something, there may be times when you want to wait and see what people say in later steps.

6. Together, decide which of the drafts the artist should develop further.

7. Ask three or more members of the intended audience to look at the next rough draft illustration(s). Ask what they see, what they think the artist is trying to say, what they like, what they do not like, and if anything offends them. Find out if the illustration communicates the story's action, intent, and emotion accurately to them or not. Recount their ideas to the artist to help the artist make an effective final illustration.

8. Check with community leaders to make sure the illustration is really final. If the illustration is of a historical event, the choice to contextualize or not (whether to make participants more local or more historical) should be made and checked with local community leaders. If another revision is needed, make changes.

Big Picture		Steps included in activity
		Steps already taken outside the activity
		Plans for future steps

✪ Activity: Promote Literacy through Local Arts Presentations

In 1969, thousands of Peruvians were moved by the story of Maria, the heroine of the soap opera *Simplemente Maria*, who enrolled in a literacy course, became a seamstress, and overcame numerous challenges to become a respected business woman. Due to the broadcast, enrollment in adult literacy classes in Peru rose dramatically. Furthermore, so many Singer sewing machines were purchased that Singer awarded the actress who played Maria a gold sewing machine. The success of the drama led Miguel Sabido, a television producer in Mexico, to develop an entertainment-education methodology that is still built upon for influential programs around the world today.[2]

Just as radio and televised dramas can instigate tremendous change within communities, so too can smaller scale programs that draw upon local arts. This activity describes how to commission literacy-promoting visual, musical, dramatic, or other performances associated with community events like dances or celebrations. People will be more likely to integrate literacy into their lives if they connect it to other domains of their lives.

Participants

Literacy experts, artists in genres chosen for activities, and community leaders.

Information You Will Need from the Community Arts Profile

The kind of art you choose to carry your message needs to be in use already in the community for carrying similar types of messages. You need to know what kinds of messages carry what kinds of meaning, and make the form match the content.

Resources Needed

Dependent on the local context.

Tasks

1. Choose a community event that would provide a good forum for promoting literacy. This could be a festival, religious gathering, sporting event, or other context.
2. Together, list possible problems for someone who does not know how to read. For example, the person (1) cannot read instructions on medicine; (2) misses a bus because he or she could not read the schedule; (3) needs legal government paperwork completed; or (4) needs to know something written but there is no one around who can read it to them, so they do not know what to do and go home without accomplishing what they need to do. Choose one of these problems as the story idea.
3. Discuss the different artistic genres of communication that exist in the community. Imagine the benefits and drawbacks of using each to communicate the story. Choose one or more genres.
4. Have experts in the chosen genre(s) lead the process of creating a new work, which may include drama, poetry, song, illustration, comic, or picture to connect with people. When they have told what happens without knowing how to read, add a verse or another act to the skit or another picture showing an alternate case where someone has learned to read and the situation unfolds differently. The person's self-esteem is improved because he can do paperwork at the government office, give the medicine correctly, take the right bus, or otherwise not be

dependent on someone else. Include information on where people can go to learn to read.

5. Discuss the possibility of presenting the promotional art to the leaders of the community.

6. Show the work to a few people from your intended audience, and ask for their feedback on how to make it better before you show it to many people.

7. Present the artistry.

8. In addition to performing works to directly show the value of reading, performances that have another goal can also provide motivation for reading if they require reading indirectly as a skill to make them. Among the Supyire of Mali, the possibility of being chosen to act in radio dramas was a major motivation to attend literacy classes, so as to be able to read scripts. Also, many people want to learn how to read so they will be able to read song books and participate more fully in choirs.

Big Picture	Meet Specify Connect Analyze / Spark Improve Celebrate	**Steps included in activity**
		Steps already taken outside the activity
		Plans for future steps

Activity: Integrate Local Arts into Methods for Teaching Reading

Arts can help people move from the known (e.g., orally communicated words in local songs or proverbs) to the unknown (visual representations of those same words). This activity shows you how to work with people involved in teaching literacy in a community to show the best ways to use local arts in their work.

Participants

Community leaders, literacy experts, and gifted and creative teachers and artists.

Information You Will Need from the Community Arts Profile

Focus on genres that have verbal ("Oral Verbal Arts in an Event," *Step 4*, Part B) and visual ("Visual Arts in an Event," *Step 4*, Part B) components. Every culture has some kinds of art forms that can lead toward literacy, by helping community members make conceptual associations between visual arts and letter shapes or movements used in making the letters. Wood burning and carving on gourds can tell a story in pictures in the Huanca Quechua area of Peru. Symbols woven or printed on cloth, scarves, or rugs carry meaning in the Middle East. Henna designs on hands carry meaning in India.

Resources Needed

Dependent on the local context.

Tasks

Literacy and other community leaders meet to list artistic resources that may help them teach more people to read. The following are a few possible ways to connect known arts to reading and writing:

1. To help teach people how to write, build on movements that they already know. Help people make the conceptual jump from three-dimensional, concrete objects and movements to two-dimensional symbols by relating the two-dimensional symbols to similar three-dimensional objects and known movements. For example, if you are teaching an Arabic letter that looks like a hand cupping three stones, have students make this motion and say the letter name.

2. Use the lyrics of songs, proverbs, stories, riddles, or other verbal arts as texts to learn to read. If using a genre with song, put the lyrics to a song on a wall in a classroom and have students sing as they follow the words.

3. Performance provides content for teaching reading. If participants act out something that has happened, such as, "Show us how old Weepy went out and speared the wild pig," the teacher can ask what words Weepy used, such as "Let's spear! Wild pig!" Then the teacher can use the vocabulary that comes out of the performance to teach reading. Teachers can write these statements on a board and ask people to read them back. This demonstrates how reading has meaning.

4. Ask local artists to illustrate a picture book or posters of community activities such as planting, growing, harvesting a crop, visiting a friend, knitting, or making a meal. Ask literacy students to tell you the steps needed to complete the activity, or the recipe for the food. Ask them to read the steps aloud together. This connects literacy with life.

5. Ask students to draw pictures of community activities and write a simple sentence about the pictures.

6. Ask students to write a song to go with pictures, events, or stories. Ask the students to read the song's words while you all sing the new song together.

Big Picture		Steps included in activity
		Steps already taken outside the activity
		Plans for future steps

 Activity: Turn Orature into Literature

People need literature in their local language on a wide range of topics to motivate them to become literate. This activity shows you how to transcribe the texts of oral arts like songs, stories, or riddles to provide motivation for reading and to broaden the range of available reading materials in the local language. This activity may work well with Bloom, an app designed to help minority communities speed up production of literature, integrating images and audio (bloomlibrary.org, accessed May 18, 2018).

Participants

Literacy specialists and experts in genres with high verbal content.

Information You Will Need from the Community Arts Profile

Familiarity with genres containing significant elements of oral verbal arts.

Resources Needed

Dependent on the local context.

Tasks

1. To make the easiest reading materials, transcribe local folk tales, songs, and proverbs people already know. Recording cultural heritage also will ensure that the next generation does not forget local wisdom.
2. Make a second level of literacy materials by recording personal stories and writing them down, or else train local authors to write their own experience stories. People can learn from each other's experiences. A calendar showing an important event that takes place each month would be a good communal experience story; for example, 'in March the rains come [or whatever happens in that month], so we . . . [whatever we do in that month].' A song also could be created to go with this.
3. Make a third level of literacy materials by asking local authors to teach new content in local terms, and also by training creative authors to

imagine stories that have not happened. People want to know many different kinds of things and imagine many different kinds of stories, so different types of materials need to be created to interest as wide an audience as possible. People can learn by imagining how things can change, and by learning new information from outside their culture, expressed by local authors in their culture's ways. People can also create new songs and dramas and write them down for performance. What community events need new songs and dramas whose words we can write down and teach?

4. Make a fourth level of reading materials by asking local translators to translate important works such as health information that comes from another culture.

5. Ask a local illustrator to illustrate all of these kinds of materials, using visual rules of the community.

6. Test all materials with a small audience of at least three people before teaching them to a larger audience. Make sure literacy materials are clear, accurate, natural, acceptable, and interesting. After testing, revise the material before presenting it to a larger audience.

7. Distribute the finished materials to literacy programs and community leaders. Make sure people know where the materials are available to access. Advertise materials via performances or media.

Big Picture		Steps included in activity
		Steps already taken outside the activity
		Plans for future steps

Activity: Integrate Local Arts into Educational Curricula

Participants

Mother-tongue teachers, local arts experts, and school directors.

Information You Will Need from the Community Arts Profile

A list of artistic genres ("Take a First Glance at a Community's Arts," *Step 1*).

Resources Needed

Dependent on the local context. See also Saurman (2010).

Tasks

1. Look together at the local school curriculum.
2. Look together at the local art forms that carry meaning within various cultural contexts.
3. Discuss and plan ways to integrate cultural knowledge and materials into specific parts of the curriculum. The following are examples of integrating a local genre that uses stitching into existing school classes:
   a. Cultural studies: Local stitching patterns and their meaning.
   b. Reading: A story about a mother stitching a traditional outfit for her daughter to wear for New Year's Day.
   c. Writing: Have a community expert come into class and talk about the traditional dress and stitching patterns, then have students write a creative story about this experience.
   d. Science: Take the students to collect leaves and berries, then demonstrate how to color cotton through local dying techniques.
   e. Math: Cut various lengths of dyed string used for stitching and have children measure the lengths.
4. Evaluate the success of these methods with teachers and other school personnel.

Big Picture	 Meet Specify Connect Analyze — Spark Improve Celebrate	**Steps included in activity**
		Steps already taken outside the activity
		Plans for future steps

Perform the Activity and Describe the Results

Do what you planned. Hold your plans lightly. Learn from mistakes. Enjoy the process. Describe what happened in the Community Arts Profile.

Notes

1. See, for example, *kwaya* contests in Tanzania, described in Barz (2003).
2. See "Entertainment-Education" (n.d.). For further study, consult Singhal and Rogers (1999).

Step

6

IMPROVE RESULTS

WHETHER LOCALLY OR internationally funded, evaluation forms a critical component of arts programs. Often evaluations are required by funders to ensure that resources were used appropriately and to demonstrate impact. Even if such evaluations are not required by funders, they are critical for helping communities understand how programs were received by targeted audiences, whether goals were met, and what might be improved for future programs. Remember that the goal of evaluating is construction, not destruction; building up, not tearing down. Note, too, that communities can minimize problems with artistic works by including key people from the beginning of the co-creative process: local leaders, expert creators, and expert performers.

The following case study helps to set the scene for our discussion on evaluation. This story comes from West Africa, where the organization Global Alliance to Immunize Against AIDS Vaccine Foundation (GAIA VF) is using "storytelling cloths" to help address contemporary issues related to health and well-being, one of the goal categories we discuss in this Guide. First, we describe one of GAIA VF's projects, an initiative in Mali focused on cervical cancer and human papillomavirus (HPV) vaccination. Second, we highlight ways in which this project demonstrates aspects of the *Make Arts* process.

The following is a summary by Kathleen and GAIA VF's Executive Director Eliza Squibb (email communication, May 13, 2016; for further details, see also Squibb 2015a; Squibb 2015b; and Global Alliance to Immunize Against AIDS 2014):

Cervical cancer rates are five times higher among women in Africa than in the US, with Mali having the highest rate in West Africa. Prevention methods such as Human Papillomavirus (HPV) vaccination and regular pelvic exams lessen cancer incidence in the US and Europe, but are not yet prevalent in Mali. A low-tech cervical cancer screening method exists in Mali, but due to lack of awareness about the disease, only a very small percentage of Malian women have received screening. Local health authorities are working with international organizations to make the HPV vaccine available in Mali. The advent of vaccination would have a significant impact on the cervical cancer burden in Mali, yet similarly to screening, the success of prevention methods will hinge on raising awareness about HPV and cervical cancer.

After completing preliminary studies on cervical cancer and HPV knowledge in Mali (De Groot et al. 2017), GAIA VF responded to this need for education through a "story-telling cloth" focused on HPV and cervical cancer. Use of textiles for communicating messages has long been common in Mali and many other parts of Africa; for example, *pagnes* (term referring to a length of printed fabric) may showcase local proverbs, promote particular political leaders, or mark national events. These fabrics are used to make clothes worn by men and women as well as accessories such as bags.

GAIA VF's initiative in Mali centered upon a *pagne* designed by artist and GAIA VF's Executive Director Eliza Squibb. On the cloth, the words "I protect myself, I care for myself, and I get vaccinated" are written across images of healthy cervixes, fallopian tubes, uteruses, and HPV viruses, which are embedded in abnormal cancerous cells. A key addition to the cloth pattern came from community members: when the imagery and significance was explained during focus groups, women mentioned a specific Malian proverb, "banakoubè kafisa ni bana foura kèyé," meaning, "it's better to prevent than to cure." This proverb was included in the final version of the pattern. Additional preliminary feedback also was incorporated into the pattern; this included color preferences, scale of the design, and changing the word in the French slogan from "immunize" to "vaccinate."

GAIA VF's educational *pagne* was the keystone of a wider initiative for cervical cancer prevention funded by the Bill and Melinda Gates Foundation. GAIA VF's goal was to maximize screening in a focused area (five clinics) while educating participants and learning about preferences for HPV vaccination. Starting in March 2015 in collaboration with the Malian Regional

Health Director, GAIA provided five clinics in Bamako, Mali, with supplies to offer free cervical exams for six months. A televised campaign launch featured the cloth and healthcare practitioners involved in the initiative. Local midwives, doctors and outreach workers tailored the story-telling cloth into fashionable outfits. Radio personalities promoted HPV vaccination and cervical cancer screening and highlighted the local proverb featured on the cloth. Community health workers used the cloth to help explain HPV and cervical cancer to women in their neighborhoods and to motivate them to attend cervical cancer screenings. Handbags made out of the cloth were distributed to patients at the participating clinics.

The results of the project were highly positive. 78% of women who participated in a clinic or neighborhood education session had seen the story-telling cloth, and the vast majority was able to correctly identify the HPV imagery. GAIA VF evaluated the effectiveness of the story-telling cloth HPV education campaign on awareness by measuring the increase in screening rates, which showed a dramatic five-fold increase over the same period in the previous year. HPV vaccination was not yet available during the six-month campaign. However, GAIA VF asked 500 (100 per clinic) of the 3,271 women screened to participate in a survey about HPV and cervical cancer. Results demonstrated that interest in the HPV vaccine was high; 92.6% of participants expressed interest in having the vaccine available in Mali, and 87.4% said that they would vaccinate their daughters. When asked why they would choose HPV vaccination for their daughters, 84% of survey participants gave an answer that related to the story-telling cloth awareness campaign: 73% mentioned "Prevention" or "Protection," and 11% responded with the exact proverb that was printed on the cloth. Participants received a bag made from the HPV cloth so that they could personally help educate others. Through the survey, GAIA VF also was able to obtain information about a number of related issues: which parent would need to give consent for vaccinations, how best to contact parents when vaccination is available, and where people prefer vaccinations to be given. This information can help ensure that future vaccination efforts are effective.

GAIA VF plans to further expand the cloth project to larger regions of Bamako. The organization also has been involved in using textiles to address other health issues in West Africa. For example, using a story-telling cloth for Ebola awareness was field-tested in Mali and Sierra Leone, and there are plans for expansion through health education programs in the countries most affected by the epidemic.

By considering this case study, we can see how particular steps in the *Make Arts* process, including evaluation, play out in a real situation. In the following, we have italicized certain phrases that link directly with the stages we discuss in this Guide.

- In the case of GAIA VF, we see how an organization has drawn upon a history of the use of textiles for educational purposes within communities to meet current needs. Organizers are aware of *the role of textiles historically in the community* and are *involving community members and health experts* in developing and evaluating the program.
- The organization has selected a particular visual genre that will be familiar to community members, yet is using this genre in *creative ways to meet contemporary needs* within communities.
- This case study shows how *new creations are being tested*; these tests, in turn, help program staff to *improve* designs and ensure that initiatives have *lasting impact* within communities. Evaluation was central to the GAIA VF project, from GAIA VF's preliminary studies of community health needs and perspectives on using textiles for educational purposes, to efforts to seek community input into the design of the cloth, and to final evaluation of the six-month project. Preliminary studies ensured that the project was meeting local needs in an effective way. Final evaluation demonstrated the high impact of the project and also provided information that can help with future roll-out of vaccinations in Mali.

In *Step 6* of this Guide, we help you to reach the following goals:

- Follow guidelines for determining whether artistic products are effective.
- Design an evaluative process using a conceptual approach.
- Design a recurring cycle of evaluation.

Just as GAIA VF built upon its preliminary research on community needs and local arts in developing the HPV cloth, you can build upon the research you performed in previous steps of the Guide. And just as GAIA sought to evaluate its program through multiple means, you too can build evaluation into your projects. Each of the processes in the following should include frequent reference to the Community Arts Profile (or its contents, stored in people's minds).

How Do We Assess a Product?

People sometimes assess events or works using words like "good" or "bad," "like" or "dislike." But how do they make these judgments? (See also *Foundations*, "What Is 'Good.'"). When, for example, someone says, "I never liked the Beatles' music," do they mean that they did not like their tunes, they did not like their lyrics, or they did not like their long hair? Sometimes people are not able to articulate what exactly they like or do not like about an artwork. This is not surprising, because artistic communication works through the production and reception of a staggering number of possible signs and their associated meanings. If you glance through all of the research activities in *Step 4*, you will see that people could be evaluating arts according to any of these kinds of signs: meter; line; syntax; enjambment; rhyme; assonance; alliteration; metaphor; simile; verses; stanzas; refrains; pulse; tempo; meter; accents; figures; motifs; phrases; tonal center; keys; intervals; modes; scales; range; tessitura; themes; contours; cadences; parallel, chordal, or polyphonic relationships between concurrent pitches; formulas; progressions; tonality; strophes; iterations; through-composition; theme variation; solo; duo; trio; choir; unison; vibrato; accompaniment; use of space; characterization; number and location of participants; blocking; plot structure; idea; dramatic premise; frames; improvisation; movements; gestures; movement phrasing; dynamics; efforts; spatial relationships; visual unity; balance; rhythm; proportion; line; shape; value; color; hue; shade; tint; texture; and so on.

Not only are the kinds of signs seemingly endless, but each group and individual may have diverse associations with any given sign. One person may smile whenever he hears Latin percussion because he met the woman who would become his wife at a party where they danced the samba. Another man may detest samba because his fiancée broke up with him at a similar event. There could be zillions of signs multiplied by zillions of associations at an artistic event, any one of which could make it fail.

Furthermore, not only does productive evaluation require us to perceive an infinite number of signs, their combinations, and their meanings, but we also need to be aware of personal relationships and social dynamics. An epic poet might perform brilliantly, but if an influential audience member is holding a grudge against him, the community might ultimately dismiss the artist's skill.

The complexity of artistic communication should keep us humble, but there are several factors that make identifying criteria for improvement possible. Here we present these factors as guidelines for designing evaluation and improvement exercises.

Trust Local Systems

Groups usually share a sense of when an artwork is good or not and have ways of communicating what needs to be fixed. Perform the research in "Aesthetics and Evaluation" (*Step 4*, Part C) to find out how correction normally works in the community. In some situations, community members may get rid of inferior products by blocking them from future presentation.

Evaluate According to Effects

In *Step 3*, the community identified the effects that new artistry should have on people in order to move them toward their goals. Observe and ask about experiencers' responses to the new bits of artistry. Did it have the effects they wanted? If an orator's performance is meant to motivate people to join a parade celebrating their ethnic identity, but participants watch distractedly and then disperse to their homes, then the oration failed.

Relax, But Keep Learning

You cannot study all of the possible signs, so do this: watch people's reactions, listen to what they say, and dip into the research activities in *Step 4* related to the genres you are working with regularly—maybe one activity a week or month. For example, if you are getting to know people who carve fruit, schedule these research activities: "Describe Spatial Relationships between an Object's Visual Features," "Document the Creation of an Object," and "Identify the Role(s) in Visual Art Creation" (*Step 4*, Part B). Then start learning to carve the fruit yourself. This education will sensitize you to factors that may prove important in the improvement of new artistry.

Identify What Kinds of Evaluation Should Happen When

Artistic activity can benefit from evaluation at two points in the co-creative process. First, when you are helping people during the act of creation, everyone can evaluate intermediate versions of the works. Second, you may help people reflect on a work after it has been presented.

Keep these bits of advice in mind as you and the community decide how to improve the artistry produced by the sparking activities in *Step 5*. The following are three approaches to designing such processes. The first, "Design an Evaluative Process Using a Conceptual Approach," provides basic principles that you and the community can draw upon to create your own system. The other two approaches offer more specific steps to follow. Read all three and decide which fits your context best, and modify them as necessary.[1]

Design an Evaluative Process Using a Conceptual Approach

Here is a process that you and community members can follow that will enhance the evaluation of artistic events:

- Identify and work through *local social structures*, and help everyone involved provide correction in locally appropriate ways (using standards of politeness, respect, indirection, roles within a social hierarchy, etc.).
- Define together the *criteria* for determining the efficacy of a work and how it could be improved. For example, a created work may be effective insofar as its features work together to effect the purposes demanded by the context of its performance and by its experiencers. These purposes could include the work's accuracy of information, ability to communicate, ability to touch people through its aesthetic quality, ability to motivate to action, etc.
- Identify the *elements* of an artistic communication event (see "Take a First Glance at an Event," *Step 4*, Part A). These should include how the work utilizes space, materials, participants, shape through time, performance features, feeling, content, themes, and community values.
- Identify the *purpose(s)* of the artistic communication event. These could include to educate, motivate to action, and so on.
- Identify *people* to include in the process of evaluation. These people need to have the knowledge, skills, and respect necessary to critique various elements.
- Identify *objects* that can provide a focal point and reference for discussion, so that you do not have to rely exclusively on memory for critique. These could include song texts, drama scripts, musical notation, masks, dance moves, photographs, and audio- and videorecordings.
- Together *affirm* the aspects of the creation that work well, and encourage the creators to *do something even better* based on the evaluation.

Figure 6.1 lists examples of evaluation in several creative contexts.

266 Make Arts for a Better Life

Kinds of Elements to Evaluate	Examples of Such Elements	Qualified to Evaluate	Example of Methods of Evaluation
Space/location, time, participants, etc.	Storytelling around a fire at night, with all ages	Genre experts, traditional leaders	With written summary of the event description: • Discuss relationship to genre.
Performance features (music, dance, verbal arts, drama, visual, etc.)	Proverb choice, movement characteristics, melody shape	Expert performers	With audio and video recordings: • Review for aesthetic/technical successes, weaknesses of performance. • Transcribe melody, lyrics, movements, poetic features, colors, etc., for analysis.
Message(s)	Medical content	Health worker	With transcriptions of texts: • Analyze texts of songs, dramas, stories (with back-translation if critiquer does not know language) according to clarity, accuracy. • Comprehension testing: ask experiencers what they understood.
Purpose(s)	AIDS education	Agenda setters for the communication event	With a summary of all aspects of the event: • discuss degrees that the event fulfilled its intended purposes and other purposes, and how the event could be improved; may use a focus group or exit interviews.

FIGURE 6.1. Ways to evaluate several kinds of artistic elements.

Design a Recurring Cycle of Evaluation

We need to check art forms in order to know if the created product is meaningful to our target audience. For example, if we draw a picture for children, we need to know if the symbols and colors in the picture are meaningful, if the overall message of the picture is clear, if the image(s) are easy for them to both understand and imitate (as best they can), if they can easily absorb and restate the meaning of the visual image, if the image clearly comes from a cultural context to which they can relate, and so on. We also want to check with some experts in the community in order to know if the art forms relate meaningfully to the community as a whole.

Here are some ideas for checking an art form, but the approach should be designed appropriately for each cultural context.

With Whom Should You Check?

- Four or five target audience members.
- At least two community experts of the artistic genre.

Use All of the Following Tests with Each of the Preceding People

It is important to write down anything you learn about the art form so that improvements can be made. Checking with each person can take anywhere from five minutes to more than 20 minutes. It is important to take time and learn as much you can about what needs to be improved.

Test for Meaning

- Show or demonstrate the artwork.
- Ask them to tell you what the artwork communicates to them.
- Listen to them and see if they seem to understand the meaning.
- If not, show them the artwork again and ask them for the meaning once again.
- Write down their responses, and write down what parts of the artwork are clear and what parts are unclear (this could be words, phrases, themes, colors, patterns, actions, etc.).

Alternate/Additional Test for Meaning

- Show or demonstrate the artwork.
- Ask them if they can reproduce some portion of the artwork back to you. This might be in the same form as the artwork (e.g., demonstrating a dance movement from a dance performance) or in a different form (e.g., drawing a picture of something that they remember from a theater production; see Greiner et al. 2007). Let them do this on their own and see what they can remember.
- If they are having some difficulty remembering, show or demonstrate the artwork again.
- Ask them again to reproduce some portion of the artwork.
- If they are still having some difficulty, you can prompt them a little, but it is wise not to prompt too much.
- Write down any comments on parts that are difficult to replicate.

Test for Ownership and Accuracy

Does the form parallel the form used by the target audience?

- Ask them how they feel about the artwork.
- Would they use it? How would they use it? Would they enjoy hearing, seeing, or experiencing the artwork? When?
- What do they not like? What would they change? What would make the art better or more meaningful for them?
- Does it feel to them as though it is their own? Does it feel as though it belongs to their community?
- Is this form consistent with
    - the listener's learning or education level?
    - local teaching methods?
    - the appropriate language and symbol or sound?

Improve the Artwork

Take the results from the arts checking to the artwork creator or meet with the creation committee and change or adjust its unclear portions.

From Good to Effective

Test again to see if you hit the target audience. Hopefully the answer is yes! If the goal has been to communicate a message or promote an art form, then you may have succeeded in your mission. However, now comes an even trickier issue. A "good" creation—perhaps one that is well researched, well developed, accepted by and meaningful to the intended audience members—still may not yield behavior change within communities. A woman who attends a performance about HIV and AIDS, for example, may come away with new facts about prevention, transmission, and treatment. However, whether she modifies unhealthy sexual practices based on these new facts depends on numerous factors, including her own sense of self-control, how much power she has to resist unwanted or unsafe advances, and how much need she has to depend on unsafe practices in order to gain income. Furthermore, if HIV and AIDS rates do decrease within a community, it may be difficult to determine whether this is due to the program you have helped develop, to other educational programs within the community, to clinics supplying additional prevention and treatment resources, or to other factors. Thus, evaluating the efficacy of arts programs can be complicated. Examples of large-scale studies and evaluations that take into account such complicating factors in their analyses are available and may be useful to consider as you plan your work.[2] No matter how large or small your program, it is important to be aware of social, cultural, and other factors that may influence changes within communities so that you can form a better picture of what is happening and how you might address problems (e.g., by ensuring that you are aware of complementary efforts within the community, that audience members know where to go for additional information or support after programs, etc.).

When Projects Fail

Sometimes projects fail. People like to report successes more than failures, so there tends to be more literature reporting on new research or project findings than on failures, but that does not mean that all projects succeed. As Jeff Todd Titon (2015:158) writes about applied ethnomusicologists: "We are experimenters, we live with uncertainty, we expect sometimes to fail, and we hope to learn from our failures." Projects may fail for a variety of reasons. Sometimes they have not been planned well: for example, project goals do not appropriately reflect local goals; projects are viewed as foreign rather than locally owned; or key stakeholders have been left out. Sometimes practical or personnel issues mean that projects do not develop as planned: anticipated funding does not become available; key participants drop out for various reasons; misunderstandings or conflicts develop between participants; or venues become unavailable. By following the methods in this Guide, you should be able to work with community members to plan projects as carefully as possible, minimizing the risk of problems at later stages. Yet surprises can still arise.

Kathleen experienced a variety of challenges with the Childlife Arts Programme described in the *Foundations* section of this Guide. Problems in that case included the following: some other organizers became upset that she could not fully fund the project, despite early discussion where she made it clear this was not possible or necessarily beneficial if the program was meant to be sustainable for the future; some organizers who were active at an early stage did not participate in later stages, meaning that the burden of work fell on only a few people; and there were few resources available for the project, meaning that organizers relied almost entirely on volunteer teaching and volunteer funding for arts materials. These challenges played a large role in why the project did not continue past the initial workshops.

Finally, projects can succeed in some regards, and fail in others. In their article entitled "Programmed to Fail? Development Projects and the Politics of Participation," Sanjay Kumar and Stuart Corbridge (2002) describe how the

Eastern India Rainfed Farming Project, a joint venture of the governments of India and the United Kingdom, was both a success and a failure. They argue that this project reflected newer efforts in the development world to avoid top-down approaches, and instead to emphasize participation and sustainability, including by involving poor populations. Assessments of the project suggest that it was successful in improving farm-based livelihoods in Jharkhand, Orissa, and West Bengal. However, the project failed to meet another goal: it did not result in increased participation of the poorest villagers. Kumar and Corbridge emphasize that this was not due to lack of sincerity or effort by participants, in particular community organizers who were charged with working with villagers. Nor was it due to lack of training of participants, or to lack of internal and external evaluation, all of which were built into the program at multiple stages. Instead, they argue that the project "[set] itself up for 'failure' because it [set] unrealistic goals" (Kumar and Corbridge 2002:76). In the end, they assert, local systems of land ownership and social exclusion meant that wealthier and more educated people were better placed to take advantage of the project; furthermore, community organizers needed the support of these people in order to work in the communities. Poorer villagers did not necessarily see value in the project; in addition, the idea that they would participate was dismissed by other community members as unlikely (Kumar and Corbridge 2002:84). Kumar and Corbridge (2002:94) argue that these results were entirely predictable considering the history of development interventions in the area.

Kumar and Corbridge remind us of two important issues:

1. When setting goals, be realistic. Any project has practical, financial, personnel or other constraints. Think creatively about how to overcome challenges, but also recognize and be realistic about constraints. Look at historical antecedents and learn from them. Consider social contexts and learn from them. Your research in setting up the Community Arts Profile will help.

2. Kumar and Corbridge (2002:95) argue that "we need a language of 'success' and 'failure' that is less oppositional." We can learn from failure, and sometimes turn that into success in the future. But also, projects may both "succeed" and "fail" in various ways; most projects probably do. Reflect on what works or does not work in the projects in which you are involved.

Notes

1. A further resource is Ane Haaland's (1984) classic manual with many examples.

2. For example, see Vaughan et al. (2000) for a description and evaluation of the effects of a long-running entertainment education radio soap opera on HIV and AIDS knowledge, attitudes, and prevention behaviors in Tanzania.

Step

7

CELEBRATE AND INTEGRATE FOR CONTINUITY

EVERYTHING THAT WE can sense or think about cycles through birth, growth, decay, and death. People, ideologies, songs, flowers, buildings, waves, customs, vehicles, wildebeests, cakes, hats, galaxies—they all come and go. Of course, the length of each cycle and stage varies widely, and sometimes the intermediate steps get skipped altogether. And occasionally part of something that has died gets resurrected, as when the forgotten works of a sixteenth-century painter are found and inspire artists centuries later. So why do we not just join the ebb and flow, the wax and wane of history? Why do we try to make some things last longer and others not? How do we know when to celebrate and integrate artistic works, and when to fold our hands and rest?

In *Step 7* we provide a few ideas that will help you wrestle with these daunting questions in your co-creative context. Specifically, we will give some pointers on how to

- choose what to integrate and celebrate;
- act to keep effective programs going; and
- understand more about how continuity works.

Choose What to Celebrate and Integrate

Your first choice here is simple: celebrate and integrate the arts that you have been engaging with in *Steps 2–6*. With a community, you have identified goals, have decided on certain kinds of artistry that can move the community closer to these goals, and have implemented actions that resulted in new bits of this artistry and then improved them. This process has ensured as much as possible that the creative processes and people you have been engaging with are the ones that should take root and flourish.

But all situations change all the time. This invigorating fact (or frustrating, depending on your personality) means that communities need to regularly reassess their present and think about the future. The constituency of a community will alter, new modes of communication will enter, government policies will evolve—so the kinds of artistic communication best suited to meet community goals will change. Here are some suggestions for initiatives in the months and years ahead.

Embed the Make Arts Cycle in Community Life

Go through the co-creative cycle in this Guide again: *Steps 1–7.* The more a community does this, the more it will become a familiar process that flows efficiently through members' lives. And the more normal it becomes to reflect and act, the more corporate wisdom to make decisions resulting in thriving will emerge.

Encourage Continuity in Arts That Are Most Fragile

Diversity and fragility are closely connected. The United Nations Educational, Scientific, and Cultural Organization (UNESCO) states that nearly 2,500 of the world's approximately 7,000 languages are in one of five levels of endangerment: unsafe, definitely endangered, severely endangered, critically endangered, and extinct (Moseley 2010). Other aspects of these communities—including artistic forms of communication—normally experience similar fragility. The disappearance of an artistic tradition diminishes its practitioners, weakens the identities of that art's home communities, dilutes knowledge and social systems the art is interwoven with, and mutes voices whose contributions to human resilience may never be heard. We should take special note of the artists and their art forms that are most in the world's margins. UNESCO is attempting to support these artists through its Intangible Cultural Heritage program (www.unesco.org/culture/ich/).

Encourage Continuity in Arts That Are Most Likely to Flourish

We want new artistry to make positive differences in a community, so innovations that spread like wildfire can be great things.

As you reflect on these guidelines, you will realize that they sometimes work counter to each other. That is the reality of life.

Act to Keep Effective Programs Going

We have encouraged you to make relationships, urge others to create, get to know and value artists, include all of the important artists and decision-makers in sparking activities, and help make artistic products and their presentation better. These activities will help ensure the efficacy of programs.

However, you might still need to plan to inject energy at strategic points. Here are a few ideas:

Celebrate

Celebrating local arts can help strengthen the esteem of a community and protect invaluable cultural heritage. By affirming local arts, you serve as an advocate for a community's unique expressions and foster conditions for further artistic flowering. You also help a community's voice (their unique stories, perceptions of the world, and values) to be heard and understood by others.

Ways to celebrate new and older art forms include the following:

- presenting them to community officials and leaders;
- disseminating recordings;
- performing at festive social events; and
- entering contests.

The "Identity and Sustainability" goals and activities (*Steps 2, 5*) offer more detailed suggestions for celebration.

Integrate

Integrating has to do with making artistic practice part of normal patterns of community life. A good place to start is to reflect with the community on the ways that they teach each other things like new songs, dances, and carving skills. If possible, their plans should include these means of transmission. In order to keep creativity going, the community may decide to repeat sparking activities such as workshops or commissioning. Existing social groups like dance associations or literacy clubs may also have motivation to keep creating. Or communities might decide to form new groups that meet regularly to help members create, such as the creators' clubs we described in *Step 5*. Each of these ideas feeds into repeated parts of community life, so that the engines of creativity keep running.

Evaluate

Every so often, look at the community's co-creative activities and see what the results are. Try to develop a milieu in which everyone recognizes that everything can be improved and everything has a life cycle. This will help in planning.

A Planning and Management Method: Results-Based Management

Our seven-step co-creative cycle is in itself a planning and management method. However, sometimes you will work with organizations that use other systems. Results-based management (RBM) is an effective tool used in a number of well-known organizations, including the United Nations, the Canadian government, and the International Committee of the Red Cross. RBM also shares many characteristics of the *Make Arts* approach.

Results-based management is a participatory and team-based approach to planning and management that focuses on achieving defined results. It is a way of viewing what we do by first looking at the hoped-for impacts and working back in time and levels of detail.

Imagine dropping a stone in a pond. The ripples spread out from the point the stone first hit the water, eventually lapping up on the pond's shoreline. RBM leads you through a process of imagining the impacts a community wants to see happen (the shoreline), thinking logically about what would need to occur backwards in time to reach that impact (the ripples), and planning activities to make those things happen (dropping the stone in the water). RBM has developed a particular vocabulary to describe this, depicted in Figure 7.1.

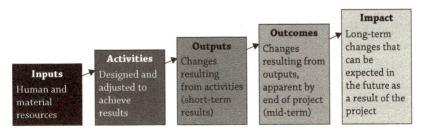

FIGURE 7.1. Results-based management logical planning sequence.

When you use RBM to plan, you create a results chain (like the ripples in a pond) based on cause-and-effect relationships:

- carrying out activities causes short-term results (outputs);
- outputs cause mid-term results (outcomes); and
- outcomes cause long-term results (impact).

Although it may at first seem paradoxical, you create this chain by starting on the right side of this diagram and working left. So, through discussion, the community

- decides on a long-term goal (impact);
- decides what mid-term changes (outcomes) would need to occur for this impact to happen;
- decides what short-term changes (outputs) would need to occur for the outcomes to happen;
- decides what activities would need to be done to produce the outputs; and
- decides what human, physical, and financial resources (inputs) they would need to perform the activities.

Figure 7.2 shows a small portion of such an arts-related results chain.

Relentless Pursuit of Vitality

In the following testimony, Neil Coulter describes how artistic materials and practices can die out in communities, and the deep pain this can sometimes cause individuals, whether members of the community or individuals connected with the community. Coulter explains (email communication, May 9, 2012; see also Coulter 2011):

I am an ethnomusicologist who lived among and performed research with speakers of the Alamblak language in Papua New Guinea from 2003 through 2006. One of the instruments I documented was the *nrwit* (*garamut* in Tok Pisin): a hollowed length of tree trunk, between 4 and 6 feet long, and between 2 and 4 feet tall, with a long, thin opening in the top. The *nrwit* player holds a beater stick, 3–4 feet long, and strikes a nodule at the edge of the slit with the blunt end of the beater. The deep, resonant sound from the *nrwit* carries over a great distance and can be used to send messages within or beyond the village. An individual nuclear family might own one *nrwit*, which rests on the ground just outside the family home, sheltered from the weather by the overhanging eaves of the roof. Alamblak people stated that previous generations used the *nrwit* to say anything that people could say, although the signaling system is not sonically imitative of the spoken language. By the time of my fieldwork, the system had fallen into disuse, and only a few older

How		What we want		Why?
Inputs	*Activities*	*Outputs*	*Outcomes*	*Impact*
Willing deaf and hearing members	Hold a series of meetings in which deaf and hearing members learn to know each other well. Emphasis should be on the hearing learning from the deaf	Deaf and hearing members of the community are growing together and learning from each other		
Connections with local deaf community	Form small groups of deaf and hearing people who help each other and involve themselves in activities in the community's deaf community			
Deaf to spoken language translators, and vice versa	Create a space in the government building that meets the needs of deaf people to perform and socialize			
Funds, designer	Hold a series of workshops in which deaf artists create poetry, visual arts, and other forms of arts			
	Hold regular coffee-house type events where deaf artists can perform, display, and discuss their work	Deaf community members feel comfortable in the government buildings	Deaf people in a community form relationships with hearing people in local decision-making bodies, based on the acceptance they feel	Deaf people are contributing to their wider community's future

FIGURE 7.2. Sample results-based management plan for improving Deaf identity.

Note: In literature in the United States, the word "Deaf" is often capitalized. "This is the form used in reference to a specific, self-defined cultural group in the United States, with a common history and language" (Mariana Portolano, http://endora.wide.msu.edu/7-1/coverweb/portolano/deaf.htm, accessed May 19, 2018). This capitalization is a strong marker of identity and respect for many in the United States.

men were able to play the signals. Other people said that they could understand some signals when they heard them but could not themselves produce *nrwit* communication. Today the primary use of the *nrwit* is announcing the death of a village resident.

Signaling on the *nrwit* has been reduced to an identity reminder for the Alamblak ethnic community. No one has more than symbolic proficiency. Recordings and documentation exist, but people are not using the signal system. Kondak, the acknowledged expert who taught me the *nrwit* patterns, died in 2010. People could, if they choose, re-learn the *nrwit* patterns, likely in an adapted form rather than the exact traditional system; at this point, it seems unlikely. As mobile phones become a larger part of communication in Papua New Guinea, people will have the option to send text messages, similar to the *nrwit* signals. But when I asked an Alamblak friend about this, he pointed out an important difference: the *nrwit* sends one message to entire villages at once, but text messages go only to one individual. Community involvement is a Melanesian ideal that is not well-suited to mobile phone communication.

The *nrwit* tradition is on the verge of extinction, which affects me personally: I have concern for my Alamblak friends and have hopes for the very best for their lives. They've lost something of great value.

Such stories motivate us to keep working alongside the increasing number of artists and communities who tell similarly sobering stories.

Change Is Not All Bad, of Course

As we have suggested, while some genres fade, others emerge. New forms of slang take hold among young generations. New sounds emanate from urban buses, sidewalk stands, nightclubs, and church halls. Bruno Nettl (2005:434) notes that "the hybrids and mixes resulting from intercultural contact could be interpreted as enrichment as easily as pollution, and old traditions as a class have not simply disappeared."[1] But many communities feel that they are indeed losing valuable artistic resources. And what is the bigger picture? If art is an expression of a people—part of their identity—then what happens to the people when that art becomes only an artifact or gradually disappears? *Closing 7* presents ways to measure the health of an art form. If you can identify the state of vitality of the art in which a community is interested, then you can target co-creative activities more wisely. The closer an art form is to extinction, the more energy is required to spark creativity.

Final Thoughts

We hope that the *Make Arts* steps that we have outlined, the questions that we have posed, and the resources and activities that we have highlighted will help readers to act more wisely, humbly, and effectively with communities in supporting the arts and promoting better lives. En avant!

Note

1. Also recall our discussion of the term "sustainability," along with concerns about preservationist stances, in *Step 2*.

Closing Matter

Closing 1: References

Adolphs, Ralph. 2003. "Cognitive Neuroscience of Human Social Behavior." *Nature Reviews Neuroscience* 4: 165–178.

'Aha Pūnana Leo. 2016. "A Timeline of Revitalization." http://www.ahapunanaleo.org/index. php?/about/a_timeline_of_revitalization (accessed March 28, 2018).

Albert, Robert, and Mark Runco. 2010. "Creativity Research: A Historical View." In *The Cambridge Handbook of Creativity*, edited by Robert Sternberg, 3–19. Cambridge: Cambridge University Press.

Alcoreza, Raúl Prada. 2013 (first translated edited edition [2011, original Spanish edition]). "Buen Vivir as a Model for State and Economy." In *Beyond Development: Alternative Visions from Latin America*, edited by M. Lang and D. Mokrani, 145–158. Permanent Working Group on Alternatives to Development. Quito: Fundación Rosa Luxemburg; Amsterdam: Transnational Institute.

Alter, Joseph S. 1999. "Heaps of Health, Metaphysical Fitness Ayurveda and the Ontology of Good Health in Medical Anthropology." *Current Anthropology* 40 (S1), Special Issue, *Culture—A Second Chance?*: S43–S66.

Alviso, J. Ricardo. 2003. "Applied Ethnomusicology and the Impulse to Make a Difference." *Folklore Forum* 34 (1–2): 89–96.

Apel, Willi. 1975 [1972]. *Harvard Dictionary of Music*. Cambridge, MA: Belknap Press of Harvard University Press.

Araújo, Samuel, and Members of the Grupo Musicultura. 2006. "Conflict and Violence as Theoretical Tools in Present-Day Ethnomusicology: Notes on a Dialogic Ethnography of Sound Practices in Rio de Janeiro." *Ethnomusicology* 50 (2): 287–313.

ARSC. 2016. "Education and Training in Audiovisual Archiving and Preservation." http://www. arsc-audio.org/etresources.html (accessed March 28, 2018).

Ball, Philip. 2012. *The Music Instinct: How Music Works and Why We Can't Do Without It.* Oxford: Oxford University Press.

Ball, William. 1984. *A Sense of Direction: Some Observations on the Art of Directing.* New York: Drama Publishers.

Bame, Kwabena N. 1973. "The Influence of Contemporary Ghanaian Traditional Drama on the Attitudes and Behaviour of Play Go-ers." *Research Review* 9 (2): 26–32.

Barber, Karin, John Collins, and Alain Ricard. 1997. *West African Popular Theatre.* Bloomington: Indiana University Press.

Barefoot Collective, and N. D. Mazin (illustrator). 2009. *The Barefoot Guide to Working with Organisations and Social Change.* http://www.barefootguide.org (accessed March 28, 2018).

Barefoot Guide Connection, The. 2017. http://www.barefootguide.org (accessed March 28, 2018).

Barz, Gregory. 2006. *Singing for Life: HIV/AIDS and Music in Uganda.* New York: Routledge.

Bauman, Richard, editor. 1992. *Folklore, Cultural Performances, and Popular Entertainments.* Oxford: Oxford University Press.

Becker, Judith. 2004. *Deep Listeners: Music, Emotion, and Trancing.* Bloomington: Indiana University Press.

Biswas, Ranjita. 2010. "Dancing Away the Pain." *The Guardian.* http://www.guardian.co.uk/world/2010/oct/12/kolkata-women-trafficking-dance-therapy? (accessed March 28, 2018).

Blacking, John. 1977. "Some Problems of Theory and Method in the Study of Musical Change." *Yearbook of the Traditional Folk Music Council* 9: 1–26.

Blacking, John. 1986. "Identifying Processes of Musical Change." *The World of Music* 28 (1): 3–15.

Bleibinger, Bernhard. 2010. "Solving Conflicts: Applied Ethnomusicology at the Music Department of the University of Fort Hare, South Africa, and in the Context of IMOHP." In *Applied Ethnomusicology: Historical and Contemporary Approaches*, edited by Klisala Harrison, Elizabeth Mackinlay, and Svanibor Pettan, 36–50. Newcastle upon Tyne, UK: Cambridge Scholars.

Boal, Augusto. 1995. *The Rainbow of Desire: The Boal Method of Theatre and Therapy.* London: Routledge.

Boerger, Brenda H., Stephen Self, Sarah Moeller, and Will Reiman. 2017. *Language and Culture Documentation Manual.* http://leanpub.com/languageandculturedocumentationmanual (accessed March 28, 2018).

Borczon, Ronald M. 2004. *Music Therapy: A Fieldwork Primer.* Gilsum, NH: Barcelona.

Brewer, William F., Clark A. Chinn, and Ala Samarapungavan. 1998. "Explanation in Science and Children." *Minds and Machines* 8: 119–136.

van Bruggen-Rufi, Monique. 2018. "Music Therapy in Huntington's Disease." PhD dissertation, Leiden University Medical Center.

Campbell, Patricia Shehan, and Lee Higgins. 2015. "Intersections between Ethnomusicology, Music Education, and Community Music." In *Oxford Handbook of Applied Ethnomusicology*, edited by Svanibor Pettan and Jeff Todd Titon, 639–668. Oxford: Oxford University Press.

Chaiklin, Sharon, and Hilda Wengrower, editors. 2015. *The Art and Science of Dance/Movement Therapy: Life is Dance*, 2nd edition. Philadelpha: Routledge.

Chapline, Jeffrey, and Julene Kay Johnson. 2016. *The National Endowment for the Arts Guide to Community-Engaged Research in Arts and Health.* Washington, DC: NEA Office of Research & Analysis. https://www.arts.gov/publications/national-endowment-arts-guide-community-engaged-research-arts-and-health (accessed March 28, 2018).

Chenoweth, Vida. 1972. *Melodic Perception and Analysis*. Ukarumpa, Papua New Guinea: Summer Institute of Linguistics.

Clift, Stephen, and Paul M. Camic. 2016. "Introduction to the Field of Creative Arts, Wellbeing and Health: Achievements and Current Challenges." *Oxford Textbook of Creative Arts, Health and Wellbeing: International Perspectives on Practice, Policy and Research*, 3–10. London: Oxford University Press.

Colombo, John, and Robert S. Bundy. 1983. "Infant Response to Auditory Familiarity and Novelty." *Infant Behavior and Development* 6 (2–3): 305–311.

Cottrell, Stephen. 2011. "The Impact of Ethnomusicology." *Ethnomusicology Forum* 20 (2): 229–232.

Coulter, Neil. 2011. "Assessing Music Shift: Adapting EGIDS for a Papua New Guinea Community." *Language Documentation and Description* 10: 61–81.

"Creativity in the Arts and Sciences: Historical Conceptions." 2015. *Science Encyclopedia*. http://science.jrank.org/pages/8871/Creativity-in-Arts-Sciences-Historical-Conceptions (accessed March 28, 2018).

Csikszentmihalyi, Mihalyi. 2013 [1996]. *Creativity: Flow and the Psychology of Discovery and Invention*. New York: HarperCollins.

Cushner, Kenneth. 2005. *Human Diversity in Action: Developing Multicultural Competencies for the Classroom*, 3rd edition. Boston: McGraw-Hill.

Davis, Matthew. 1999. "Health through Song: Outreach Workers in Benin and Guatemala Use Lyrics to Promote Health." *Harvard Medical Alumni Bulletin* 73: 36–41.

De Groot, Anne S., Karamoko Tounkara, Mali Rochas, Sarah Beseme, Shahla Yekta, Fanta Siby Diallo, J. Kathleen Tracy, Ibrahima Teguete, and Ousmane A. Koita. 2017. "Knowledge, Attitudes, Practices and Willingness of Vaccination in Preparation for the Introduction of HPV Vaccines in Bamako, Mali." *PLoS ONE* 12 (2) (February). https://www.researchgate.net/publication/313688252_Knowledge_attitudes_practices_and_willingness_to_vaccinate_in_preparation_for_the_introduction_of_HPV_vaccines_in_Bamako_Mali (accessed March 22, 2018).

Delton, Andrew W., and Aaron Sell. 2014. "The Co-evolution of Concepts and Motivation." *Current Directions in Psychological Science* 23 (2): 115–120.

DESA, Development Policy and Analysis Division. "Report of the UN System Task Team on the Post-2015 Development Agenda." http://www.un.org/en/development/desa/policy/untaskteam_undf/report.shtml (accessed March 28, 2018).

DESA, Office for ECOSOC Support and Coordination. "Millennium Development Goals and post-2015 Development Agenda." http://www.un.org/en/development/desa/oesc/mdg.shtml (accessed March 28, 2018).

Dooley, Robert A., and Stephen H. Levinsohn. 2001. *Analyzing Discourse: A Manual of Basic Concepts*. Dallas: SIL International.

Doty, Mark. 1998. *Sweet Machine*. New York: HarperCollins.

Dreger, Alice. 2011. "Darkness's Descent on the American Anthropological Association." *Human Nature* 22 (3): 225–246.

Duffy, William. 2014. "The Oral Poetics of Professional Wrestling, or Laying the Smackdown on Homer." *Oral Tradition* 29 (1): 127–148.

Dutton, Denis. 2009. *The Art Instinct: Beauty, Pleasure, and Human Evolution*. New York: Bloomsbury Press.

Easterbrook, Gregg. 2018. *It's Better Than It Looks: Reasons for Optimism in an Age of Fear*. New York: PublicAffairs.

Edge, John T. Twitter post. February 12, 2010, 6:49 a.m. http://twitter.com/johntedge/status/9009036481.

Edwards, Andrés R. 2010. *Thriving Beyond Sustainability: Pathways to a Resilient Society*. Gabriola Island, British Columbia: New Society Publishers.

The English Oxford Living Dictionaries. 2018. "Good." https://en.oxforddictionaries.com/definition/good (accessed March 28, 2018).

"Entertainment-Education." N.d. http://mediaimpact.org/entertainment-education/ (accessed March 28, 2018).

Feld, Steven. 1984. "Sound Structure as Social Structure." *Ethnomusicology* 28 (3): 383–409.

Feldman, Edmund B. 1992. *Varieties of Visual Experience*, 4th edition. New York: Adams.

Ferraro, Gary, and Susan Andreatta. 2014. *Cultural Anthropology: An Applied Perspective*, 10th edition. Belmont, CA: Wadsworth.

Finnegan, Ruth. 2014. *Communicating: The Multiple Modes of Human Communication*, 2nd edition. London: Routledge.

Frakes, Jack. 2005. *Acting for Life: A Textbook on Acting*. Colorado Springs: Meriwether.

Franken, Robert E. 1993. *Human Motivation*, 3rd edition. Pacific Grove, CA: Brooks/Cole.

Frith, Uta. 2013. "Are There Innate Mechanisms That Make Us Social Beings?" *Neurosciences and the Human Person: New Perspectives on Human Activities*. Vatican City: Pontifical Academy of Sciences, *Scripta Varia* 121. www.pas.va/content/dam/accademia/pdf/sv121/sv121-frithu.pdf (accessed March 28, 2018).

Gates, Bill. 2018. "What Gives Me Hope About the World's Future." *Time Magazine*. http://time.com/5086907/bill-gates-nancy-gibbs-interview/ (accessed March 26, 2018).

Giurchescu, Anca, and Eva Kröschlová. 2007. "Theory and Method of Dance Form Analysis." In *Dance Structures: Perspectives on the Analysis of Human Movement*, edited by Adrienne Kaeppler and Elsi Evancich Dunin, 21–52. Budapest: Akadémiai Kiadó.

Global Alliance to Immunize Against AIDS. 2014. "The Story-Telling Cloth—or How We Use Textiles as Social Media to Improve Vaccine Uptake." http://www.gaiavaccine.org/blog/2014/11/4/the-story-telling-cloth-or-how-we-use-textiles-as-social-media-to-improve-vaccine-uptake (accessed March 28, 2018).

Goldbard, Arlene. 2017. *Art Became the Oxygen: An Artistic Response Guide*. US Department of Arts and Culture. https://usdac.us/artisticresponse (accessed March 28, 2018).

Goodridge, Janet. 1999. *Rhythm and Timing of Movement in Performance: Drama, Dance and Ceremony*. London: Kingsley.

Grant, Catherine. 2014. *Music Endangerment: How Language Maintenance Can Help*. Oxford: Oxford University Press.

Grant, Catherine. 2017. "Vital Signs: Toward a Tool for Assessing Music Vitality and Viability." *The International Journal of Traditional Arts* 1 (1). http://tradartsjournal.org/index.php/ijta/article/view/4 (accessed March 17, 2018).

Graves, James Bau. 2005. *Cultural Democracy: The Arts, Community, and the Public Purpose*. Urbana: University of Illinois Press.

Greenwald, Michael L., Roger Schulz, and Roberto Dario Pomo. 2004 [2001]. *The Longman Anthology of Drama and Theater: A Global Perspective*. New York: Longman.

Greiner, Karen, Arvind Singhal, and Sarah Hurlburt. 2007. "'With an Antennae We Can Stop the Practice of Female Genital Cutting': A Participatory Assessment of *Ashreat Al Amal*, An Entertainment-Education Radio Soap Opera in Sudan." *Investigación y Desarrollo* 15 (2): 226–259.

Grimes, Joseph E. 1975. *The Thread of Discourse: Janua Linguarum*. The Hague: Mouton.

Guest, Ann Hutchinson. 2005. *Labanotation: The System of Analyzing and Recording Movement*. New York: Routledge.

Guest, Ann Hutchinson, and Tina Curran. 2008. *Your Move: The Language of Dance Approach to the Study of Movement and Dance*. Abingdon, UK: Taylor & Francis.

Guest, Kenneth. 2015. *Cultural Anthropology: A Toolkit for a Global Age*. New York: W. W. Norton.

Haaland, Ane. 1984. *Pretesting Communication Materials: With Special Emphasis on Child Health and Nutrition Education: A Guide for Trainers and Supervisors*. Rangoon: UNICEF.

Hackney, Peggy. 2000. *Making Connections: Total Body Integration through Bartenieff Fundamentals*. New York: Routledge.

Hammer, Mitch. 2011. "Additional Cross-Cultural Validity Testing of the Intercultural Development Inventory." *International Journal of Intercultural Relations* 35: 474–487.

Harada, Yasuko. 2012. "Performing Arts and Conflict Transformation in Acholiland, Northern Uganda." MA dissertation, University of Sheffield.

Harris, Robin P. 2017. *Storytelling in Siberia: The Olonkho Epic in a Changing World*. Urbana-Champaign: University of Illinois Press.

Harrison, Klisala, Elizabeth Mackinlay, and Svanibor Pettan, editors. 2010. *Applied Ethnomusicology: Historical and Contemporary Approaches*. Newcastle upon Tyne, UK: Cambridge Scholars.

Harrison, Klisala, and Svanibor Pettan. 2010. "Introduction." In *Applied Ethnomusicology: Historical and Contemporary Approaches*, edited by Klisala Harrison, Elizabeth Mackinlay, and Svanibor Pettan, 1–20. Newcastle upon Tyne, UK: Cambridge Scholars.

Hart, Geoff. 2007. "Some Thoughts on Visual Vocabulary, Grammar, and Rhetoric." *Intercom Journal of the Society for Technical Communication* 54 (5): 36–38. http://www.geoff-hart.com/articles/2007/visual.htm (accessed March 17, 2018).

Hatcher, Jeffrey. 2000 [1996]. *The Art and Craft of Playwriting*. Cincinnati: Story Press.

Herrmann, Fritz-Gregor. 2007. "The Idea of the Good and the Other Forms in Plato's Republic." In *Pursuing the Good: Ethics and Metaphysics in Plato's Republic*, edited by Douglas Cairns, Fritz-Gregor Herrmann, and Terry Penner, 202–230. Edinburgh Leventis Studies 4. Edinburgh: Edinburgh University Press.

Higgins, Lee. 2012. *Community Music: In Theory and Practice*. New York: Oxford University Press.

Higgins, Lee, and Lee Willingham. 2017. *Engaging in Community Music: An Introduction*. London: Routledge.

Higher Education Funding Council for England. 2016. "REF Impact." http://www.hefce.ac.uk/rsrch/REFimpact (accessed March 28, 2018).

Hill, Harriet, Margaret Hill, Dick Baggé, and Pat Miersma. 2016. *Healing the Wounds of Trauma: How the Church Can Help*, revised edition. Philadelphia: American Bible Society.

Hill, Juniper. 2012. "Imagining Creativity: An Ethnomusicological Perspective on How Belief Systems Encourage or Inhibit Creative Activities in Music." In *Musical Imaginations: Multidisciplinary Perspectives on Creativity, Performance and Perception*, edited by David Hargreaves, Dorothy Miell, and Raymond McDonald, 87–104. Oxford: Oxford University Press.

Hofman, Ana. 2010. "Maintaining the Distance, Othering the Subaltern: Rethinking Ethnomusicologists' Engagement in Advocacy and Social Justice." In *Applied Ethnomusicology: Historical and Contemporary Approaches*, edited by Klisala Harrison, Elizabeth Mackinlay, and Svanibor Pettan, 22–35. Newcastle upon Tyne, UK: Cambridge Scholars.

Hood, Mantle. 1960. "The Challenge of Bi-Musicality." *Ethnomusicology* 4: 55–59.

Hughes-Freeland, Felicia. 1999. "Dance on Film: Strategy and Serendipity." In *Dance in the Field: Theory, Methods and Issues in Dance Ethnography*, edited by Theresa J. Buckland, 111–121. New York: St. Martin's Press.

Human Relations Area Files. 2018. http://hraf.yale.edu/resources/reference/outline-of-cultural-materials/#outline-of-cultural-materials8211-online (accessed March 28, 2018).

Huron, David. 2008. *Sweet Anticipation: Music and the Psychology of Expectation*. Cambridge, MA: MIT Press.

Hutchinson, Sydney. 2003. "Confessions of a Public Sector Ethnomusicologist." *Folklore Forum* 34 (1–2): 79–87.

Hutchinson Guest, Ann. 2005. *Labanotation: The System of Analyzing and Recording Movement*. New York: Routledge.

Hutchinson Guest, Ann, and Tina Curran. 2008. *Your Move: The Language of Dance Approach to the Study of Movement and Dance*. Abingdon, UK: Taylor & Francis.

Impey, Angela. 2002. "Culture, Conservation and Community Reconstruction: Explorations in Advocacy Ethnomusicology and Participatory Action Research in Northern Kwazulu Natal." *Yearbook for Traditional Music* 34: 9–24.

"IUF 1000: What Is the Good Life." 2018. http://undergrad.aa.ufl.edu/uf-quest/iuf-1000-what-is-the-good-life/ (accessed March 28, 2018).

Johnston, Clay, and Carol J. Orwig. 1999. "Your Learning Style and Language Learning." *LinguaLinks 1999*. Dallas: SIL International. https://www.sil.org/resources/publications/entry/67412 (March 28, 2018).

Jourdain, Robert. 2008. *Music, the Brain, and Ecstasy: How Music Captures Our Imagination*. New York: William Morrow Paperbacks.

Journal of Applied Arts and Health. 2016. http://www.ingentaconnect.com/content/intellect/jaah (accessed March 28, 2018).

Jules-Rosette, Bennetta. 1985. "Ecstatic Singing: Music and Social Integration in an African Church." In *More than Drumming: Essays on African and Afro-Latin American Music and Musicians*, edited by Irene V. Jackson, 119–144. Westport, CT: Greenwood.

Juslin, Patrick, and John A. Sloboda, editors. 2010. *Handbook of Music and Emotion: Theory, Research, Applications*. New York: Oxford University Press.

Kahunde, Samuel. 2012a. "Our Royal Music Does Not Fade: An Exploration of the Revival and Significance of the Royal Music and Dance of Bunyoro-Kitara, Uganda." PhD thesis, University of Sheffield.

Kahunde, Samuel. 2012b. "Repatriating Archival Sound Recordings to Revive Traditions: The Role of the Klaus Wachsmann Recordings in the Revival of the Royal Music of Bunyoro-Kitara, Uganda." Special Issue: Ethnomusicology, Archives and Communities: Methodologies for an Equitable Discipline. *Ethnomusicology Forum* 21 (2): 197–219.

Kaplan, Frances, editor. 2006. *Art Therapy and Social Action: Treating the World's Wounds*. Philadelphia: Jessica Kingsley.

Kaufman, James C., and Ronald A. Beghetto. 2009. "Beyond Big and Little: The Four C Model of Creativity." *Review of General Psychology* 13 (1): 1–12.

Kirby, Michael. 1972. "On Acting and Not-Acting." *The Drama Review: TDR* 16 (1): 3–15.

Kodish, Debora. 2013. "Cultivating Folk Arts and Social Change." *Journal of American Folklore* 126 (502): 434–502.

Koen, Benjamin D., Gregory Barz, and Kenneth Brummel-Smith. 2008. "Introduction: Confluence of Consciousness in Music, Medicine, and Culture." In *The Oxford Handbook* of *Medical Ethnomusicology*, edited by Benjamin D. Koen et al., 4–17. Oxford: Oxford University Press.

Krüger, Simone, and Ruxandra Trandafoiu, editors. 2014. *The Globalization of Musics in Transit: Music Migration and Tourism*. New York: Routledge.

Krüger, Simone. 2008. "Ethnography in the Performing Arts: A Student Guide." https://www.heacademy.ac.uk/resource/ethnography-performing-arts-student-guide (accessed March 28, 2018).

Kumar, Sanjay, and Stuart Corbridge. 2002. "Programmed to Fail? Development Projects and the Politics of Participation." *The Journal of Development Studies* 39 (2): 73–103.

Kushnir, J., A. Friedman, M. Ehrenfeld, and T. Kushnir. 2012. "Coping with Preoperative Anxiety in Cesarean Section: Physiological, Cognitive, and Emotional Effects of Listening to Favorite Music." *Birth Issues in Perinatal Care* 39 (2): 121–127.

Language Archive, The. 2018. "ELAN." http://tla.mpi.nl/tools/tla-tools/elan (accessed March 28, 2018).

Lauer, David A., and Stephen Pentak. 2015. *Design Basics*, 9th edition. Boston: Wadsworth.

Lederach, John Paul. 2005. *The Moral Imagination: The Art and Soul of Building Peace*. New York: Oxford University Press.

Lester, P. M. 2003. *Visual Communication: Images with Messages*, 4th edition. Stamford, CT: Thomson-Wadsworth.

Levine, Ellen G., and Stephen K. Levine, editors. 2011. *Art in Action: Expressive Arts Therapy and Social Change*. London: Jessica Kingsley.

Levitin, Daniel J. 2007. *This Is Your Brain on Music: The Science of a Human Obsession*. New York: Dutton/Penguin.

Lewis, M. Paul, and Gary Simons. 2017. *Sustaining Language Use: Perspectives on Community-Based Language Development*. Dallas: SIL International. http://www.leanpub.com/sustaininglanguageuse (accessed March 28, 2018).

Lipoński, Wojciech. 2003. *World Sports Encyclopedia*. St. Paul, MN: MBI.

Longacre, Robert E. 1996. *The Grammar of Discourse*, 2nd edition. New York: Plenum.

Longacre, Robert E., and Stephen H. Levinsohn. 1978. "Field Analysis of Discourse." In *Current Trends in Textlinguistics*, edited by Wolfgang U. Dressler, 103–122. Berlin: Walter de Gruyter.

Lord, Albert. 1960. *The Singer of Tales*. Cambridge, MA: Harvard University Press.

Maletic, Vera. 2004. *Dance Dynamics: Effort and Phrasing Workbook*. Columbus, OH: Grade A Notes.

Malher-Moran, Melinda. 2016. "Research on the Efficacy of Dance/Movement Therapy is Growing." https://adta.org/2016/03/19/research-efficacy-dancemovement-therapy-growing (accessed March 26, 2018).

Margolis, Joseph. 1965. *The Language of Art and Art Criticism: Analytic Questions in Aesthetics*. Detroit: Wayne State University Press.

Marshall, Alex. 2018. "Can You Tell a Lullaby from a Love Song? Find Out Now." *New York Times*, January 25.

McKee, Robert. 1997. *Story: Substance, Structure, Style, and the Principles of Screenwriting*. New York: HarperCollins.

McKinney, Carol. 2000. *Globetrotting in Sandals: Field Guide to Cultural Research*. Dallas: SIL International.

McLaughlin, Buzz. 1997. *The Playwright's Process: Learning the Craft from Today's Leading Dramatists*. New York: Back Stage Books.

Mehr, Samuel, Manvir Singh, Hunter York, Luke Glowack, and Max M. Krasnow. 2018. "Form and Function in Human Song." *Current Biology* 28 (3): 356–368.

Minkler, Meredith, Nina Wallerstein, and Nance Wilson. 2008. "Improving Health Through Community Organization and Community Building." In *Health Behavior and Health Education: Theory, Research, and Practice*, 4th edition, edited by Karen Glanz, Barbara Rimer, and K. Viswanath, 288–312. San Francisco: Jossey-Bass.

Mlama, Penina. 1994. "Reinforcing Existing Indigenous Communication Skills: The Use of Dance in Tanzania." In *Women in Grassroots Communication*, edited by Pilar Riaño, 51–64. London: Sage.

Moseley, Christopher, editor. 2010. *Atlas of the World's Languages in Danger*, 3rd edition. Paris: UNESCO Publishing. http://www.unesco.org/culture/languages-atlas/ (accessed March 28, 2018).

Mpofu, Elias, Kayi Ntinda, and Thomas Oakland. 2012. "Understanding Human Abilities in Sub-Saharan African Settings." *Online Readings in Psychology and Culture* 4(3). https://dx.doi.org/10.9707/2307-0919.1036 (accessed March 28, 2018).

Mpofu, Elias, Kathleen Myambo, Andrew Mogaji, Teresa-Anne Mashego, and Omar Khaleefa. 2006. "African Perspectives on Creativity." In *The International Handbook of Creativity*, edited by James Kaufman and Robert Sternberg, 456–489. New York: Cambridge University Press.

Myers, Helen. 1992. "Fieldwork." In *Ethnomusicology: An Introduction*, edited by Helen Myers, 21–49. New York: W. W. Norton.

Neil, Martin. 2010. "Bugs, Bribes and Bamboo Buildings." http://www.voicesfromthenations.org/2010/08/18/bugs-bribes-and-bamboo-buildings#more-1835 (accessed March 28, 2018).

Nettl, Bruno. 1956. *Music in Primitive Culture*. Cambridge, MA: Harvard University Press.

Nettl, Bruno. 2005. *The Study of Ethnomusicology: Thirty-One Issues and Concepts*. Urbana: University of Illinois Press.

Niu, Weihua, and Sternberg, Robert. 2006. "The Philosophical Roots of Western and Eastern Conceptions of Creativity." *Journal of Theoretical and Philosophical Psychology* 26: 18–38.

Nketia, J. H. Kwabena. 1974. *The Music of Africa*. New York: W. W. Norton.

Noble, Gabriel. 2013. "A Soccer Ball That Is Lighting the World!" http://news.yahoo.com/blogs/the-upbeat/soccer-ball-lighting-world-142857214.html (accessed March 28, 2018).

Ó Briain, Lonán. 2014. "Minorities Onstage: Cultural Tourism, Cosmopolitanism, and Social Harmony in Northwestern Vietnam." *Asian Music* 45 (2): 32–57.

Padilha, José. 2010. *Secrets of the Tribe*. Distributed by Documentary Educational Resources, Watertown MA. (Film).

Pereira, Carlos Silva, João Teixeira, Patricia Figueiredo, João Xavier, São Luis Castro, and Elvira Brattico. 2011. "Music and Emotions in the Brain: Familiarity Matters." *PLoS ONE* 6 (11): e27241. https://doi.org/10.1371/journal.pone.0027241 (accessed March 28, 2018).

Pettan, Svanibor. 2008. "Applied Ethnomusicology and Empowerment Srategies: Views from Across the Atlantic." *Muzikološki Zbornik/Musicological Annual* 44 (1): 85–99.

Pettan, Svanibor, and Jeff Todd Titon, editors. 2015. *The Oxford Handbook of Applied Ethnomusicology*. Oxford: Oxford University Press.

Pinker, Stephen. 1994. *The Language Instinct: How the Mind Creates Language*. New York: William Morrow.

Pinker, Stephen. 2018. *Enlightenment Now: The Case for Reason, Science, Humanism, and Progress*. London: Allen Lane.

Plucker, Jonathan, Rafael Beghetto, and Gayle Dow. 2004. "Why Isn't Creativity More Important to Educational Psychologists? Potential, Pitfalls, and Future Directions in Creativity Research." *Educational Psychologist* 39: 83–96.

Polson, Tod. 2013. *The Noble Approach: Maurice Noble and the Zen of Animation Design*. San Francisco: Chronicle Books.

Powell, John. 2010. *How Music Works : The Science and Psychology of Beautiful Sounds, from Beethoven to the Beatles and beyond*. 1st US edition. New York: Little Brown.

Ranger, Terence, and E. J. Hobsbawm. 2012 [1992]. *The Invention of Tradition*. Cambridge: Cambridge University Press.

Ravier, Sophie. 2014. "The Role of Music in Post-Conflict Reconciliation in Mali." MA dissertation, University of Sheffield.

Reigersberg, Muriel Swijghuisen. 2010. "Applied Ethnomusicology, Music Therapy and Ethnographically Informed Choral Education: The Merging of Disciplines during a Case Study in Hopevale, Northern Queensland." In *Applied Ethnomusicology: Historical and Contemporary Approaches*, edited by Klisala Harrison, Elizabeth Mackinlay, and Svanibor Pettan, 51–74. Newcastle upon Tyne: Cambridge Scholars.

Reigersberg, Muriel Swijghuisen. 2011. "Research Ethics, Positive and Negative Impact, and Working in an Indigenous Australian Context." *Ethnomusicology Forum* 20 (2): 255–262.

Renkema, Jan. 1993. *Discourse Studies: An Introductory Textbook*. Amsterdam: Benjamins.

Reyero, Verónica. 2017. "Smartphone Ethnography." http://antropologia2-0.com/en/smartphone-ethnography (accessed March 28, 2018).

Richards, Paul. 1972. "A Quantitative Analysis of the Relationship between Language Tone and Melody in a Hausa Song." *African Language Studies* 13: 137–161.

Ricoeur, Paul. 1984. *Time and Narrative*, vol. 1. Chicago: University of Chicago Press.

Roder, Beverly J., Emily W. Bushnell, Anne Marie Sasseville. 2000. Infants' Preferences for Familiarity and Novelty During the Course of Visual Processing. *Infancy* 1 (4): 491–507.

Rosati, Connie S. 2008. "Objectivism and Relational Good." *Social Philosophy and Policy* 25 (1): 314–349.

Rovai, Alfred. 2002. "Building Sense of Community at a Distance." *International Review of Research in Open and Distance Learning* 3 (1). http://www.irrodl.org/index.php/irrodl/article/view/79/153 (accessed March 17, 2018).

Rubin, Judith Aron. 2016. *Approaches to Art Therapy: Theory and Technique*, 3rd edition. Oxfordshire: Routledge.

Sadler, Blair, and Anjali Joseph. 2008. "Evidence for Innovation: Transforming Children's Health Through the Physical Environment. Executive Summary." Alexandria, VA: National Association of Children's Hospitals and Related Institutions. http://www.premiersafetyinstitute.org/wp-content/uploads/evidenceforinnovation-execsum-small.pdf (accessed March 26, 2018).

Saucier, Gerard, Thalmayer, Amber Gayle, and Bel-Bahar, Tarik S. 2014. "Human Attribute Concepts: Relative Ubiquity across Twelve Mutually Isolated Languages." *Journal of Personality and Social Psychology* 107 (1): 199–216.

Saurman, Mary. 1995. "The Effect of Music on Blood Pressure and Heart Rate." *EM News* 4 (3): 1–2.

Saurman, Mary Beth. 2010. "Culturally Relevant Songs: Teaching Tools in Education Programs." Paper presented at the joint conference of the Sixth Symposium of the International Council for Traditional Music Study Group on Music and Minorities and the Second Symposium of the International Council for Traditional Music Study Group on Applied Ethnomusicology, Hanoi, Vietnam, July 19–30.

Saurman, Mary Beth, and Todd Saurman. 2004. "Applied Ethnomusicology: The Benefits of Approaching Music as a Heart Language." *Journal of Language and Culture* 23 (2): 15–29. Institute of Language and Culture for Rural Development, Mahidol University.

Saville-Troike, Muriel. 2002. *The Ethnography of Communication: An Introduction*. Malden, MA: Blackwell.

Schechner, Richard. 2006. *Performance Studies: An Introduction*, integrated media edition. New York: Routledge.

Schiffrin, Deborah, Deborah Tannen, and Heidi E. Hamilton, editors. 2003. *The Handbook of Discourse Analysis*, new edition. Oxford: Blackwell.

Schippers, Huib. 2010. "Three Journeys, Five Recollections, Seven Voices: Operationalising Sustainability in Music." In *Applied Ethnomusicology: Historical and Contemporary Approaches*, edited by Klisala Harrison, Elizabeth Mackinlay, and Svanibor Pettan, 150–160. Newcastle upon Tyne, UK: Cambridge Scholars.

Schippers, Huib. 2015. "Applied Ethnomusicology and Intangible Cultural Heritage: Understanding 'Ecosystems of Music' as a Tool for Sustainability." In *The Oxford Handbook of Applied Ethnomusicology*, edited by Svanibor Pettan and Jeff Todd Titon, 134–156. Oxford: Oxford University Press.

Schippers, Huib, and Catherine Grant, editors. 2016. *Sustainable Futures for Music Cultures: An Ecological Perspective*. New York: Oxford University Press.

Schrag, Brian. 1998. "Mono Creativity: The Commissioning and Composition of Three Songs." *Research Review* (Legon, Ghana) Supplementary Issue No. 10.

Schrag, Brian. 2005. "How Bamiléké Music-Makers Create Culture in Cameroon." PhD dissertation, University of California, Los Angeles.

Schrag, Brian. 2013a. *Creating Local Arts Together: A Manual to Help Communities Reach Their Kingdom Goals*. General editor, James R. Krabill. Pasadena: William Carey Library.

Schrag, Brian. 2013b. "How Artists Create Enduring Traditions." In *Resiliency and Distinction: Beliefs, Endurance and Creativity in the Musical Arts of Continental and Diasporic Africa. A Festschrift in Honor of Jacqueline Cogdell DjeDje*, edited by Kimasi L. Browne and Jean N. Kidula, 415–444. Richmond, CA: MRI Press.

Schrag, Brian. 2015a. "A Triple Insider's Take on Arts Therapy, Arts-based Community Development, and Huntington's Disease." *Voices* 15 (3). https://voices.no/index.php/voices/article/view/822/694 (accessed March 28, 2018).

Schrag, Brian. 2015b. "Motivations and Methods for Encouraging Artists in Longer Traditions." In *Handbook of Applied Ethnomusicology*, edited by Jeff Todd Titon and Svanibor Pettan, 317–347. Oxford: Oxford University Press.

Schrag, Brian. 2016. "Music in the Newer Churches." In *The Wiley-Blackwell Companion to World Christianity*, edited by Lamin Sanneh and Michael McClymond, 359–367. Hoboken, NJ: Wiley Blackwell.

Schwab, Klaus, Nicholas Davis, and Satya Nadella. 2018. *Shaping the Fourth Industrial Revolution*. Cologny, Switzerland: World Economic Forum.

Seeger, Anthony. 1992. "Ethnography of Music." In *Ethnomusicology: An Introduction*, edited by Helen Myers, 88–109. New York: W. W. Norton.

Seeger, Anthony. 2006. "Lost Lineages and Neglected Peers: Ethnomusicologists Outside Academia." *Ethnomusicology* 50 (2): 214–235.

Seeger, Anthony, and Shubha Chaudhuri, editors. 2004. *Archives for the Future: Global Perspectives on Audiovisual Artchives in the 21st Century*. Calcutta: Seagull Books.

Shanahan, Joanne, Meg E. Morris, Orfhlaith Ni Bhriain, Daniele Volpe, Tim Lynch, and Amanda M. Clifford. 2017. "Dancing for Parkinson Disease: A Randomized Trial of Irish Set Dancing Compared With Usual Care." *Archives of Physical Medicine and Rehabilitation* 98 (9): 1744–1751.

Shelemay, Kay Kauffman. 2001. *Soundscapes: Exploring Music in a Changing World*. New York: W. W. Norton.

Singer, Milton. 1972. *When a Great Tradition Modernizes: An Anthropological Approach to Modern Civilization*. New York: Praeger.

Singhal, Arvind, and Everett M. Rogers. 1999. *Entertainment-Education: A Communication Strategy for Social Change*. Mahway, NJ: Lawrence Erlbaum.

Skinner, Jonathan. 2014. "Applied and Social Anthropology, Arts and Health: Introduction: Cross-Border Interventions." *Anthropology in Action* 21 (1): 2–3.

Slobin, Mark. 1992. "Ethical Issues." In *Ethnomusicology: An Introduction* (Vol. 1), edited by Helen Myers, 329–336. New York: W. W. Norton.

Society for Ethnomusicology. 2001. *A Guide for Documentation, Fieldwork and Preservation for Ethnomusicologists*, 2nd edition. Bloomington, IN: The Society for Ethnomusicology.

The Society for Ethnomusicology's Music and Social Justice Resources Project. 2018. https://ethnomusicology.site-ym.com/page/Resources_Social (accessed March 28, 2018).

Spradley, James. 1980. *Participant Observation*. New York: Holt, Rinehart & Winston.

Squibb, Eliza. 2015a. "Exciting Opportunities in Sierra Leone." https://www.globalgiving.org/projects/story-telling-cloth-for-ebola-education/ (accessed March 28, 2018).

Squibb, Eliza. 2015b. "Reimagining Traditional Textiles for Health Education." *West African Research Association* (Spring Newsletter): 14–15.

Stanford Encyclopedia of Philosophy. 2017. "Plato." https://plato.stanford.edu/entries/plato/ (accessed March 17, 2018).

Staricoff, Rosalia Lelchuk. 2006. "Arts in Health: The Value of Evaluation." *Journal of the Royal Society for the Promotion of Health* 126 (3): 116–120.

Sternberg, Robert J., and Todd Lubart. 1999. "The Concept of Creativity: Prospects and Paradigms." In *Handbook of Creativity*, edited by Robert Sternberg, 3–15. New York: Cambridge University Press.

Stillman, Sarah. 2014. "Ebola and the Culture Makers." https://www.newyorker.com/news/daily-comment/ebola-culture-makers (accessed March 28, 2018).

Stone, Ruth M. 1979. "Communication and Interaction Processes in Music Events among the Kpelle of Liberia." PhD dissertation, Indiana University.

Stone, Ruth M. 2000. "African Music in a Constellation of Arts." In *The Garland Handbook of African Music*, edited by Ruth M. Stone, 7–12. New York: Garland.

Sweers, Britta. 2010. "Polyphony of Cultures: Conceptualization and Consequences of an Applied Media Project." In *Applied Ethnomusicology: Historical and Contemporary Approaches*, edited by Klisala Harrison, Elizabeth Mackinlay, and Svanibor Pettan, 215–232. Newcastle upon Tyne, UK: Cambridge Scholars.

Tatarkiewicz, Władysław. 1980. *A History of Six Ideas: An Essay in Aesthetics*. Translated from the Polish by Christopher Kasparek. The Hague: Martinus Nijhoff.

Tillis, Steve. 1999. *Rethinking Folk Drama*. Westport, CT: Greenwood Press.

Titon, Jeff Todd. 1997. "Knowing Fieldwork." In *Shadows in the Field: New Perspectives for Fieldwork in Ethnomusicology*, edited by Gregory Barz and Tim Cooley, 87–100. New York: Oxford University Press.

Titon, Jeff Todd. 2015. "Sustainability, Resilience, and Adaptive Management for Applied Ethnomusicology." In *The Oxford Handbook of Applied Ethnomusicology*, edited by Svanibor Pettan and Jeff Todd Titon, 157–195. Oxford: Oxford University Press.

Titon, Jeff Todd. 2018. "Sustainable Music: A Research Blog on the Subject of Sustainability and Music." http://sustainablemusic.blogspot.co.uk/ (accessed March 28, 2018).

United Nations. 2008. "United Nations Declaration on the Rights of Indigenous Peoples." United Nations. http://www.un.org/esa/socdev/unpfii/documents/DRIPS_en.pdf (accessed March 22, 2018).

United Nations. 2016a. "Sustainable Development Goals: 17 Goals to Transform Our World." http://www.un.org/sustainabledevelopment/sustainable-development-goals (accessed March 28, 2018).

United Nations. 2016b. "We Can End Poverty: Millennium Development Goals and Beyond 2015." http://www.un.org/millenniumgoals (accessed September 13, 2017).

United Nations. 2018. "The Sustainable Development Agenda." http://www.un.org/sustainabledevelopment/development-agenda/ (accessed March 17, 2018).

Unseth, Peter. 2008. "How to Collect 1,000 Proverbs: Field Methods for Eliciting and Collecting Proverbs." *Proverbium* 25: 399–418.

Van Buren, Kathleen. 2007. "Partnering for Social Change: Exploring Relationships between Musicians and Organizations in Nairobi, Kenya." *Ethnomusicology Forum* 16 (2): 303–326.

Van Buren, Kathleen. 2010. "Applied Ethnomusicology and HIV and AIDS: Responsibility, Ability, and Action." *Ethnomusicology* 54 (2): 202–223.

Vaughan, Peter W., Everett M. Rogers, Arvind Singhal, and Ramadhan M. Swalehe. 2000. "Entertainment-Education and HIV/AIDS Prevention: A Field Experiment in Tanzania." *Journal of Health Communication* 5 (Supplement): 81–100.

Vrekalić, Andreja, Orfhlaith Ni Bhriain, Amanda Clifford, Jennie Gubner, and Brian Schrag. 2017. "Continuing a Conversation: Ethnomusicology's Contributions to Arts Therapies." Unpublished statement of intent. International Council for Traditional Music World Congress, Limerick, Ireland.

Waldinger, Robert. 2015. "What Makes a Good Life? Lessons from the Longest Study on Happiness." https://www.ted.com/talks/robert_waldinger_what_makes_a_good_life_lessons_from_the_longest_study_on_happiness#t-747115 (accessed March 28, 2018).

Wallas, Graham. 2014 [1926]. *The Art of Thought*. Turnbridge Wells, UK: Solis Press.

Wates, Nick. 2014. *The Community Planning Handbook*, 2nd edition. London: Routledge.

Webb, Nancy Boyd, editor. 2004. *Mass Trauma and Violence: Helping Families and Children Cope*. New York: Guilford Press.

World Health Organization. 2018. "Infant Mortality." http://www.who.int/gho/child_health/mortality/neonatal_infant_text/en/ (accessed March 28, 2018).

Closing 2: Glossary

AGENCY   The capacity of a group or an individual to exert power, usually in terms of making decisions.

ANALYTICAL PERFORMANCE   Presentation designed by a researcher in order to isolate features of artistic production. Also known as analytical enactment.

ARTISTIC COMMUNICATION   An act of conveying messages marked by heightened attention to form and visceral and emotional impact.

ARTISTIC DOMAIN   A category of special communication determined by the nature of its production. In the Guide, we use this term to refer to Euro-American categories, including music, dance, drama, oral verbal arts, and visual arts. Other communities organize their thoughts and words about arts differently.

ARTISTIC ENACTMENT   An instantiation of an artistic genre during an event. Although essentially identical in meaning to *performance*, we use the term *enactment* whenever possible to acknowledge visual arts. Referring to a sculpture as a *performance*, for example, confuses the clear meaning we wish to convey.

ARTISTIC EVENT   Something that occurs in a particular place and time, related to larger sociocultural patterns of a community, containing at least one enactment of an artistic genre. It is divisible into shorter time segments. Examples: festival, church service, birthday party, and rite of passage.

ARTISTIC GENRE   A community's category of artistic communication characterized by a unique set of formal characteristics, artistic enactment practices, and social meanings. It can draw on multiple artistic domains.

ARTS   A general term that refers to forms of communication marked by patterns that differ from a community's everyday communication.

ARTS ADVOCATE   Anyone who encourages the use of local arts for a community's benefit. Sometimes referred to as an *ethnoarts advocate*.

CATALYST   Someone or something that starts an action that continues on its own.

COMMUNITY   A group of people that shares a story, identity, and ongoing patterns of interaction, and that is constantly in flux.

CONTEXTUALIZATION   Adapting an outside cultural form or idea into a society or culture.

CULTURAL DOMAIN   A broad category of cultural meanings or phenomena that includes smaller categories.

CULTURAL THEME   Any principle that recurs in several cultural domains and defines relationships among sets of cultural meanings.

EMIC   A viewpoint from inside a culture being studied.

ETHNOARTS   Study of the artistic communication in a group that strongly identifies itself as an ethnolinguistic community.

ETHNOCENTRISM   An attitude in which one evaluates aspects of a different culture based on values and assumptions from his or her own.

ETHNOGRAPHY   A description of a community based on observation of and interaction with living people over a prolonged period of time. A *performance (or enactment) ethnography* relates how sounds, movements, dramatizations, and other artistic products are conceived, created, and received, and how they influence other individuals, groups, and social and artistic processes.[1]

ETHNOMUSICOLOGY   The study of music in and as culture.

ETIC   A viewpoint from outside a culture being studied.

GATEKEEPER   A person who exerts significant influence on whether a community accepts an innovation or not, and who has a personal or social stake in its success or failure.

GENRE   A community's category of communication characterized by a unique set of formal characteristics, performance practices, and social meanings. Examples of genre include *olonkho* (Siberia), Broadway musical (New York City), *kanoon* (Cameroon), *huayno* (Peru), *haiku* (Japan), praise and worship (Euro-America), *qawwali* (South Asia), and *mola* (Central America). See also *artistic genre; artistic enactment*.

INTEGRAL PERFORMANCE CONTEXT   An environment that has many social and artistic components that are familiar to the enactors.

LABANOTATION   A system for transcribing dance movements.

LANGUAGE DEVELOPMENT   The series of ongoing, planned actions that a language community takes to ensure that its language continues to serve its changing social, cultural, political, economic, and spiritual needs and goals.

LOCAL ART   An artistic form of communication that a community can create, perform, teach, and understand from within, including its forms, meanings, language, and social context.

MERISTEM   The region in a plant in which new cells are created; the growth point.

MUSIC   Humanly organized and heightened sound.

ORALITY   The way of accessing and passing on information by nonliterate means.

ORATURE   A body of works communicated orally, such as stories, myths, and folklore.

ORGANOLOGY   The study of musical instruments.

PARTICIPANT OBSERVATION   An investigative practice used in ethnographic research in which the researcher engages in life activities with the participants of the study.

POLYSEMY   The ability of one form or symbol to hold multiple meanings.

QUALITATIVE RESEARCH An approach in which the researcher collects open-ended, emerging, and evolving data with the primary intent of developing themes from the data. The results tend to focus on meanings and experiences.

QUANTITATIVE RESEARCH An approach that focuses on specific variables and the testing of specific hypotheses, that employs strategies such as experiments and surveys, and that yields statistical data. The results tend to focus on numbers and frequencies.

REFLEXIVITY The acknowledgment that representations of reality are constructions of the researcher and are informed by his or her own choices and viewpoints.

REVITALIZATION/CULTURAL REVITALIZATION Bringing something back to life again, through research, creation, and use of indigenous resources.

RULE OF THIRDS In photography, a frame can be divided into three vertical and three horizontal sections. Many photographers propose that an object appears more prominent if it is not in the center of the frame.

SPARKING ACTIVITY Anything anyone does that results in the creation of new artistry; a catalyst.

SUSTAINABILITY A desired characteristic whereby what is initiated in a community will be continued or further developed; often discussed in development projects.

TACIT KNOWLEDGE Information held by culture-bearers (cultural insiders) that is not easily expressed.

TAXONOMY A set of categories organized on the basis of a single semantic relationship that shows the relationships of all the terms in a domain.

TRANSCRIPTION Graphic representation of aspects of artistic communication.

NOTE

1. Inspired by Anthony Seeger (1992).

Closing 3: Sample Research Documents

Sample Information Letter (Adapt to Local Needs)

INFORMATION LETTER for
PROJECT TITLE:
RESEARCHER and AFFILIATION:
TELEPHONE CONTACT FOR RESEARCHER:
EMAIL CONTACT FOR RESEARCHER:

Introduction

You are invited to participate in a research project on [   ]. Please take time to read the following information, and ask any questions that you might have. You are free to choose whether or not to participate in the project.

Background on the Project

The aims of this project are [ ]. Settings for research may include [ ]. Participants include [ ]. The project will last from [date] to [date].

Results

Data collected during this research will be stored [   ] and will be used for [   ]. Fieldwork data as well as any subsequent products will be made available to participants upon request.

Requirements for Participants

If you agree to participate in the project through interviews, audio- or videorecordings, or photographs, you will be asked to sign a separate consent form. You will be given the option to remain anonymous if preferred.

Potential Risks or Benefits for Participants

[Consider whether there are any physical, psychological, or other risks to participants. Also state whether there are any financial or other benefits for participants.]

Ethics Review Procedure

[If your research has been through an ethics review process at an organization or institution, indicate this here.]

Queries

If you have further queries or concerns about the project, please do not hesitate to contact me by email at [   ] or telephone at [   ].

Thank you for your interest!

Sample Permission Form (Simplify and Adapt to Local Needs)

RELEASE FORM for

PROJECT OR EVENT:

DATE(S):

_____

Name of Individual Researcher or Organization Representative:

_____

Name(s) of Participant(s):

_____

_____

_Mailing Address of Participant(s):_____

_Phone Contact of Participant(s):_____

_Email Contact of Participant(s):_____

Participant(s), please circle your responses below:

• My/our performance may be videorecorded.   YES   NO

• My/our performance may be audio recorded.   YES   NO

• I/we may be photographed for the project.   YES   NO

• I wish to be acknowledged in any related publication as (circle one):

  1. Name as written above.

  2. This name: (please print) _____.

  3. I wish to remain anonymous.

I/we the undersigned authorize the [_organization or person name_] to publish these materials in written, visual, audio, and video form, for noncommercial, nonprofit research and educational purposes. I/we understand that no royalties will be paid to anyone and that no one will personally profit from these recordings without the express consent of participants.

_____   _____

Participant Signature   _Researcher/Organization Representative_
                                           Signature

_____   _____

Date   _Date_

Additional participants may sign below, as needed:

_____

_____

_____

_____

Closing 4: Sample Community Arts Profile Outline

We have created a file that provides spaces to describe and capture the results of activities that you and a community engage in related to the Guide. Essentially, it restates many of the Guide's sections so that you know where to include results of activities you perform. In the file, you will replace the capitalized words with words appropriate to your context. For example, COMMUNITY NAME would be substituted with the name of the community you are working with, such as Sakha, the Bach clan, or *l'Eglise Catholique de Tchinga*. You are free to modify the structure, categories, and content of your Community Arts Profile however you would like. What follows is an example of the table of contents of a Community Arts Profile yet to be filled in.

Community Name

Name of arts advocate(s):
Dates of work represented by this document:

Summarize plans, activities, results

- *Make Arts* projects: Steps completed (to any degree). Note that the *Make Arts* process can be performed multiple times in the same community, for different goals, and drawing on different genres. You can number these for easy reference.
- List of events and genres researched (to any degree)

Make Arts Process: NUMBER, for GOAL(S)

Number refers here to the reference number or code being used to specify the particular *Make Arts* project you are describing. We suggest a simple *year* plus *number* code, such as 2019:2: you began performing this *Make Arts* process in 2019, and it is the second *Make Arts* project you completed that year. *Goals* refers to the goals chosen by the community.

Step 1: Meet COMMUNITY and its Arts

- Take a first glance at a community
- Take a first glance at a community's arts
- Start exploring a community's social and conceptual life
- Summarize results and challenges of this step

Step 2: Specify Goals for a Better Life

- Help a community discover its goals
- Describe one or two goals to focus on now
- Summarize results and challenges of this step

Step 3: Connect Goals to Genres

- Describe the desired effects of the new artistry
- List the genre, content, and events that will produce the effects the community desires
- Summarize results and challenges of this step

Step 4: Analyze Genres and Events

- Decide what research you will perform
- Perform research, entering results in "Descriptions of Artistic Genres" (see following section of *Closing 4*)
- Summarize results and challenges of this step

Step 5: Spark Creativity

- Think about what a sparking activity is
- Prepare to draw on familiar methods of composition
- Identify opportunities to capitalize on and barriers to overcome
- Decide on the type of activity
- Design a new activity or modify an existing activity
- Summarize results and challenges of this step

Step 6: Improve Results

- Choose and modify an approach to evaluation and improvement
- Perform the approach to evaluation and improvement
- Summarize results and challenges of this step

Step 7: Celebrate and Integrate for Continuity

- Choose what to celebrate and integrate
- Plan actions to ensure effective programs continue
- Summarize results and challenges of this step

Descriptions of Artistic Genres: GENRE NAME

The following is an outline for one genre, and could be repeated for other genres.

A: Event Analysis: EVENT NAME

- Brief description
- First glance at an event
- Performance lenses on an event

B: Artistic Aspects of an Event

- Music
- Drama
- Dance
- Oral verbal arts
- Visual arts
- Interrelationships between formal elements of an event

C: Broader Cultural Context of an Event

- Artists
- Creativity
- Ownership and rights
- Language
- Transmission and change
- Cultural dynamism
- Identity and power
- Aesthetics and evaluation
- Time
- Emotions
- Subject matter
- Community values
- Communal investment

Closing 5: Index of Artistic Domain Research Activities

Closing 6: Index of Sample Sparking Activities

Closing 7: Suggestions for Guide Users

Suggestions for Educators

Make Arts for a Better Life can provide structure for projects, workshops, classes, and curriculum development. In the following, we discuss principles and examples that you can adapt to educational contexts.

Pedagogy

The seven steps in the *Make Arts* process can range in scale from a one-hour project to a lifetime endeavor. This almost infinite variability allows students to interact with arts and arts makers in any community. However, it also can lead to a lack of direction and a sense of never quite doing the right thing. Here are some principles that can help you make your students' experiences clear and rewarding.

Pour the Make Arts Process into Your Instructional Framework

You can modify elements of the process to fit the scale of your teaching context in several ways. First, for each project or class, you may specify the amount of time students are required to spend on activities related to each step. Since there is always more to do, somewhat arbitrary time frames should not detract students from learning the processes and concepts. Second, reduce or expand the depth and breadth of results required. For shorter projects, have students focus on activities named "Take a First Glance at . . . ." Third, ensure you set realistic expectations for the validity and generalizability of your students' projects. For most educational environments, you will not have the resources, time, or expertise to apply rigorous social science research standards to projects. For example, gathering a verifiably representative sample of community members in identifying goals (*Step 2*) and measuring impact (*Step 7*) will likely be beyond the scope of your institutional capacities.

Expect Some Disorder

The seven steps constitute a flexible framework, whose order may or may not match the context of a particular project. A project with a community that has already chosen an artistic genre to create for an upcoming festival will not require a detailed process of choosing a genre. Tell students that they should start trying to go through the steps from 1 to 7, modifying their order when justified. In other words, every project should include activities from every step, but students need not perform them in consecutive order.

Prepare Students to Interact Well with Communities

We have woven respect for communities into the fabric of the Guide. Two critical approaches are: adopting a learner's stance at all times, and expecting to find value in every community. Students will vary in their capacities to adopt this stance and foster this expectation. Alternative approaches to helping often include applying predetermined solutions to new contexts, which can undermine the learner's orientation. In addition, every student—and instructor—sees people through unique lenses that both clarify and obscure their complexity and beauty.

To increase the likelihood of positive experiences for both students and communities, develop a strategy to identify and resolve potential problems. One systemic approach would be to require a class in cultural anthropology or cross-cultural communication before yours; we have found that students usually emerge with a strong expectation of cultural relativity and humility. You also may decide to meet with each student to gauge his or her attitudes toward people outside his or her usual relationships. The meeting could include questions and prompts such as:

- Tell me about someone you have met recently who is different from people you normally interact with. In what ways does he or she differ from you culturally?
- Do you think that some cultures are better than others? Do you think that some cultures have right or wrong beliefs and ways of living? Do you believe that your culture is superior or inferior to others?
- Do you believe that most people are basically the same in terms of their beliefs and behaviors?
- Do you believe that different cultures are fundamentally similar/different?

A conversation like this can be awkward, so you may want to administer formalized tools like the Inventory of Cross-Cultural Sensitivity (ICCS; Cushner 2005) and the Intercultural Development Inventory (IDI; idiinventory.com). The for-profit IDI has proven particularly effective in analyzing cultural competences in secondary and university students in several countries, and provides strategies to help people move toward more curious and exploratory states (Hammer 2011).

Sample Project

Notes to Instructor

- Before assigning this project, have students read "Foundations." Discuss the content together, exploring how each section might affect students' interactions with communities new to them.
- Connect students with communities through two basic approaches. First, you can prearrange communities for students by drawing on your or your institution's networks. Second, you can place most of the responsibility of finding groups on the students, relying on their networks, interests, ingenuity, and initiative. Diverse urban populations often develop systems of highlighting ethnic communities that can help in this process, such as cultural heritage organizations and arts councils.
- Have students take notes on each step in a notebook, a Community Arts Profile (see *Closing 4*), or another data-gathering and analysis system.
- Help students fulfill all ethics requirements for your context.
- Draw upon activities in this Guide in developing assignments. Additional assignments are described in the following.

Assignment: Make Arts with a Community

Overview

The student should engage a local community in the seven steps of the *Make Arts* process, documenting the progress of the project through a written journal and culminating in a multimedia presentation with textual support. The student should complete *Steps 1–4*, and as much of *Steps 5–7* as possible given time constraints. He or she should approach this as a pilot project, an initial endeavor that could be built upon in the future. The student should include community members in every step, if possible.

In addition to assignments listed, the student should make a summary of the project by replacing and expanding on the italicized words with items from his or her project:

> *Community* will prepare
> *event* that includes enactment of
> *genre or activity* with
> *content* to produce
> *effects* that help *community*
> move toward *goal for a better life.*

Step 1: Meet a Community and Its Arts
Activities from the Guide

- Take a first glance at a community.
- Take a first glance at a community's arts.

Notes

- After exploring the community, help the student restrict the scope of his or her project.

Step 2: Specify Goals
Activities from the Guide

- Read descriptions and examples of categories of goals: identity and sustainability, health and well-being, and human rights.
- Steps to specifying goals: Before performing this activity, discuss ways that it should be adapted to this community's context.

Step 3: Select Communication Genre and Content
Activities from the Guide

- Choose the desired effects of new artistry.
- Choose the content of new artistry.
- Choose a genre or genres that have the capacity to communicate the content and produce the desired effects.
- Imagine events that could include the performance of new works in the genre(s) that would produce the effects in its experiencers.

Step 4: Analyze the Genre and Event
Activities from the Guide

- A. Take a first glance at an event.
- B. Not required. If questions arise related to the artistic features of an enactment, scan Part B for research activities that address those questions.
- C. Relate the event's genre(s) to its broader cultural context. Choose one activity from two or three of these categories.

Step 5: Spark Creativity
Activities from the Guide

- Identify opportunities to maximize and barriers to overcome.
- Decide on the type of activity.
- Design a new or modify an existing activity.
- Perform the activity and describe the results.

Step 6: Improve New Works
Activity from the Guide

- Follow guidelines for determining whether artistic products are effective.

Step 7: Integrate and Celebrate Artistic Works
Activities from the Guide

- Choose what to integrate and celebrate.
- Imagine ways to "act to keep effective initiatives going."

Suggestions for Project Leaders

Make Arts for a Better Life can provide direction and data for projects overseen by large development organizations—like UNESCO, UNICEF, DfID, and USAID—as well as smaller, regional or local nongovernmental groups and community based groups.

Make Arts' Unique Contributions

Intrinsic to the *Make Arts* process are participatory methods of engaging, listening to, and discussing community goals from the beginning; research into the forms and meanings of local arts; and recognition of the benefits of piloting small projects before making large investments of time and money. Organizations do not always allow for these priorities. Some, for example, have a particular solution to a problem that they want a community to embrace, without first learning whether it is appropriate to that context. Perhaps you can integrate some on-the-ground research in situations like these.

Propose and Manage a Better Project

Each organization has unique proposal requirements, management structures, and financial accountability processes with which they engage. Virtually all project funders, however, insist on well-conceived rationales based on sound research, clearly defined objectives and goals, strategies to meet those goals that include feasible activities, clear expectations of results of the activities, identification of people and resources necessary to complete the activities, indicators of success or failure of the project, thorough review after implementing the project, and a proposal for next steps. Figure C7.1 summarizes some of the typical elements of a planning cycle: *Assess* a community's situation, make a *plan* to reach goals for improvement,

FIGURE C7.1. Common project life cycle.

implement the plan, *monitor* it, *evaluate* how well the plan worked in reaching the goals, *assess* the changed situation, and make a *new plan* to reach modified goals. The *Make Arts* process can contribute substantially to each of these.

Exploratory Planning to Inform Your Project Proposal

To gain the most from *Make Arts* during the proposal process, perform all seven steps during an exploratory planning phase. *Steps 1–4* will guide you through research necessary to propose plans in *Steps 5–7*. See Figures C7.2 and C7.3.

Performing these activities	Provides data for
Step 1 • Take a first glance at a community • Take a first glance at a community's arts	Situation analysis—social, geographical, stability
Step 2 • Read categories of goals - Identity and sustainability, health and well-being, and human rights • Adapt "Steps to Specifying Goals" to the community	Long-term impact and shorter-term goals
Step 3 • Choose the desired effects of new artistry • Choose the content of new artistry • Choose a genre or genres that have the capacity to communicate the content and produce the desired effects • Imagine events that could include performance of new works in the genre(s) that would produce the effects in its experiencers.	Initial strategy: Activities with local artistic resources that result in attaining goals. Create skeletal logical framework.
Step 4A • Take a first glance at an event **Step 4C** • Relate the event's genre(s) to its broader cultural context	Verify validity of initial strategy by researching meanings and social embeddings of chosen arts. Identify potential risks based on status of arts chosen, gatekeeper attitudes, availability of experts and resources to perform chosen arts.

FIGURE C7.2.   Project planning research steps.

Based on your research in Steps 1-4, complete the proposal.	
Step 5	Plan activities to perform. Development process for activities includes risk assessment, identification of indicators of success, and finances and other resources required. You can modify this planning step to integrate your organization's preferred methods and tools, such as SWOT (Strengths, Weaknesses, Opportunities, Threats).
Step 6	Analyze results of activities using local evaluation methods. Since *Make Arts* integrates evaluation organically into the process, you may plan to review, modify, and redo activities.
Step 7	Complete initial logical framework.

FIGURE C7.3.   Completing the proposal.

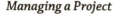

Managing a Project

Once a project has been approved, *Make Arts* can contribute to its implementation in ways listed in Figure C7.4.

Step 4	Return to Step 4 to research hidden elements of artistry exposed by confusion, ambiguity, or conflict that arises throughout implementation of the plan.
Step 5	Perform activities.
Step 6	Measure outcomes using chosen indicators.
Step 7	Review results in terms of sustainability.

FIGURE C7.4. Implementing the plan.

Suggestions for Researchers

Make Arts for a Better Life can serve as a touchstone for researchers performing ethnographic and artistic form research, whether you are working explicitly in development or not. In fact, nearly half of this volume consists of research activities, mostly contained in *Step 4*, Parts A, B, and C.

We have included so much research guidance for two main reasons. First, we want to do all we can to ensure that students and project leaders can enter any community in the world and find research help in the guide. This requires an event-based, flexible model that accounts for phenomena associated with as many artistic domains as possible. *Step 4* provides a compendium of paths you can follow to learn about the particular artistry with which you are engaged.

Second, although we (Brian and Kathleen) were both educated as ethnomusicologists, we have been highly motivated to explore arts that are not primarily musical. We have encountered contexts where our training kept us from noticing aspects of artistry that were crucial to a robust understanding. Fortunately, the field of ethnomusicology planted the seeds of the more encompassing approach you find here. To bring this approach to maturity, we engaged with scholars representing performance studies, folklore, creativity studies, anthropology, ethnography of communication, communication studies, linguistics (especially, pragmatics), ethnochoreology, ethnopoetics, philosophy of the arts, theater arts, aesthetics, community development, and more.

We include research activities that address formal and ethnographic phenomena as exhaustively as possible, because anything less is incomplete, perhaps erroneous. As a scholar, you should have time for extended research that development personnel might not.

Summaries of the primary research sections of this guide follow.

Step 1: Meet a Community and Its Arts

Step 1 sets the basic groundwork for subsequent research. "Take a first glance at a community" and "Take a first glance at a community's arts" ask for information usually readily available or quickly attainable. We ask readers to begin gathering data in a Community Arts Profile, which could consist of a series of paper notebooks, electronic text file, or relational database. We also summarize basic ethnographic research methods such as interviewing, participant observation, and recording.

Step 4: Analyze Genres and Events

In the introduction to *Step 4*, we define and describe interactions between the two entry points of our approach: events and genres. Foundational to our approach is the goal of describing events and genres in their own terms. We do not guide you, for example, in an attempt to categorize each of a community's arts as music or dance or drama. Rather, we help you list a community's arts, then describe each in terms of its unique musical, movement, dramatic and other features.

Step 4, Part A: Describe the Event and Its Genre(s) as a Whole

Step 4, Part A introduces seven lenses through which you can explore events and genres: *space, materials, participant organization, shape of the event through time, performance features, content,* and *underlying symbolic systems*. We provide research questions and activities for each lens. All but *performance features* and *underlying symbolic systems* are common categories of event analysis.

Step 4, Part B: Explore the Event's Forms through Artistic Domain Categories

We have included research activities organized into five artistic domain categories common to Euro-american music and arts academies: *music, drama, dance, oral verbal arts,* and *visual arts. Oral verbal arts* refers to genres exhibiting features found in storytelling, proverbs, and poetry, and is not normally found in a conservatory setting. We have organized each artistic domain section by the same seven lenses used in *Step 4*, Part A, providing coherence in your ultimate description of the event as a whole. Analyzing an event through additional artistic domains such as architecture or food is a conceptually straightforward process.

Step 4, Part C: Relate the Event's Genre(s) to Its Broader Cultural Context

Step 4, Part C, provides research activities in a dozen or so ethnographic categories especially relevant to artistry. Examples include *creativity, identity and power, aesthetics,* and *emotion.*

Closing 8: Measuring Artistic Genre Vitality

International scholarly and nongovernmental organizations have noted a widespread increase in the disappearance of artistic traditions. *Closing 8* outlines some of their efforts to understand causes and develop solutions.

Identifying Factors Crucial to a Genre's Continuity

Linguists have tried to understand the rapid rate of language death in the world today, thereby developing models that can be applied to artistic communication. From Lewis and Simons (2017), we see that strength in five strong social dynamics (Figure C8.1) is critical for the ongoing life of an art form.

1. *Function*	Concerns solidifying or creating social uses for artistic activity. The more uses an art form has, the higher status it enjoys. Without status, no one will want to make or experience an art form.
2. *Acquisition*	Consists of the ways that the skills, competencies, and knowledge associated with an art form are passed on to others. Without acquisition, no one new will ever learn to create in the form, and it will die.
3. *Motivation*	Determines why people choose to use certain arts for social functions.
4. *Environment*	Affects how the surrounding society supports the use of an art form or not.
5. *Differentiation*	Societal norms must clearly delineate the functions assigned to an artistic form, marking it as distinct from the uses of other arts and communication genres.

FIGURE C8.1. Conditions for sustainable use of a genre.

Schippers and Grant (2016) propose a different, music-focused set of important domains. From 2009 to 2014, Huib Schippers oversaw an ambitious research program entitled "Sustainable Futures for Music Cultures: Toward an Ecology of Musical Diversity." Drawing on extensive exploration of music genres from nine diverse contexts, Schippers and Grant (2016:10–13) extract five primary domains influencing genres' sustainability: (1) systems of learning music; (2) musicians and communities; (3) contexts and constructs; (4) regulations and infrastructure; and (5) media and the music industry. One outcome of the project is a website that anybody can use to search for guidance on increasing the vitality of music genres they know; the website, www.MusicEndangerment.com, guides the user through a series of questions that can lead to the genre's description according to each of the five domains. The site then suggests activities that other communities with similar situations have used to increase musical vitality.

Tools to Assess a Genre's Health

Frameworks like these help us think about artists and their genres in categories that are likely to uncover characteristics supporting or detracting from sustainability. Scholars have also developed tools to measure the health of genres in ways that inform plans to encourage more vitality. In Figure C8.2, we present a slightly modified version of Harris's Graded Genre Health Assessment (2017:112). This assessment draws primarily on strength of transmission patterns and social embeddings to gauge genres' vitality on a global stage.

From her work in Siberia, Harris (2017) traced the life, near-death, and rebirth of the Sakha's *olonkho* epic song-story genre through this framework. She found that solo performance of *olonkho* enjoyed a Vigorous (3) level of health in Sakha communities in the early twentieth century, which dropped to Threatened (4) during the imposition of Soviet cultural policy in the mid-twentieth century and to Stressed (6) by the end of the Soviet period. When UNESCO named *olonkho* a "Masterpiece of the Oral and Intangible Heritage of Humanity" in 2005, Sakha people began actively to support its revitalization. Due to their robust investment of energy, time, and resources, the solo form of the *olonkho* genre is showing signs of strengthening. A lack of living tradition bearers, however, currently restricts its recovery to a level of Locked (5), with modern performances largely memorized, rather than improvised. On the other hand, related genres such as theatrical *olonkho* have experienced a clear resurgence. Harris identifies transmission and interaction between stable and malleable elements of the *olonkho* genre as key to producing resilience.

Grant (2014) developed the Music Vitality and Endangerment Framework (MVEF) to assess music genres' health. She uses a set of questions for each factor to assign its level of strength. You can explore MVEF more at Grant (2017). In Figure C8.3, we adapt it slightly to embrace all arts.

These tools may provide insights crucial to designing interventions to increase an art form's resilience. Fundamental to fostering better futures through arts is the existence of local arts. Work on endangerment is crucial.

Level of Health	Description
1. *International*	An international "community of practice" forms around the artistic genre. Ideally, international participation will include live enactment as well as consumer engagement.
2. *National or regional*	The genre's reputation grows beyond the home community. Community members may receive financial or other types of support from the national or regional level. People outside the home community learn to perform the genre, and the enactment becomes iconic of the nation or region. Although not the ultimate goal of the genre's revitalization, this level of vitality can increase confidence in the home community. The genre's high profile might open doors for community development in other domains.
3. *Vigorous*	The pivotal level for artistic vitality. Oral transmission and largely traditional contexts of education are intact and functioning. People have sufficient opportunities for enactment, and young people are learning through observation, participation, and appropriate educational contexts. A genre can exist comfortably at this level without needing to move higher.
4. *Threatened*	The first level that hints at endangerment. Although still performed, the genre is undergoing noticeable changes: diminishing enactment contexts, increased time given to more recent introductions, and more rural-urban movement.
5. *Locked*	The genre is known by more people than just the grandparent generation, but its enactment is restricted to tourist shows or other contexts that are not integrated into the everyday life of the community. The enactment repertoire is fixed, with no new additions. Participation and creative energy decline noticeably.
6. *Stressed*	The grandparent generation is proficient in this genre, but fewer contexts exist for passing it on to younger people. The younger people may not express interest, or older generations may presume a lack of interest from the youth. The genre is not dead or endangered at this level, and can be revitalized, but signs indicate likely endangerment.
7. *Dormant*	Functional contexts for enactment are gone, but recordings and other ethnographic descriptions exist. A community could reacquaint itself with the genre, but its rebirth would likely take on a different character from the original.
8. *Extinct*	No one in the community is capable of creating or performing in this genre. Probably no enactment has occurred in the lifetime of anyone currently living. This stage occurs fairly rarely, as most genres grow into other styles or their stylistic elements are perpetuated in related styles.

FIGURE C8.2. Graded Genre Health Assessment.

Factor 1.	Intergenerational transmission
Factor 2.	Change in number of proficient artists
Factor 3.	Change in number of people engaged with the genre
Factor 4.	Change in the art and artistic practices
Factor 5.	Change in performance contexts and functions
Factor 6.	Response to mass media and arts industries
Factor 7.	Availability of infrastructure and resources for arts practices
Factor 8.	Knowledge and skills for arts practices
Factor 9.	Governmental policies affecting arts practices
Factor 10.	Community members' attitudes toward the genre
Factor 11.	Relevant outsiders' attitudes toward the genre
Factor 12.	Amount and quality of documentation

FIGURE C8.3. Arts Vitality and Endangerment Framework.
Adapted from Grant (2014:125).

Closing 9: Quick Reference

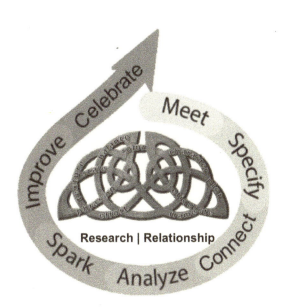

The *Make Arts for a Better Life* **Process**

The arts advocate(s) assisting with this process could be a member of the community or a friend of the community. Our goal is for community members to take the lead in decision-making and implementing plans.

1. *Meet a Community and Its Arts*: Explore artistic and social resources that exist in the community. Performing *Step 1* allows you to build relationships, involve and understand people within the community, and discover the artistic treasures of the community.

2. *Specify Goals for a Better Life*: Discover the goals that the community wishes to work toward. Performing *Step 2* ensures that you are helping the community work toward aims that they have agreed on together.

3. *Connect Goals to Genres*: Consider artistic genres and events that can help the community meet its goals, and activities that can result in purposeful creativity in this genre. Performing *Step 3* reveals the mechanisms that relate certain kinds of artistic activity to its effects, so that the activities you perform have a high chance of succeeding.

4. *Analyze Genres and Events*: Describe an event and its genre(s) as a whole, and its artistic forms as arts and in relationship to broader cultural context. Performing *Step 4* results in detailed knowledge of the art forms that is crucial to sparking creativity, improving what is produced, and integrating it into the community.

5. *Spark Creativity*: Implement activities that the community has chosen to spark creativity within the genre they have chosen. Performing *Step 5* produces new artistic works for events.

6. *Improve Results*: Evaluate results of the sparking activities and improve them. Performing *Step 6* ensures that the new artistry exhibits the aesthetic qualities, produces the impacts, and communicates the intended messages at a level of quality appropriate to its purposes.

7. *Celebrate and Integrate for Continuity*: Plan and implement ways that this new kind of creativity can continue into the future. Identify more contexts where new and old arts can be displayed and performed. Performing *Step 7* makes it more likely that a community will keep making its arts in ways that produce positive effects long into the future.

Index